# Race, Politics and Social

Social and political relations in Britain and other industrial societies have been formed against a background of ongoing change and transformation in the politics of race. Attention has tended to be focused on the racist and extreme nationalist movements which have emerged in Europe, but most studies have given little thought to a variety of processes which have given new meaning to the political language of race. Within minority communities, in particular, there have been dramatic transformations in terms of their political mobilisation, an issue now too great to be ignored by the major national parties.

*Race, Politics and Social Change* focuses on the detailed empirical research of the authors' five-year study in Birmingham. They thus improve upon the general and abstract analyses of other theorists of race, providing the reader with substantial theoretical arguments located within the context of particular situations. Their conclusions contain important and original insights into the changing political discourses about race and the role of black politicians in both the Labour and Conservative Parties.

**John Solomos** has written many texts on key aspects of race relations. Among his publications are *Race and Racism in Britain* and *Racism and Migration in Western Europe*. **Les Back** has researched widely on popular culture, youth culture and the politics of race. He has just published *New Ethnicities and Urban Culture*.

# Race, Politics and Social Change

# Race, Politics and Social Change

John Solomos and Les Back

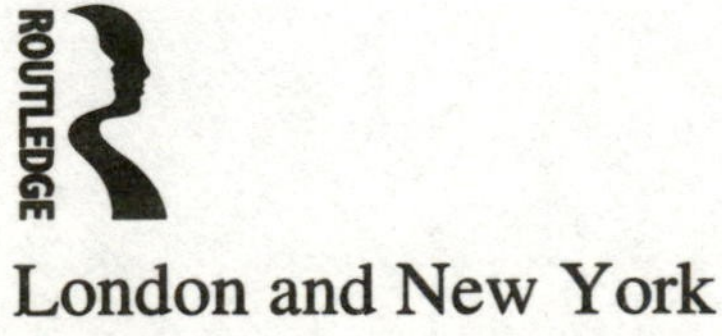


London and New York

First published 1995
by Routledge
11 New Fetter Lane, London EC4P 4EE

Simultaneously published in the USA and Canada
by Routledge
29 West 35th Street, New York, NY 10001



Typeset in Times by LaserScript, Mitcham, Surrey
Printed and bound in Great Britain by
Mackays of Chatham PLC, Chatham, Kent



*British Library Cataloguing in Publication Data*
A catalogue record for this book is available from the British Library

*Library of Congress Cataloguing in Publication Data*
A catalogue record for this book has been requested

ISBN 0–415–08577–2 (hbk)
ISBN 0–415–08578–0 (pbk)

**For Nikolas Stephen Solomos and Stephanie Joy Back,**
**with much love and hope for the future**

# Contents

# Preface

In the present political environment a key question, both from a conceptual and practical perspective, is the following: How can we explain the power of ideas about race and ethnicity in shaping political mobilisation and participation? In one way or another this is a question that is being asked today by social scientists in all the major advanced industrial societies. It is also the issue that has preoccupied us in the course of our research and in the process of writing this book. Indeed, it is interesting to note that even in the short period during which we have worked on this project important transformations have taken place that have highlighted the complex ways in which race and ethnicity have become volatile political symbols in our postmodern political environment.

Within the spatial boundaries of Europe the extent of the transformations has taken many commentators by surprise. The growing role of racist and extreme nationalist social movements in both Eastern and Western Europe is perhaps the most noticeable aspect of these processes (Balibar, 1991; Miles, 1993; Wrench and Solomos, 1993). But it is also important to note that in practice a variety of localised, national and supranational processes have helped to give meaning to the political language of race and ethnicity and to create spaces for new forms of racial and ethnic 'identity' (Goldberg, 1993; Gilroy, 1993a). Moreover, it is worth noting that during the past decade we have seen a major transformation in forms of political mobilisation within minority communities, often in directions that have not been fully anticipated.

*Race, Politics and Social Change* has been written against this background of ongoing change and transformation of the politics of race in Britain and other industrial societies. It provides an account of the development and transformation of political debates about race and ethnicity through an analysis of the changing dynamics of racialised politics in Birmingham and in British society as a whole. Its major concern throughout is to remedy a marked absence in existing research by focusing on the dynamics of race, politics and social change over the past three decades. It is because of this concern that we have chosen to focus specifically on analysing processes of change and political mobilisation.

The book's key arguments derive from our study of the everyday processes that have produced new forms of political discourse and mobilisation around the issue of race in Birmingham. The focus is therefore on contemporary British society, though we have tried throughout to bring out similarities and differences with other advanced industrial societies. The advantage of this approach is that it allows us to go beyond abstract speculation and examine in some detail the political discourses, institutions, mobilisations and policy changes that characterise the present situation. Additionally, by concentrating on everyday processes and debates we have attempted to provide a flavour of the dynamics of racialised political mobilisation. Many critical theorists of race have largely been concerned with global and somewhat abstracted analyses of contemporary racial and ethnic relations. Our focus is rather different: it is on the dynamics of racialised political mobilisation within the context of particular situations. This allows us to explore this dimension of contemporary political life in all its rich detail, and to provide an insight into how the politics of race has been fashioned in the context of the major transformations that we have seen in the past few decades.

This approach also stands in marked contrast to the deep-seated tendency to see the politics of race as fixed and unchanging. Such a tendency is evident in the arguments of both radical researchers, who work from a monolithic conception of contemporary forms of racism (Sivanandan, 1990b) and in the bulk of the mainstream research on the politics of race, which takes as its starting point a narrow definition of political institutions and forms of participation and mobilisation (Saggar, 1992; Layton-Henry, 1992). Yet what recent events in Britain, Europe and the United States have shown is that contemporary forms of racialised politics are inherently unstable and subject to new forms of political mobilisation. Why this instability? How have new forms of mobilisation helped to change the face of political institutions and generated new means of involvement and participation in the political system? What role and impact do minority politicians have within the political system? These are some of the questions that we seek to address from both a theoretical and an empirical perspective in this book. These are also the questions that have received little or no attention in Britain, though there are numerous studies that examine the politics of race in the United States over the same period.

The research on which this book is based originated from our concern to explore the dynamics of these changes and to outline their implications for the future. Drawing on our detailed study of the changing patterns of the politicisation of racial and ethnic identities in the city of Birmingham, we have sought to produce an analysis that has pertinence to a broader range of situations and historical circumstances. In order to contextualise the material about Birmingham in a wider political and social context we have drawn on our own research into the politics of race, nation and identity in Britain and other societies (Solomos, 1988, 1993; Wrench and Solomos, 1993). A key starting point of this research is that there is a need to go beyond a narrow analytical framework and to engage in a dialogue with the research agendas and conceptual frameworks utilised across the whole spectrum of social scientific research on forms of racialisation and ethnicity. Aspects of this dialogue are to be found throughout this volume as we attempt to come to terms with the main characteristics of contemporary forms of mobilisation based on race and ethnicity.

In combining an account of the specific and the general we are seeking to challenge the predominantly static conception of the politics of race that pervades much of the literature. We want to show that any rounded analysis of the politics of race has to be able to deal with the complex intertwining of national, local and everyday processes of racialisation. In this sense we are covering the range of issues that has been raised recently in theoretical discussions of the ways in which categories such as race and ethnicity work to 'define population groups and, by extension, social agents as self and other at various historical moments' (Goldberg, 1993: 80). Rather than remain at the level of theoretical exegesis, however, we have chosen to combine a detailed study of the politics of race in a specific socio-political situation with our broader analytical concerns.

It is also worth emphasising, as a number of recent critical studies have done, that it is worse than useless in the present political environment to assume a single monolithic conception of race that exists in the same form in every society (Miles, 1989, 1993; Goldberg, 1993; Gilroy, 1993a). Indeed, it is part of the objective of this book to show how ideas about race and its political significance have actually changed over time, and how these changes have linked up to broader processes of social and political change in British society. In attempting to explore the changing forms of political identities which have, in one way or another, been shaped by racialised processes, we are hoping to show that any critical understanding of these processes needs to question simplistic notions that see contemporary discourses about race as uniform and linear in their course of development.

As we try to make clear in the substantive parts of the book we do not see the account provided in *Race, Politics and Social Change* as having relevance from a purely academic perspective. From our vantage point it seems both pertinent, and practically useful, to develop an understanding of racialised politics that attempts to explain the development of the present situation and which explores the dynamics of trends that are likely to come to the fore in the future. We want, in other words, to make two kinds of interventions through this book. First, we are interested in providing a critical perspective on the changing politics of race in the present political environment. We feel uncomfortable with static and unchanging conceptions of the political system which do not allow room for the impact of political mobilisation and action on processes of representation, and this explains our focus in this volume on the dynamic of politicised racialised identities as they are formed and reformed. Second, we want to address questions which are of some importance to all attempts to develop a truly multiracial society, namely: How can we ensure individuals and groups with different ethnic, racial, gender or religious identities are recognised as equals and treated as equals in politics? How can political institutions allow claims to representation on the basis of particular identities and at the same time protect basic civic rights for all?

We do not pretend that these questions are easy to answer. Far from it, since it seems clear from recent public debates in a number of advanced industrial societies that questions about multiculturalism and race and ethnicity are both troubling and difficult to come to terms with. The rise of racist and nationalist movements in both majority and minority communities is a sign of the massive dangers ahead. But we hope that our exploration of some of the key aspects of racialised political mobilisation allows us to provide some kind of constructive input into current and future debates. In particular we want to intervene in current debates about the politics of identity and 'new ethnicities' which have become a major theme in the literature on the postmodern condition. Rather than remain within the parameters of the rather abstract ways in which these issues are usually debated, however, we have chosen to provide a rigorous and contextualised account of a particular situation. We then explore some of the broader conceptual and political questions from this grounded perspective.

In conducting the research on which this study is based we have been assisted in a number of ways by colleagues and friends. First and foremost we wish to acknowledge the support of the Economic and Social Research Council (Award no. R000231545), which funded the research over the period from October 1989 to April 1992. This enabled Les Back to devote himself full time to the research in Birmingham. The whole project was therefore made possible by the generous support of the ESRC. Robin Cohen, then Director of the Centre for Research in Ethnic Relations at the University of Warwick, kindly provided us with a base in the Centre and this proved to be an invaluable location throughout the project. At another level numerous individuals, in Birmingham and elsewhere, helped us in carrying out the research, and we take this opportunity to thank them for their time and generosity. Numerous local politicians, activists, officers and others gave generously of their time to talk to us about our research. We hope our findings will be of interest and of some value to them and to others outside academic research. In particular we would like to thank the following for their incisive observations and critical comments on the research: Ashfaq Ahmed, Amir and Zarina Khan, Phil Murphy, John Tyrell, Gurdev Manku, Barbara Guinnett, Rose Anderson, Patricia Davidson, Adrian Collins, Raghib Ahsan and Maurice Birioti. Also thanks to Paul Smith at Birmingham City Council and Patrick Baird at Birmingham Central Library. Throughout the course of our research a number of academic colleagues helped show us that despite the constant pressures of academic life there is still some time for discussion and reflection in our communities of scholars. Participants in the Workshop on the Politics of Racism, particularly Clive Harris, Syd Jeffers, Michael Keith and Karim Murji, provided a lively forum for exploring tentative ideas and thoughts. We have also benefited greatly from various other conferences and seminars at which we have attempted to give some coherence and order to our ideas on these issues. To all who helped us with various aspects of the book a big thank you. During the course of this study Harriet Lodge, Joanne Winning and Terry Mayer have helped to deal with all the administrative demands of a project such as this. Joanne and Terry also read parts of the book and made valuable suggestions. The arduous task of transcribing the interview tapes was carried out efficiently and with good humour by Charlene McGroarty. Her work was indispensable and made our own task much easier.

Our families provided important emotional support and other forms of sustenance throughout. They helped us to see the project through by putting up with the demands of conducting the research and writing this book.

Watching the Baggies return to the good times provided a different kind of distraction and excitement during the writing of this book, with particularly fond memories of Wembley in May 1993, the stupendous victories over the Wolves in September 1993 and February 1994, and the beach party in Portsmouth in May 1994. The London Supporters Branch provided nice company during various trips to home and away games. Boing! Boing! Baggies! Baggies!

# Introduction

Why have questions about race and ethnicity become such key themes in contemporary political debates? What impact have mobilisations based on racialised identities had on the development of policies and programmes to deal with forms of racial inequality and discrimination? These and other questions reflect the increasing concern in many societies regarding the role of ideas about race and ethnicity in political life. This issue was a relatively neglected topic until the 1980s, but since then it has been a growing concern of scholars and political activists (Solomos, 1993; Miles, 1993). Whether we look at contemporary Europe, the United States or South Africa the role of racism in shaping political life is the subject of both research and increasingly volatile public political debate. Yet it is also clear that if we are to understand fully how the construction of racialised politics has come about we need more detailed accounts of the processes that have led to the growing politicisation of debates about race in specific socio-political contexts.

An additional and disturbing factor in recent years is the resurgence of movements that use racial and national symbols to mobilise political support. Such movements have not necessarily been successful in all specific national contexts, but it can be argued that they have helped to highlight the potential for conflict that surrounds questions of race in our changing global environment (Brubaker, 1992; Castles and Miller, 1993; Wrench and Solomos, 1993). In this sense it can be said that there are few social and political issues that are as high on the political agenda as questions about race and immigration. What is striking, however, is that little research has been carried out to explore the ways in which political mobilisations around questions of race and ethnicity actually take place, the meanings attached to them and the role of minorities themselves as agents of political action and participants in the political system.

It is against this wider background that we undertook the research on which this book is based. When we started our research in 1989 it was already clear that the political debates around race and immigration in the period since the 1950s had produced an environment in which all aspects of what are commonly called race relations in British society have become highly charged and politicised. Numerous studies have highlighted the variety of ways in which debates about immigration have influenced political institutions and shaped policy development in areas such as education, employment, housing and policing (Layton-Henry, 1992; Saggar, 1992; Solomos, 1993). What was also clear, however, is that we were still some way from a clear understanding of the complex and changing dynamics of racialised politics in British society. In particular we felt that there was a marked lack of theoretically grounded ethnographic studies of what one may call the everyday dynamics of racialised politics. It was also clear that some key aspects of contemporary racialised politics, e.g. the emergence of black politicians as a significant phenomenon, had received little or no attention within the mainstream of research in this field (Solomos and Back, 1991b).

With this in mind we sought first and foremost to use our research as a means of exploring the political processes that have helped to shape the current situation as well as looking forward to trends and developments that are likely to shape the situation over the next two decades or so. This has necessitated a focus on more recent processes and developments, and we do not in the context of this study provide a detailed account of the overall historical background. There is much work that obviously remains to be done on the history of race and ethnic relations in Birmingham and elsewhere and we do not want to deny that this is an important aspect of the issues we are looking at. Indeed, this is something we discuss in some detail in the course of this study. But we have chosen to concentrate on the history of the present in order to remedy the clear lack of studies that address the question of the changing politics of race and ethnicity in the present confused environment. By focusing on recent trends and developments we hope to raise questions of relevance to different political contexts and to suggest avenues for more systematic cross-country comparisons. But we also want to explore the processes of change that we are seeing at the present and the likely directions of future political mobilisations.

The arguments to be found in this book reflect this concern on our part to move beyond a descriptive account of the history of political debates about race and immigration and provide a theoretically informed account of the complex ways in which ideas about race and ethnicity actually work in everyday politics. Rather than retrace the familiar story of how British political life became increasingly racialised over the past four decades or so, we have chosen to provide an account that focuses on the role that political actors and institutions have played in the construction of a new politics of race.

## CONTEXTUALISING THE RESEARCH

As we have already made clear, the starting point of this book is the concern to break with the tendency in much of the research in this field to see the political meanings and values attached to ideas about race as static. But what does this actually mean in a substantive sense? Putting it briefly, it means that we are concerned with three intertwined processes. First, the processes that have brought about the political understandings of race that have shaped our political culture and institutions. Second, the mechanisms which ethnic minorities have used to mobilise themselves politically. Third, the responses of political parties and institutions to racial and ethnic questions. In tackling all three processes we have sought to utilise the case study of Birmingham to illustrate how constructions of race need to be located within particular discursive contexts. This in turn ties up with wider theoretical and conceptual dilemmas that we seek to tackle in the introductory and concluding chapters.

A key feature of this book is that we explore in some detail the political ideas and values of politicians and activists about race. This is because we feel that it is precisely this aspect of the contemporary politics of race that needs to be at the core of any rounded attempt to understand the situation we now face. For example, it has become clear in recent years that minority groups are playing an increasingly active role in the shaping of political and policy agendas within national and local political institutions. This phenomenon has certainly become important at the level of local politics, with the election of a sizeable number of black local councillors over the past decade. But it is also becoming an issue within the context of national party politics and within Parliament. It is of some relevance, therefore, to ask why we have seen relatively little serious research about this question.

This is a study of the dynamics of race, class and social change. It is informed by three kinds of conceptual and empirical input. The first input derives from a series of studies we have been carrying out over the past decade about the changing politics of race, ethnicity and nation in British society. The second and most important input is a study of racialised politics in Birmingham, a conurbation that has played a vital role in the shaping of the politics of race in British society. This research has focused specifically on recent changes in the involvement of minorities in the political system, the emergence of new political forces and movements and the responses of the main political parties to issues such as the representation of black minorities and the emergence of black politicians. The third input derives from our ongoing attempt to provide a theoretical framework for the analysis of the interplay between the development of racial identities and wider socio-political processes.

These issues have, surprisingly, received little or no attention within the main body of research on race, politics and ethnicity. This is partly because there have been few theoretically informed studies of political mobilisation and activism that have sought to explore the role of race in shaping political identities, party politics and political representation in the context of British society. Most studies have analysed political processes from a very narrow perspective, which has meant in practice ignoring the wider social and cultural environment within which ideas about race have been formed. Or they have lacked an in-depth analysis of how political actors and institutions have attempted to come to terms with the racialisation of political life in the current situation. It is to remedy this imbalance that we have conducted research that combines an interdisciplinary theoretical perspective with an ethnographic analysis of the everyday processes that help to mould political debates about race and ethnicity in contemporary societies.

## ETHICAL AND POLITICAL ISSUES

Before moving on to discuss the substantive findings of the research, however, we want to use the rest of this chapter to say something about the ethical and political dilemmas we faced in conducting this research and the practical pressures we had to grapple with. This is all the more necessary because there is surprisingly little discussion of the ethical and political dilemmas of conducting research in this field.

Part of the agenda of doing research on the politics of racism must be a continual process of self-critical awareness and a sensitivity that research can have both intended and unintended political consequences. Ethical and political dilemmas are an integral element of research on race and ethnic issues (Ladner, 1973; CCCS, 1982; Rich, 1986; Stanfield and Dennis, 1993). Studies of race and ethnic issues inevitably, though not always in a clear fashion, confront two sets of questions. First, questions are asked about what the research is for. In the context of the 1980s and 1990s the hidden text behind such questions is the suspicion that much of the research in this field has had very little political or policy relevance. Second, questions arise about the likely impact of the research on the issues or the groups that are being researched. This second area of concern links up quite closely with the first and serves to highlight the politicised and often controversial nature of research in this field.

Both sets of questions give rise to their own problems, and it has to be said that they are not easy to deal with. But it is impossible in the present environment not to address and at least attempt to come to terms with these questions in one way or another. This is something that we were keenly aware of before we started our research on this project, but over the whole period in which we conducted our field-work we were confronted with various issues related to these questions on an almost daily basis. This did not surprise us, though our preparedness for these questions did not necessarily make it easier for us to deal with them in practice. In fact, it also rapidly became clear to us that in the course of our research we were bound to confront other ethical and political dilemmas, and ones that we were not in a position to deal with in an easy manner.

We were aware from the earliest stages of our research that the questions we were exploring did not merely amount to a matter of dealing with abstract intellectual issues. Rather, the question of defining 'the research problem' and how we should ask questions was part of our daily dilemma in carrying out our field-work. As a number of researchers have noted, minority communities in Britain, the United States and elsewhere have felt over-studied and have become wary of answering questions to outside and mainly white researchers. For us this meant that we needed to think carefully about what kinds of questions we wanted to ask, to whom and why. In short, we had to reckon with the politics of conducting research on race in a context that was intrinsically politicised and in which there were likely to be suspicions about why we were conducting our research.

Within Britain discussion about the politics of race relations research has in many ways followed debates in the United States. The issues much debated in North America since the 1960s have been concerned with what kind of academic research was being conducted, the relations between such research and the state, and the place of white social scientists in such research (Staples, 1976; Geschwender, 1977; Marable 1983). In the British context these issues were echoed in the debates and conflicts that took place inside and outside of academic life from the early 1970s onwards. More recently the focus of the criticisms has been on what objectives research on race relations should have, e.g. whether the main focus of research should be on minority communities and their cultural and family networks or on the institutions of white racism. In addition, the politicisation of race over the last two decades has raised a number of complex ethical and political dilemmas that confront any researcher working in the field. In this kind of context researchers have found it necessary to give some account of the place and function of race relations research. This is what we refer to as 'speaking positions'.

Many of the early researchers of race relations in Britain emphasised the need for their work to be seen as autonomous in terms of ideological and political commitments, or at best having only a tangential link with existing debates about racism (Patterson, 1969; Rose *et al.*, 1969; Deakin, 1970). Another version of this approach does not eschew the need to look at the political or policy aspects of race relations, arguing instead that the way to influence legislative and administrative branches of government is not through political analysis but through the presentation of factual statistical information about discrimination in such areas as housing, employment and social services. This approach is particularly associated with the work of the Policy Studies Institute and the Centre for Research in Ethnic Relations. The end result of this approach may be said to be an emphasis on race research as either a neutral academic discipline or as uncommitted policy research that aims to present policy-makers with the facts on which they could base new policy initiatives.

A more complex variation on the academic autonomy argument is found in the work of John Rex (Rex, 1973, 1979, 1981). Rex is one of the most important political sociologists working in the field of race relations and has an international reputation. His work was of direct interest to us since over the past three decades he has conducted two very influential studies of race relations in Birmingham (Rex and Moore, 1967; Rex and Tomlinson, 1979). His position is much more sophisticated than that of the work mentioned above. Taking his starting point from Myrdal's (1969a, 1969b) important discussion of how American research on race relations tended to be based on certain taken-for-granted assumptions and untested hypotheses, Rex argues that similar biases can be found in much of the race relations literature in Britain. He notes, for example, the tendency in the literature to assume that various inadequacies in the culture or family life of West Indian and Asian immigrants are responsible for the social problems brought about by racism, unemployment, low wages, menial occupations, poor housing and bad schools. Whilst accepting, however, the reality of this tendency to blame the victim, he argues forcefully against the reduction of social science research on race to the demands of special interests, whether those of the policy-makers or those of the black communities or political activists themselves. Rex maintains that there is a need to defend academic enquiry that is more than a neutral study of the facts of racial disadvantage but does not fall into the trap of political rhetoric.

The sources of Rex's methodological position need to be understood in terms of the epistemological grounding of his sociology. Much of Rex's objection to the idea of politicised research is derived from what he views as the fundamental folly of Marxism and the superior explanatory power of Weberian sociology. His essential criticism of post-war Marxist thought is that it contains an a priori quality. His main objection to structural Marxism is the tendency to conflate cause and effect without rigorous testing:

> Such metaphysical speculation is interesting enough, but when it claims to have the validity of science, it often becomes little more than dogma.
>
> (Rex, 1979: 305)

Rex's way out of this trap is to adopt Weber's heuristic theoretical tool – the ideal type. The ideal type in Weber's metaphysics is necessarily a fiction. There are perhaps some interesting parallels here between this assertion and some of the more recent debates within postmodernism and anthropology (Clifford and Marcus, 1986). Thus theoretical constructs attempt to identify social relations that are essentially invisible. Rex provides the example of how class-based social relations cannot be observed as having an external quality, rather they remain a hidden guiding force that affects social action. Thus ideal types are necessary to characterise what is essentially encoded within the ebb and flow of social life. They are theoretical yardsticks against which social reality is measured and it is thus the quest of the sociologist to lessen the distance between ideal-typical formulations and empirical evidence. Rex suggests that this approach provides a 'salutary warning against the dangers of metaphysical dogmatism' (1979: 306).

Rex offers a typology of social thinking which divides science from ideology, utopia and myth. He attributes his enquiry to the status of scientific knowledge and designates other forms found within Marxism and radical black sociology as utopian. He is perhaps most damning when he identifies the explanations given by some of his informants as confined within the realm of myth. Writing on some of the explanations offered by black people in Handsworth, Birmingham, he states:

> These are manifest distortions and untruths which one can understand as part of the way in which the underclass is recruited and mobilised. It is unfortunate that the picture of the world which they create is one which is sometimes dignified with the name black radical sociology. In fact, a radical perspective on politics requires precisely the capacity amongst some political leaders to transcend myths like these and understand more objectively the structure and dynamics of their situation so as to be better able to control it.
>
> (Ibid.: 311)

Rex claims that by setting up theoretical yardsticks against which reality can be measured, an account of social reality can be offered which is superior to what he identifies as myth and utopia. Thus, in this context, political and moral choices are quite separate from sociological analysis. His position can be summed up in the following passage:

> It is all too common today for sociologists to assert that their sociology is critical, non-value-free or reflexive, and having done so to abandon any attempt to conform to the sorts of standards of reasoning and proof which are characteristic of scientific thought.
>
> (Ibid.: 314)

He concludes in his study of Handsworth:

> While we have tried already to make our own social position and perspective clear, we also believe our work should have some content. What we present here, we hope, is a self-consciously reflexive sociology of race relations in Birmingham.
>
> (Ibid.: 320)

From this perspective the role of social research is to assist in uncovering the social processes that have helped to structure the social and political meanings attached to the notions of race and ethnicity in particular historical contexts. This is at the heart of his opposition to approaches that do not maintain the autonomy of social researchers in the field (Rex, interview: 7 August 1990).

There have been a range of criticisms of Rex's position (CCCS 1982; Miles 1982) and on the ways research has been carried out in black communities (Bourne, 1980; Gilroy, 1980; Lawrence, 1981, 1982; Parmar, 1981; Phillips, 1983). However, we want to concentrate on a number of issues that relate directly to Rex's position. One clear problem is that while he maintains that his work is 'reflexive' there is little account of how his own research on Sparkbrook and Handsworth was actually conducted. There are only a few glimpses of the relationship between the researchers and their informants within these two influential studies. For example, although Rex and Tomlinson offer us a 'sociological' explanation of Handsworth's character which they see as superior to that of those who live within the 'mythic' world of common sense, they actually tell us little about their own interactions with the communities they researched. While Rex offers an eloquent defence of his own epistemology, there exist glaring absences in his empirical and theoretical writing that seem to us to limit the utility of his methodological approach.

In contrast to Rex, some recent studies on the politics of race have attempted to advocate more explicitly a direct relationship between research and political interventions. One important example of this is the speaking position advocated by Ben-Tovim *et al.* in their book *The Local Politics of Race* (1986). This is a study that can be seen as a radical departure from the perspectives outlined above. The authors argue for a mutual intertwining of research and political action. In this situation researchers should be activists and activists should be researchers and research should be placed in the forefront of political action. While there are absences and inconsistencies in their argument, this position has been very influential on the way research in this field has developed, including the way we framed our research in Birmingham.

*The Local Politics of Race* concentrates on how race policy has been developed and transformed in two localities, namely Wolverhampton and Liverpool. Its explicit aim is to consider the possibilities for action leading to the achievement of racial justice. Ben-Tovim *et al.* make it explicit that their research was focused primarily on voluntary and campaigning organisations outside the local state. This was partly a result of the resistance they encountered from local politicians and government officers. They comment:

> The problems we encountered with central and local government were in direct contrast to our experience of working in and with local organisations. In fact through our involvement in these organisations we found we were gaining a wealth of detail about how local government worked and didn't work. . . . The nature of our involvement entailed such activities as attending meetings to engage in debates about strategies and objectives; writing policy papers and using them for the discussion and lobbying; doing local research for the use of organisations and attending and organising conferences.
>
> (Ben-Tovim *et al.*, 1986: 3)

Thus they argue for an approach to research that is intimately involved with pressure group politics. They criticise two academic traditions within the analysis of racism, namely the sociology of race relations and academic Marxism. They argue that research needs to be consciously politicised and that to defend the 'value- free' stance is merely to defend the status quo:

> Widespread condemnation of racism and discrimination amongst academics sits uncomfortably alongside a commitment to objectivity in the production and use of research findings. . . . So long as it [a political stance] is not there, there will remain a fundamental incompatibility between an ethical stance condemning racism on the one hand and a commitment to objective or apolitical research on the other.
>
> (Ibid.: 5)

They also claim that academic Marxism has been equally guilty of absolving itself from political struggles. Thus critical writing on racism has gained itself a respectable academic niche where individual careers are advanced by hijacking a moral high ground. Marxism, like the sociology of race relations, takes a stance that is remote and not engaged with political struggles. Ben-Tovim *et al.* claim that both of these genres end up legitimising the very thing they set out to undermine:

> Race relations research which appears ostensibly committed to anti-racism or the elimination of racial discrimination but which is not explicitly designed to effect any change in those directions, effectively serves to maintain if not to

> endorse the status quo and sometimes. albeit unwittingly, to legitimise further inequalities.
>
> (Ibid.: 9)

Thus they are openly critical of the bulk of research in this field, which they see as largely unable to deal with the real dynamics of the politics of race. Their critique of much academic writing on race relations is valuable and we would go along with many of their sentiments. However, there are some important tensions within their speaking position and a good deal is left unsaid on the subject of exactly how their research was harnessed to political engagements and struggles.

One problem within the position advocated by Ben-Tovim *et al.* is that the authors end up with a stance that is closer to that of John Rex than they probably would care to admit. Like Rex, first, they give little account of the actual nature of field-work relations and how the research was conducted. Second, they end up by arguing that they are speaking from the perspective of a privileged narrative. What they do in effect is to swap John Rex's rhetoric of the superiority of sociological investigation for a form of radical credentialism that is justified by the researcher's participation in political struggles. Ultimately, the researchers set themselves up as advocates for oppressed groups because they maintain they are part of an alliance galvanised through political action.

This stance is tantamount to saying that the researcher can become a kind of representative of or spokesperson for the oppressed group. Our own doubts about this do not arise because we see ourselves as outside the political domain, or because we hold to some notion of value-free research, but rather they result from our uncertainty about the utility of reducing all the voices of oppressed groups and their allies to a single voice. Thus, while there is much value in critiques of race relations research and the call made by political activists for researchers to help change the current situation rather than just to study it, it is a huge step to take from accepting the need for committed research to saying that researchers can actually 'speak' for minorities.

Such an assumption is problematic on a number of grounds, not least because there is no way in which a researcher can assume that all minority communities have one voice or interest, or that it is possible to speak for such communities as though they could not speak or struggle for themselves. The plausibility of such radical credentialism does not stand up, particularly when we bear in mind the complex social and political histories of the various black communities in Britain. Thus, while we share the criticisms of politically disengaged scholarship expressed by Ben-Tovim *et al.*, we find their ultimate position – that of advocates – deeply problematic. In this sense the 'insiderism' that pervades their writing is open to question and can lead to both ethical and practical problems in the actual research environment.

## METHODOLOGY AND THE BIOGRAPHY OF THE RESEARCH

Bearing the above points in mind, we sought from the outset to avoid the trap of a speaking position that was either based on an uncritical disengaged scholarship or which could ultimately be reduced to a form of advocacy. We have preferred an approach that is concerned with understanding the ideologies and practices that have shaped the changing politics of race in Birmingham. Initially at least, we adopted a position which shifted the focus of analysis from the study of the powerless to an analysis of those who influenced and determined race policy and political outcomes in Birmingham. We set out to examine the processes that shaped racialised political identities and the role of white and black political actors involved in political action aimed at developing new forms of representation and involvement for minority communities.

It is important here also to point towards a key difference between the work of Rex and Ben-Tovim *et al.* and the approach that we have adopted in our study of the changing politics of race in Birmingham. Ben-Tovim *et al.*, for example, did not get access to the politicians, officers and bureaucrats within the local authorities they studied. In a sense, this meant that they could only focus on those groups who were mobilising for political change from the outside. In our own research in Birmingham we wanted specifically to gain access to those actors within the local state who were in positions of influence, to those political actors seeking to gain such positions and to black and white politicians who were in one way or another involved in the political process. Such access was not without its problems. For example, at the beginning of our research one of the key areas we wanted to explore was the impact of the growing number of black politicians on the political system. However, in approaching this issue we were concerned to locate the phenomenon of black councillors within the wider structures and processes of local politics within the city and the national politics of race. We were not only concerned to interview the seventeen black Labour councillors who were in office when we started the research; we also wanted to know how these politicians were positioned within patterns of political patronage. For this reason we decided to interview as many of the elected representatives as possible, drawing our sample from all political parties. This decision immediately meant that we had to deal with some important ethical and practical dilemmas inherent in our research.

In addition to targeting the councillors we also decided to interview the key council officials, ranging from those people working within the established race relations structures to chief officers for all the major departments that serviced the key committees within the council structure. We also decided that we would talk to as many people as possible who were active within mainstream and community politics. The intention here was to get an idea of how the Birmingham City Council was viewed from within the wider community. Given this range of objectives we inevitably had to confront rather different methodological dilemmas from those faced by researchers with more limited research agendas.

This is the context from which our original ideas about the research evolved. The bulk of the research on which we draw in the substantive chapters of this study was carried out during the period from 1989 to 1992, and it involved detailed explorations of the key dimensions of racial politics in Birmingham through archival research, qualitative interviews, regular discussions with key political actors and participant observation (see the description in Appendix 1). From the beginning the research involved dialogues and interactions with political activists, local politicians, council officers and community representatives. Many of these interactions took place with Les Back, who had previously conducted research with young people in South London focused mainly on the configurations of adolescent racism as part of his doctoral research. It is important here to understand that the dialogues and interactions that took place within the interview context were with a white male researcher. We are not suggesting that this is a fixed or simple identity. We do, however, think it is important to establish that this fact did have implications for the kind of field-work dilemmas we are going to talk about, as can be seen if we refer to some of the everyday ethical and political issues we confronted in the course of the research. We consistently sought to get access to a wide variety of political actors and to discuss their views in both formal and informal contexts. Gaining access to the primary sample of politicians and local government officers was complex and our experience of contacting each of these groups varied. Generally, city councillors and political activists were easy to contact and open about discussing these issues. We simply wrote to the individual councillors and then contacted them on the telephone to set up interviews. This meant that it was relatively easy to interview a considerable proportion of local politicians, sometimes a number of times. This did not mean that there were no problems in conducting interviews with local politicians. On the contrary, we faced a number of important ethical and practical dilemmas, as we shall discuss later on.

Initially at least, we confronted a different set of problems in conducting interviews with officers working for the Council. The response of local government officers was very different. We wrote to all the appropriate council officers in the authority, including chief officers, asking if they would participate in our research. We wrote to close to one hundred people in the authority. A small proportion of those people contacted wrote back and agreed to participate in the research. These included officers from the Education Department, Social Services, Urban Renewal and Housing. However, a large number of our letters were redirected to the Race Relations Unit. This in itself seemed to indicate that many departments saw the whole area of racial equality as outside their remit. We received a letter from the head of the Unit, which said:

> We are somewhat surprised at the 'blitz' of correspondence from you to the City Council over this issue [the research] when you could have just written one letter to the authority as a corporate entity. My colleagues have referred your letters to me and have indicated that it would be appropriate for me to respond to your request on their behalf to give a corporate view.
>
> (Personal communication, 13 March 1991)

As a result we met the head of the Unit, and we found out at this meeting that the chief officers in the authority had asked him to vet our research. They had informed him that he should get a list of names of the people to whom we wanted to speak and establish some way of finding out who had been responsible for any comments on the authority that might appear in print. We said at the meeting that we would be unwilling to give a list of names because we did not want to jeopardise the confidentiality of those people who spoke to us. The irony of the situation was that we were actually conducting interviews while these negotiations were taking place. A number of people had agreed to meet us after the first round of letters. So we decided that we would ask to see the chief officers and contact other people in the authority through informal networks. We then gave the head of the Unit a list of the chief officers that we felt we needed to interview for our research.

We were also told at this meeting that our requests had arrived at a crucial time. The structure of the local authority was under review. Up until this point the Race Relations Unit had fallen under the remit of the Personnel Department in the City Council. Many claimed that the work of the Unit was being blocked by senior officers in Personnel. The head of the Unit was accused of soliciting our research as a way of placing more pressure on the authority to change his line manager. There was, of course, no relationship at all between the timing of our request and the shifts occurring within the authority. The salient point is that in order to gain access to people within the authority we had to adopt a combination of overt and covert strategies.

An important issue to stress here is that many of the people who saw us 'unofficially' at various stages of our research were in practice placed in a vulnerable position. We felt this was particularly acute when it came to black officers within the authority. The reason for this was because there were simply fewer black people in senior officer positions within the authority and, as a result, they were identifiable by deduction. In this situation we tried to make available transcripts of our interviews, so that people in particularly vulnerable positions would have some control over how their sentiments were used in our texts. On one occasion a black officer phoned us after receiving a transcript and said:

> I don't want to deny any of the things that you have written down – that is the truth as far as I can see it. But if you were to print that my bosses could easily figure out that it was me that said that. It could easily jeopardise my job here.

We gave this person assurances that we would show them copies of our work for approval. The reply this person gave was telling:

> That's fine. You see we have to be careful, there are a lot of people ready to jump on the race band wagon. They get their five minutes of glory and the rest of us have to suffer with the consequences in our working lives.

This raises questions about the whole basis of our speaking position, i.e. the desire to study the powerful. While we may be scrutinising the practices of powerful white people, it is ridiculous to defend a position that implicitly suggests that this has no impact on black people. The structures of local government are not exclusively white domains. In this setting it is vital to speak with black people within these structures, but this raises important ethical dilemmas about how to protect the identity of officers who may already feel that they are in a marginal and vulnerable position.

Thus, for researchers to speak rhetorically about their mission to study white racism and institutions contains a subtle sleight of hand. While superficially this seems more credible, other important issues emerge. On one occasion Les Back offered an account of our 'studying the powerful speaking position' to a long-established black activist. He reminded Les that to do so would be comparable to studying slavery by speaking only to the slave masters. It was at this point context that the rhetoric of our position broke down. We simply could not conduct this research by focusing only on white people with influence, since this would ignore the important role of black politicians and activists within the political system. This in turn highlighted the issues of what kinds of relationship we had with the black people who contributed to our research and whether those people had advance warning and information about how their sentiments were going to be used. In practice this was not a problem we found easy to resolve and, as we shall show at various points in the course of the book, this had a profound effect on the conduct of our research and our position in the context of specific political disputes.

There is another issue that remains hidden in the speaking position we adhered to at the beginning of our research. This relates to the whole question of the interactional politics of interviewing. We do not view the accounts generated in interviews as inert information-gathering occasions but as interactional samples produced through a dialogue with a white male interviewer. Thus, we built into each account an interrogation of each statement as a product of particular social circumstances. We maintain, therefore, that the analysis of interviews should be a closely reflexive endeavour. However, issues were raised through doing the research that we did not account for or anticipate.

This leads us to another dimension that has been much discussed among researchers both in Britain and the United States. This is the question of the ability of white and black researchers to understand and empathise with black experiences of racism. An influential line of argument is that white researchers cannot fully comprehend the experiential consequences of racism. It has to be remembered, however, that in a research context such as ours this is only part of the story. While the experiential argument may be true at a certain level, it is also the case that white researchers in the course of their work do experience the transmission of racist ideas and formulae. This is an important distinction in research within political contexts. For example, a question that was often raised in the course of our research was: What does one do in situations where racist ideas are communicated to the researcher? To say nothing in response to them may be seen to imply the legitimisation of these ideas through silence (Back, 1992). This particular dilemma was experienced by Les Back in numerous contexts. Often assertions would be offered to him with the expectation that there would be agreement. On one particular occasion a Conservative politician asked Les Back what he felt about what the politician had been saying. There was an awkward silence, eventually broken by the councillor, who said: 'Well, I guess you are not the one being interviewed, are you?' Thus we found that in the interview context the identity of the interviewer was also being constructed by the interviewee. Repeatedly it was assumed that Les Back's whiteness would mean that he would agree with assertions that were often informed by racism. What exactly does the researcher do in this situation? Les Back often felt dishonest and unethical for not confronting these comments, yet on occasions where disagreement was voiced, this so radically transformed the interactional context in which the interview was taking place that the interview could not continue.

It became apparent that maintaining 'racial' symmetry in the interview setting (i.e. a white researcher interviewing other whites) in no way meant that the political issues over research in this area were resolved. Far from it; a whole series of other issues were raised, including whether or not a consistent ethical position could be sustained for all the people who participated in the study regardless of their position within racialised politics.

The point that we want to emphasise here is that our own ethical stance with regard to access to findings and accountability was profoundly ambivalent. While, on the one hand, we promised accountability to all the people we interviewed, eventually we had to make decisions as to how much access we would allow our participants to the research material and our findings. These decisions were made on both ethical and political grounds. There was pressure on us to explain how we would use interview material and what measures we would take to protect those of our contacts who were in vulnerable positions. This applied in particular to many of our black contacts, to whom we felt obliged to show transcripts of interviews for their comments. This was not something we could offer to all the politicians, officers and activists who we interviewed. Thus, we can quite rightly be accused in this setting of not adhering to a uniform ethical standpoint. Rather, we were making strategic judgements as to the relative need for open access to our research, judgements that were linked to a shifting political terrain.

One of the features of the debate on ethical questions and the study of racism is that it has focused on the principles of research at an abstract level. There are very few discussions that transcend the statement of 'a position' and discuss frankly the tangible dilemmas that researchers in this field have raised (Keith, 1992). We hope that what follows will offer something of a departure from the rhetoric of establishing the 'correct credentials', in that we attempt to make clear throughout our own starting point and the problems and dilemmas that we have sought to come to terms with.

## STRUCTURE OF THE BOOK

This book is organised in chapters that cover key aspects of our concerns in a thematic manner. Chapter 1 outlines the main conceptual arguments that lie at the heart of our understanding of the changing forms of racial politics in the present political environment. It explores recent theoretical debates about the evolution of the key concepts of race and racism in contemporary social theory. In recent years there has been a phenomenal growth in research and writing on theoretical perspectives in this field, covering diverse academic disciplines and taking in a range of paradigms. This chapter attempts to provide an overview of this complex range of questions and to outline the framework we have sought to develop from our own research. Chapter 2 then moves on to examine the complexities of the interplay between race, politics and social change. It seeks to show that the political construction of racial identities needs to be seen against the background of social and political changes and the role they play in shaping racialised politics in specific contexts.

The rest of the book concentrates more explicitly on an account of the development of new debates and forms of political mobilisations around questions of race and ethnicity in the context of Birmingham. Chapter 3 explores the dynamics of the relationship between political mobilisation and processes of racial formation. This links the theoretical issues touched upon in the previous chapter to the more specific concerns of this study, and it allows us to provide a tentative account of the key issues that will be addressed in the rest of the book. Chapter 4 examines the impact of the new politics of race on political parties and processes of representation and participation. This is an area that has received little attention, despite the important role that racialised political debates and mobilisations play in influencing both local and national processes. Chapter 5 continues the analysis of the previous chapter by exploring in greater depth the articulation of political discourse about race. There is a tendency in much of the literature to assume that racial discourses are monolithic and unchanging. In this chapter we seek to challenge this assumption through an exploration of the transformations in the political discourse of Labour and Conservative politicians about racial and related issues.

Chapter 6 pursues a theme that has been little analysed in the bulk of the existing literature in this field, namely the growth of new forms of minority politics and their impact on the political system. It looks at the constructions of new forms of black politics during the past two decades that have been brought about by the notable growth in the number of black political representatives and increased pressures for greater access to political power.

Chapter 7 takes up the question of the impact of the trends analysed in previous chapters on the development of policy initiatives about equal opportunities and anti-racism. This is an area in which there has been much debate in recent years, particularly in relation to the limits of current policies and the contradictions that are inherent in the ideologies of multiculturalism and anti-racism. Here we explore the political environment of policy change and the impact of new forms of political involvement on the evolution of local political interventions.

Finally, Chapter 8 concludes the book by looking at prospects for the future. In particular, we explore the new politics of race and ethnicity which has emerged out of the trends outlined in the rest of the book and the possibilities this has for the development of new identities and new forms of political representation. Our hope is that in exploring these issues we shall be able to shed some light on the options that confront us and on possible routes towards developing an agenda for change.

# 1 Theoretical and conceptual issues

One of the most thorny problems in theorising about race and ethnicity is the question of how political identities are shaped and constructed through the meanings attributed to race, ethnicity and nation. This is partly because the question of how to conceptualise the interplay between race and political action is not purely an academic matter. It is connected with a wider political culture in any given historical conjuncture. Any book concerned with the politics of race and social change must come to terms with the highly politicised nature of this field and the problems that this gives rise to in developing a theory of the interrelationship between race, politics and society. It is perhaps not surprising, therefore, that we have seen a growing interest in this question in recent years at the same time as we have seen important changes in forms of political mobilisation among minorities in British society.

This growth of interest in the study of the politics of race has helped to clarify some questions, but others remain to be addressed. Take, for example, the following, seemingly simple, questions: What explains the role of race in political mobilisations and conflicts in contemporary advanced industrial societies? How does political agency connect with social structure in shaping what is popularly called the politics of race? These questions are also at the heart of the main theoretical debates about the changing politics of race and ethnicity which have developed in recent years. Such debates have focused particularly on how we can understand the relationship between race, politics and social change in the present environment. Yet despite some progress in clarifying issues raised by these questions, we still (i) lack a clear analytic framework for analysing the interrelationship between race, politics and social change, and (ii) know relatively little about key features of contemporary racialised politics.

This is why before moving on to developing our own account of the politics of race and social change it is important that we at least provide an outline of the theoretical framework we have used in dealing with these questions. This is what the rest of this chapter attempts to do. It begins by looking at some of the main bodies of work that have addressed this issue in the past two decades. It then moves on to recent criticisms of these perspectives and explores some of the gaps to be found in the dominant paradigms in this field. This links up with the analysis of Chapter 2, which outlines more explicitly our own analytic framework and the key issues that will be explored in the rest of the book.

## RACE, POLITICS AND SOCIETY

Theorising about questions of race, ethnicity and nationhood has become a key concern of social theorists in recent years. Whereas critical theorists in the early 1980s were bemoaning the lack of analytical clarity about what constituted the politics of race or what was meant by the notion of racism in contemporary societies, today there is a wealth of theoretical and conceptual work going on in this field. This has taken various forms. First, there have been various attempts to construct theoretical models for explaining the increasing role of race as a symbol for political mobilisation, the role of racial ideologies in national and local agendas, and the impact of ideas about race on the development of government policies and programmes. This has led to the emergence of various schools of thought and there have been many valuable research studies produced in recent years. We shall be exploring some of the key approaches in the course of this chapter. Second, in recent years there has been a growing interest in the roles that race and ethnicity play in the affirmation of a politics of identity in advanced industrial societies. Stimulated to some extent by the growing literature on the condition of post-modernity, a number of writers have sought to go beyond the limits of existing theories in this field and explore the complex ways in which identities articulated in terms of race and ethnicity are expressed in contemporary social relations. This has led to important interventions from researchers working in the fields of cultural studies, literary theory and political theory.

In the midst of this growth of interest in the politics of race it is also clear that crucial theoretical and conceptual issues have remained untheorised and, perhaps most importantly, under-researched. Certainly, when we undertook this research we found relatively little previous material to guide us in our attempts to give some conceptual and analytical substance to our stated concern to study the politics of race and social change in Birmingham. Although in some of our previous work we had looked at the question of how to conceptualise the issue of racialised forms of political action and their changing expression in contemporary Britain (Solomos, 1988, 1993), we felt there was a need to develop a theoretically grounded analysis of the everyday processes through which race and ethnicity have become an integral part of political life. What little research there was we found to be both rather dated and lacking a strong theoretical framework. This situation is partly the result of (i) the abstract and generalised nature of many of the theoretical debates that have developed in recent years, and (ii) the lack of theoretically informed research on the dynamics of racialised politics in the contemporary period. Both of these points may seem surprising, at first sight, particularly when we take into account the highly politicised nature of research on race and ethnic issues in recent years. But these are not surprising when we take into account that much of the research on the politics of race in British society is relatively recent and has been concerned with either local case studies or very specific studies of policy formation and the impact of policies on 'racial' issues.

This picture changed somewhat when we broadened our search and took on board the wide range of research on race and politics in the United States of America. Here we found a wealth of research on key issues that tied up with our own concerns, in particular, urban politics and race, the role of minority politicians, race and public policy, and the dynamics of racialised politics. In this sense we found the American literature more relevant to our own concerns, although we were conscious that the issues and processes it addressed were in some sense specific to the political institutions and culture of American society and could not therefore be seen as directly relevant to the situation in Britain or other European societies. The earlier development of American research in this field can partly be explained by the impact of black and Hispanic politicians on political institutions in the United States since the mid-1960s (Marable, 1985). During the past three decades there has been a rapid growth in the number of elected black officials at all levels of American political life, leading to what some commentators have called a 'new black politics'. Additionally, in recent years politicians such as Jesse Jackson have sought to use this growth of minority representation as one of the means of building a 'rainbow coalition' of various excluded groups in order to challenge the established political order.

It is in the context of this growth of a vibrant minority political culture that we have seen over the past two decades the development of an extensive body of research on black and minority political mobilisation in the United States. Much of this research has been concerned with two key issues. First, the growth of black political empowerment in the aftermath of the civil rights movement and the urban uprisings of the 1960s. Second, the emergence of new forms of black and minority political mobilisation in the United States, particularly during the 1980s and 1990s. Both of these trends have led to wide-ranging research on the dynamics of black and minority political mobilisations, the role of alliances in changing the relative powerlessness of minority communities and the growth and role of black political elites.

An influential American study that links up with some of our own concerns is that by Browning, Marshall and Tabb (1984) entitled *Protest is Not Enough*, which examines the politics of Hispanic and black mobilisation in ten northern Californian cities. The authors' aim was to develop a 'conception of minority political action and position that linked mobilisation to policy, that demonstrates the connection between the passions, interests and actions of mobilisation and the government response – if any'. Browning *et al.* (1984) suggest a simple sequence of political activity: mobilisation – incorporation – responsiveness. They identify two kinds of mobilisation: demand-led protest and electoral. Their model is concerned with the outcome of and response to political mobilisation. It is this perspective that is directly relevant to the Birmingham research. Their conclusion is provocative:

> The key to higher levels of responsiveness was not representation but coalition: minority inclusion in a coalition that was able to dominate a city council

> produced a much more positive government response than the election of minority council members who were not part of the dominant coalition.
>
> (Browning, Marshall and Tabb, 1986: 576)

They also point out that white support for minority incorporation was not a matter of benign altruism because the existence of these coalitions depended on the support of black and Hispanic politicians. The attraction of this model is that it focuses on the political system as a whole, rather than narrowly focusing on the activities of minority politicians. The responsibility for change is placed squarely within the political system itself. It also captures the dynamic nature of the political process where any advance may be subject to what they refer to as 'roll backs' (Browning, Marshall and Tabb, 1984: 262–263).

There are of course problems in applying the American experience to Britain. Perhaps the most important of these is the ideological character of party politics and individual parties' preoccupation with discouraging caucusing along sectional interests. This is evident in the response of the Labour Party in the late 1980s to the black sections movement in the party. In this sense the pluralist model which is found within the American situation cannot simply be applied. Nevertheless, there are elements of the account given by Browning, Marshall and Tabb for American cities that link up with the transformations which we have seen over the past two decades in both national and local politics in British society. This is something that we shall return to in the course of the substantive discussion of political mobilisation in this study. Before doing so, however, it is necessary to look at some of the key themes to be found in research on race and politics in Britain.

## RACE AND POLITICS IN BRITAIN

It is clear that from the 1950s onwards political processes and institutions have played a key role in the construction of racial and ethnic questions in British society. Research at both the national and local political level has highlighted the changing political strategies and ideologies that have helped to shape policies on issues such as housing, employment, education, policing and equal opportunities. This research has shown clearly that over the years political and ideological processes have played a very important role in the construction of popular images of minorities and in shaping the development of particular types of policy intervention. What has also become clear in recent years, however, is that minority groups are themselves playing an active role within national and local political institutions. This phenomenon has certainly become important at the level of local politics, with the election of a sizeable number of black local councillors over the past decade. But it is also becoming increasingly important within the context of national party politics and within Parliament (Solomos and Back, 1991b).

What is surprising at first sight, however, is that there have been few attempts to produce detailed accounts of the processes that may help to explain these changes. Our own awareness of the need for a fuller theorisation of these issues is related to our experience of attempting to develop a conceptual framework to research the relation between race, politics and social change. One of the starting points of this research was the hypothesis that race is first and foremost a political construct. From this starting point we wanted to locate the racialisation of politics within processes of social regulation and identity formation, within specific political cultures and discourses and within wider processes of social and economic change. In the course of our research, however, it became clear that ideas about race and ethnicity manifest themselves in plural and complex forms within political institutions. In this context, unitary or simplistic notions about race and political action become hard to sustain.

Yet it is clear that within the main strands of literature in this field little attempt has been made to develop a theoretical discussion of the processes through which ideas about race gain political salience and have an impact on patterns of political mobilisation. Most studies have been largely descriptive and atheoretical – they have not sought in any meaningful sense to provide a theoretical framework for the analysis of race and political action. This has resulted in a number of useful descriptive accounts of the role of race in electoral politics, the impact of racialised agendas on public policy and case studies of specific events or cities. But within this body of work the political processes involved in the making of racial politics have received little or no attention, either from a theoretical or empirical perspective. Indeed, it is surprising to see how little research has explored in any detail the contemporary dynamics of racial politics. This has resulted in serious lacunae in the analysis of racial politics in contemporary British society. More significantly, little attention has been paid either to forms of political and social mobilisation among minorities or to the responses of political institutions to minority struggles for empowerment.

## RACE, COMMUNITY AND CONFLICT

There are some exceptions to this general trend. For example, the work of John Rex, to whom we have already referred in the Introduction, can be seen as an attempt to develop a political sociology of racial relations in British society. Rex and his associates have from the 1960s onwards attempted to analyse the politics of race in a systematic fashion. The empirical focus of Rex's research has been on Birmingham and for this reason it is of direct relevance to our own work. But it is also important because it represents an early attempt to develop a conceptual framework for the analysis of the politics of race in contemporary Britain. Rex's starting point in his early work was that the position of ethnic minority communities must be understood primarily in terms of their status as migrants. Rex combined a Weberian notion of class analysis with elements of the urban sociology developed by the Chicago School and what he has termed in his later work a 'loose Marxism' (Rex, 1989). He attempted to provide a sociologically based explanation for racial discrimination and conflict by identifying inequalities in 'market situations' which fuel conflicts between indigenous workers and newcomer populations (Rex, 1973: 32).

This approach was exemplified in his early work with Robert Moore in Sparkbrook, an inner city area of Birmingham. In this study they analysed the way in which differential access to housing provision created a hierarchy of class situations in the Weberian sense (Rex and Moore, 1967). These classes provided a basis for conflict between actors located in different market situations which were comparable to those that occur in the workplace (Rex and Moore, 1967: 273; Rex, 1968, 1973). The existence of exclusive allocation practices within council housing provision discriminated against newcomer populations. In addition, migrants were positioned in varying locations within this housing class system, e.g. 'Pakistani landlords' occupied a 'pariah position' in a different housing class to those who lodged with them, who were predominantly 'West Indian' (Rex and Moore, 1967: 165). Running alongside this process of housing discrimination was the development of 'immigrant colonies'. The development of such colonies was a response to the 'anomie' and 'personal demoralisation' which migrants were subjected to in the city. It is in this context that community and immigrant organisation took on political meanings (Rex and Moore, 1967: 277).

In a later study Rex refers to the political work that took place in (i) organisations within immigrant 'colonies' and (ii) the development of organisations which acted for housing class interests (Rex, 1973: 4). He argues that it is through such forms of political mobilisation that minority communities attempted, in the period after their arrival in Britain, to establish their social and economic position, as well as to ensure a degree of access to political institutions.

In the study conducted by Rex and Tomlinson in Handsworth during the mid-1970s this type of analysis was further developed to take account of the changing social and political situation (Rex and Tomlinson, 1979). The basic research problem of this study was structured by the objective of researching the extent to which immigrant populations shared the class position of their white neighbours and white workers in general. The substance of the analysis outlined a class structure in which white workers had been granted certain rights which had been won through the working-class movement and the Labour Party. The result was, argued Rex and Tomlinson, that by the 1970s a situation of 'class truce' developed between white workers and the dominant social groups. Basing their analysis on Marshall's account of the welfare state, in which the salience of a shared citizenship outweighed the political importance of class as a source of political action (Marshall, 1950), they argued that the development of welfare state institutions provided an important mechanism for shaping political mobilisation within the working class.

For Rex and Tomlinson the position of migrant workers and their communities was one where they were located outside this process of negotiation that had taken place between white workers and capital. They experienced discrimination in all the areas where the white workers had made significant gains, i.e. employment, education, housing. It followed from this that the position of migrant workers placed them outside the working class, in the position of an underclass:

> The concept of underclass was intended to suggest . . . that the minorities were

> systematically at a disadvantage compared with their white peers and that, instead of identifying with working class culture, community and politics, they formed their own organisations and became effectively a separate underprivileged class.
>
> (Rex and Tomlinson, 1979: 275)

From this point Rex and Tomlinson developed a model of political action and even a political agenda for black populations as they become a 'class for themselves' (Rex, 1990). This highlighted the ways in which immigrant minorities are forced into a series of reactive or defensive political strategies in order to deal with their exclusion from full citizenship in all the key economic and social arenas.

Drawing on their research in Handsworth, Rex and Tomlinson argued that this process of political mobilisation was likely to take on different forms within Asian and West Indian communities. Within Asian communities it resulted in a concentration on capital accumulation and social mobility. In the West Indian community it took the form of withdrawal from competition altogether, with an emphasis on the construction of a black identity. This all led to what Rex refers to elsewhere as the 'politics of defensive confrontation' (Rex, 1979). Rex and Tomlinson identified a number of tiers in the political process in which minority politics operated. First, there were government-sponsored paternalistic agencies, such as the Community Relations Councils. In many ways this tier of political involvement acted as a buffer which kept the issue of race outside the mainstream political arenas. Second, there existed community-led projects based in specific localities. These organisations were aimed explicitly at promoting 'racial harmony'. Third, there existed numerous self-help organisations which developed within the minority communities themselves. Amongst West Indians this took the form of independent black political action, black cultural development and identity groups. Within Asian communities there existed the various Indian Workers' Associations, kinship-based organisations and elite negotiations with the host society (Rex and Tomlinson, 1979: 240–274).

It was on the basis of this model that Rex and Tomlinson claimed in their study of Handsworth in the mid-1970s that West Indian political action was not in the main channelled through the Labour Party, although their normative class position as workers led them to give electoral support to the Labour Party and become members of trade unions. They also claimed that the community politics in operation within self-help groups was not articulated within mainstream politics of the left. Labour's relationship to Asian communities was characterised in a very different way. Here the labour movement as a whole, and kinship, played a more important role in meeting the needs of Asians in all areas of community life. This resulted in a situation where Asian community organisations were engaged in constant negotiations with the host society, with Labour politics and left politics in general (Rex and Tomlinson, 1979: 250).

The notion that ethnic minority communities form distinct classes which exhibit distinct political interests has informed all of Rex's later theoretical work

(Rex, 1986a, 1986b, 1988). This is perhaps his most interesting contribution, for in this idea of separate class interests there exists a model of political action which reflects the class structure of metropolitan urban systems. Interestingly enough, Rex uses the Weberian notion of ideal types to describe forms of minority political structure and action (Rex, 1970). He defends this methodology as a way of 'defining concepts, of refining them in the course of historical studies, of arguing about them, and then applying them again as yardsticks against which reality can be measured' (Rex, 1979: 306).

One of the key problems of his work, however, which a number of critics have highlighted, is that in the process of constructing a series of ideal types Rex runs dangerously close to reiterating stereotypical statements about the culture and history and organisation of migrant groups. One of the great weaknesses of Rex's sociology of race relations is that he refers to minority communities as if they possessed unitary cultures which have some kind of informing spirit that is sociologically and even politically meaningful. In this sense Rex reproduces an essentially idealist view of culture which is at worst stereotypical and at best a part-truth. His paradigm in no way addresses the material and historical specificity of cultural production (Hall and Jefferson, 1976; Gilroy, 1987). Culture for him becomes an explanatory concept in itself, and not in relation to political and economic conditions. There exists a tension in Rex's work between this kind of culturalism and his utilisation of a Weberian conceptual framework which locates relationships between ethnic groups and social structures in sets of class and market situations.

What is perhaps more surprising is that with regard to minority politics Rex's work includes little in the way of detailed analysis of specific political activity and involvement of minority politicians and communities. Rather, what we find is a series of sociological frameworks where specific movements and incidents are either dealt with briefly or remain unexplored. While many of Rex's formulations can be criticised as being both narrow and somewhat stereotypical (Lawrence, 1981; Gilroy, 1982), there are a number of useful insights in his analysis of minority politics and culture. Perhaps the most useful ideal type that comes from his sociology is the hypothesis that migrant workers and their children occupy a distinct class position within British society that will ultimately lead to distinct forms of political engagement. This framework at least allows for the possibility of new and autonomous forms of minority political mobilisation.

The main weakness of Rex's analysis, however, is that it tells us little about the development of new forms of political engagement since the mid-1970s. Rather, he seems to think that his analysis of the situation in Handsworth in the early 1970s is an adequate model for the present situation. As we shall attempt to show, however, it is important to retain some analytical flexibility in order to comprehend the rapidly changing political cultures within political institutions and minority communities.

## RACE, CLASS AND POLITICS

If the question of the class basis of black political action is at the heart of Rex's model of minority political action, it has also been a key concern in political writings that can be referred to as falling broadly within neo-Marxist and post-Marxist thinking. Although there are clear differences of approach in terms of defining what is meant by 'class analysis', the relationship between class formation and racial formation has been an important concern of both Rex and Marxist writers working on these issues. A case in point is the work of Robert Miles, which represents perhaps the most consistent attempt to develop a class analysis of racialised politics. Miles has consistently opposed the notion that race is a useful analytical category, preferring what he sees as a Marxist analytical framework in which racism is viewed as integral to the process of capital accumulation (Miles, 1982, 1989). For Miles, the idea of race refers to a human construct, an ideology with regulatory power within society:

> The influence of racism and exclusionary practices is always a component of a wider structure of class disadvantage and exclusion.
>
> (Miles, 1989: 9)

Within this framework race constitutes an idea that should be seen as having no analytical value as such. It is here that Miles diverges from Rex's approach. While Rex is concerned with models of social action (i.e. for Rex it is enough that race is utilised in everyday discourse as a basis for social action), Miles is concerned with the analytical and objective status of race as a basis of action (Miles, 1982: 42). While Miles would agree that the struggle against racism is a vital political issue confronting contemporary societies, he argues that race in itself is not a scientifically valid medium for political action. Race is an ideological effect, a mask which hides 'real' socio-economic relationships (Miles, 1984). Thus the forms of class consciousness which are legitimate for Miles must ultimately be seen in terms of class relations, which are hidden within the regulatory process of racialisation. A good example of the way this framework is applied to empirical situations is the study by Miles and Phizacklea (1984) of 'working-class racism', where they argue that black and white workers share significant political commonalities within specific class locations. Using this framework the political usages of race as a mechanism for political mobilisation only makes sense within an analysis of the class and ideological relations that shape the meaning of notions of race in specific societies. To signify this process of the social construction of the category of race within specific social relations Miles uses the concept of racialisation.

For Miles, processes of racialisation are intertwined with the material conditions of migrant workers and other racialised groups. Its effects are the result of the contradiction between 'on the one hand the need of the capitalist world economy for the mobility of human beings, and on the other, the drawing of territorial boundaries and the construction of citizenship as a legal category which sets boundaries for human mobility' (Miles, 1988: 438). Within the British setting this ideological work is conducted primarily by the state and acts as a means of crisis management (Hall *et al.*, 1978; CCCS, 1982; Miles and Phizacklea, 1984). From this perspective Miles argues that the construction of political identities which utilise 'racial' consciousness play no part in the development of a 'progressive politics'. In this sense he views black political movements as ultimately operating on false premises, and he disputes the analytic value of talking about the politics of race.

Interestingly enough, there exists a paradox in Miles's thinking with regard to the kinds of political mobilisation in which black and migrant workers have participated. On the one hand he applauds the participation of black workers in the labour movement, while at the same time he is cynical of the political fruits of the labour movement, i.e. the Labour Party and the trade unions. This is particularly apparent in his appraisal of the election of black Labour MPs to the House of Commons (Miles, 1988: 456). It seems that all current forms of political participation are viewed as reformist, regressive and ultimately untenable. For Miles it appears that any form of political incorporation results in a form of co-option that merely legitimises the British social formation and capitalist democracy. There is a sense in which Miles seems to be striving for a theoretically defensible form of political action. However, it could be argued that his concentration on the illusory and repressive nature of racial ideology ultimately leads to a situation where all forms of action are dissolved into class-based terms of reference (Gilroy, 1987: 25).

Miles's work has been a major influence in contemporary debates about race and racism, and the limits of political strategies based on race. But it says surprisingly little about the issue of how we can explain the development of political action and mobilisation within migrant communities which is based on ideas about racial and ethnic identity. A key argument that could be derived from his analysis is that black and minority politics are really distillations of class conflict. If this is true, any movement away from class-based political action (i.e. movements towards black community politics) is doomed to failure (Miles, 1988, 1989). If one takes this argument further, class-based political action is ultimately in opposition to any sort of sustained political organisation around a notion of race. This is largely because for Miles the politics of race is narrowly confined to the struggle against racism. This is neatly captured in the way he reformulates Hall's famous statement on the relationship between class and race (Hall, 1980: 341). Reversing Hall's argument, Miles concludes that it is not race but 'racism [which] can be the modality in which class is "lived" and "fought through"' (Miles, 1988: 447).

## DYNAMICS OF RACIAL FORMATION

Another major influence in recent debates about the politics of race can be traced to the work of authors who have at one time or other been associated with the Birmingham Centre for Contemporary Cultural Studies (CCCS). This research was stimulated in many ways by the publication of Hall's programmatic essay on

'Race, articulation and societies structured in dominance' (1980). Hall's most important argument was that while racism cannot be reduced to other social relations, neither can it be explained autonomously from them. Thus, racism commands a relative autonomy from economic, political and other social relations. Taking as their theoretical starting point Hall's rather abstract and programmatic argument, a number of attempts were made by writers associated with the CCCS to re-theorise the significance of the nature of racism within British society (CCCS, 1982; Gilroy, 1987; Solomos, 1993). The works of these writers explored the changing political dynamics of race in the environment of the 1980s by focusing on the emergence and impact of new discourses and political agendas about race.

While Hall essentially initiated a reconceptualisation of race within Marxist theory at CCCS, this position achieved a more developed expression in the work of the Race and Politics Group, resulting in the publication of *The Empire Strikes Back* (CCCS, 1982). This volume initiated a fierce controversy when it was first published and it still occupies a controversial position in the history of studies of race in British society. It sought to use Hall's theoretical insights to analyse race and politics in British society, but it can be seen as differing from his work in two significant ways. First, it placed a greater emphasis on the role of authoritarian state racism, especially in managing a British social formation that was undergoing a period of crisis. Second, the degree of autonomy given to race from class social relations was reworked (Solomos *et al.*, 1982; Gilroy, 1982). It is this second development which is most significant with regard to the study of political action and social change. It is also the key area where the approach of these writers can be seen as differing from the analytic framework about the relationship between race and class proposed by Miles among others.

A key theme of *The Empire Strikes Back* is that the working class in Britain does not constitute a continuous historical subject; and that black communities can constitute themselves as a politically conscious 'racially demarcated class fraction'. It is in this sense that class cannot always be assumed to be the primary political force in any specific conjuncture. Thus, black communities can act as autonomous political forces in specific situations where their interests are threatened or attacked.

In recent years this kind of approach to the analysis of the role of racial politics has become more influential. Significant analytical frameworks which have foregrounded a political analysis of race are to be found in the work of British writers such as Paul Gilroy and Michael Keith and American writers such as Michael Omi, Howard Winant and David Goldberg. Although all of these writers can be seen as starting out from within a neo-Marxist or post-Marxist analytical framework, their works also engage with other approaches emanating from post-structuralism and post-modernism. Without wanting to ignore the obvious differences between these writers, it can fairly be said that their work reflects (i) an uneasiness with the limits of the Marxist model represented by Miles and other researchers, and (ii) a concern to investigate the mechanisms through which race is constructed through social, cultural and ideological processes.

Gilroy has developed this line of analysis further in *There Ain't No Black in the Union Jack*, where he moves more clearly towards a perspective which he calls race formation (Gilroy, 1987). Rejecting the various analytical arguments associated with a neo-Marxist analysis of race and class, Gilroy emphasises the need to conceive of race as the key aspect of the black experience in British society. In developing this argument he rejects any argument that prioritises class over race in the analysis of political change. He argues forcefully:

> The proletariat of yesterday, classically conceived or otherwise, now has rather more to lose than its chains. The real gains which it has made have been achieved at the cost of a deep-seated accommodation with capital and the political institutions of corporatism.
>
> (Gilroy, 1987: 246)

There is, perhaps surprisingly, a great deal of similarity between Gilroy's notion of the relationship between class and race and Rex's theoretical conclusions (Rex and Tomlinson, 1979; Rex, 1988). Both authors argue that the continuous historical project of working-class struggle has been fractured, leaving a number of classes or class/race fractions involved in specific struggles. Equally, Gilroy and Rex both emphasise that their formulations are models of social action. It is essential to both positions that the significance of race is located within the salience that this term of reference has developed in the world of political actors.

It is here that Gilroy utilises the concept of race formation, a notion he shares with the analysis of Omi and Winant (1986) in the United States. The notion of race formation emphasises above all that race is not simply a concept that can be dispensed with. Gilroy, for example, accepts that the meaning of race as a social construction is contested and fought over. In this sense he is suggesting something close to a Gramscian position on ideology whereby race is viewed as an open political construction where the political meaning of terms like 'black' are struggled over. He makes the case for the existence of an inclusive black community in which political identities are formulated that address numerous but linked everyday struggles against racism (Gilroy, 1987: 38). It is this political possession of race by actors that leads to a social movement located around notions of racial identity:

> Collective identities spoken through 'race', community and locality are, for all their spontaneity, powerful means to co-ordinate action and create solidarity.
>
> (Gilroy, 1987: 247)

Gilroy, like a number of other authors working in this field, utilises the literature on social movements (Touraine, 1981; Castells, 1983; Melucci, 1989) to provide theoretical support for an interpretation of 'non class-motivated' political action. Gilroy argues that it is in this context that both black community politics in general and the black sections movement within the Labour Party take on a political meaning of their own outside of specific class locations (Gilroy, 1993b).

Along with Gilroy, a number of other researchers have sought to develop an analytical model to simultaneously incorporate a number of political engagements without necessarily having to attempt to qualify these sites of struggle in terms of a class reductionism. Within this model of political action a multiplicity of political identities can be held. For example, an inclusive notion of black identity can prevail and at the same time allow heterogeneity of national and cultural origins within this constituency (Hall, 1991a; Rattansi, 1992; Brah, 1993). Omi and Winant's analysis of the United States provides a good example of this kind of approach to the question of political mobilisation. Taking as their starting point the changing politics of race in the period since the 1960s they argue for the need to see processes of racial formation as the outcome of the unique social, cultural and political processes that have characterised the United States over the past three decades (Omi and Winant, 1986). In this sense their model of the United States' experience ties up quite closely with a key strand in the theoretical literature on the politics of racialised mobilisation in Britain and other European societies.

While these accounts of racial formation are at one level perceptive and contain important theoretical insights into the politics of race, there are some serious omissions. The most important of these are (i) that there is no substantive analysis of the impact of black and minority participation in the political system, and (ii) there is little analysis of the transformation of political discourses about race. Such conceptual and theoretical discussions have provided an important contribution to the debate on political agency and race, but they have shed little light on processes of minority mobilisation within political institutions. Gilroy, for example, is ambivalent about the possibility of applying the notion of race formation to the electoral arena and party politics. On the question of establishing alliances within the Labour Party and promoting greater black representation he points out:

> The campaign to secure parliamentary places for black MPs and for the development of 'black sections' inside the Labour Party has been one of the very few voices holding the idea of Afro-Asian unity although in their case, the political basis for this alliance remains vague.
>
> (Gilroy, 1987: 40)

Two questions come to mind: Why is the political basis for alliances of this nature vague? Would it be impossible to conceive of electoral politics connecting with the kinds of politics of race and community that is identified by Gilroy and other writers? Neither of these questions can be adequately dealt with on the basis of abstracted assumptions. Given the important changes in the forms of black and ethnic minority political involvement over the past decade, it is of some importance to address these questions on the basis of research in the context of everyday political situations.

As yet we have seen little of this kind of research, and this has meant that we know surprisingly little about the new forms of black and ethnic minority political mobilisation. Additionally, it is important to note that little research has been done on the everyday processes of political change and conflict within political institutions. Key questions about the role of party politics, claims to representation, pressures on the policy agenda, and the role of black and minority politicians remain largely unexplored. Whatever the merits of attempts to question the limits of class-based models of the politics of race, it has to be said that as yet they have not provided a rounded analysis of the complex ways in which racialised political identities have been constructed and reconstructed in recent years. It is also interesting to note that all the approaches we have discussed say very little about the whole issue of democratic politics and the role of minorities in party politics. Indeed, it is clear that writers as diverse as Rex, Hall, Miles and Gilroy hold little hope that an oppositional politics can be developed within the arena of representative democracy, and they therefore say very little about what is perhaps the key aspect of new forms of black political involvement in British society over the past decade.

Gilroy, for example, views pressure group strategies which have evolved out of community struggles that utilise a specifically black political vernacular as the way forward. Along with Miles, he has reservations about the possibility of political participation within the institutions of the labour movement. In particular, he questions the degree to which the Labour Party can effect a defensible strategy on racial equality. He has also developed important critiques of the anti-racist initiatives that were implemented during the 1980s within local government agencies (Gilroy, 1993b). But arguments such as this leave a number of questions unanswered. For example: How have racialised political identities been shaped by political ideologies and party politics? What explains the emergence of minority politicians within mainstream party politics? What impact have mobilisations such as the Black Sections movement had on the political agenda? To what extent can political institutions in societies such as Britain be described as multicultural?

It is precisely these questions that we have sought to address in our research in order to construct an account of the role of political discourses and institutions in the formation of the racialised politics that characterises contemporary British society. This book seeks above all to explore the changing political languages about race and politics, and the mobilisations and shifting involvements that characterise the contemporary period. In so doing we are also providing a basis for rethinking and moving the rather limited research agendas that we have evaluated above.

## SUMMARY AND CONCLUSION

The discussion in this chapter has touched on some aspects of the complex sets of issues that need to be thought through in developing a theoretical framework for the analysis of the changing politics of race and ethnicity. Its main theme has been that the frameworks developed to analyse race and political action have important limitations. We are suggesting that the theoretical engagements of these frameworks cannot adequately conceptualise the political transformations and debates about race and politics which have taken place in recent years and which are likely to proceed apace during the 1990s. The political struggles that underscored the debates of the 1970s and 1980s have moved on. In many ways the turn towards the conceptualisation of culturally defined racisms and the politics of identity has been led by political events which have shaped the political environment since the late 1980s. In particular, the continuing hegemony of the Conservative right in Britain has challenged theorists to reappraise the usefulness of many of the conceptions of politics they have worked with in the past. This is perhaps best exemplified by the debate over the 'new times' thesis, which suggests that a range of sites for social antagonism and resistance exist within contemporary Britain cannot be conceptualised within a conventional class analysis (Hall and Jacques, 1989; Sivanandan, 1990a). Equally, in the context of the complex forms of identity politics, the semantics of race cannot be confined to the politics of regulation (Miles, 1989). The controversy over the publication of Salman Rushdie's book *The Satanic Verses* (1989) has provided a warning that the politics of culture cannot easily be appreciated within the conceptual language of class in any narrow sense. In this situation there is a need to rethink our research agendas to meet the challenges we are likely to face over the next decade in analysing the changing politics of race and racism.

This is what the rest of this volume aims to do through a combination of engagement with theoretical debates and an analysis of the changing terms of political mobilisation around race and ethnicity. This is by no means an easy task, but we believe that it is essential for any analysis of the contemporary politics of race and ethnicity to come to terms with the everyday processes and practices which help to give some meaning to ideas which articulate a politics of race. This necessitates an analysis which can take on board the need to locate the complex set of relations that go to make up our understanding of ideas about race, politics and social change.

# 2 Race, politics and social change

In exploring the theoretical paradigms that have influenced much of the contemporary debate about the politics of race we have so far not dealt with one of the key questions that has bedevilled much of the recent research in this field. Namely: How does the anatomy of contemporary racism link up to the changing dynamics of political, social and economic relations? Although much of the literature in this area touches on the issue in one way or another it remains one of the most difficult issues to deal with, and it is perhaps not surprising that contemporary theories of race and ethnicity have failed to address it fully from either a conceptual or an empirical point of view. Indeed there is surprisingly little discussion in much of the literature on the politics of race and racism about the linkages between racial exclusion and the changing morphology of urban social and economic change.

It is to this set of issues that we now turn, specifically in the context of addressing some of the questions that link our theoretical concerns to the analysis of national and localised processes of racial formation and mobilisation. We begin by exploring some of the key conceptual issues and how they tie in with the concern we have in analysing the changing politics of race, culture and identity in contemporary British society. In particular we want to explore some of the key problems which are raised by any attempt to theorise the complex variety of socio-political processes that go to make up the morphology of contemporary forms of racialised politics. We then move on to introduce some of the underlying questions about the interrelationship between localities and the formation of political identities that we shall analyse from a more empirical perspective in the following chapters. This leads us into a dialogue with the attempts to theorise racism within the context of the construction of particular spatial and historically specific political identities.

## CONCEPTUALISING SOCIAL AND POLITICAL CHANGE

The interrelationship between the changing politics of race and wider processes of social, economic and cultural change was one of our main concerns when we embarked on this research. By exploring the changing morphology of political debates and conflicts about the politics of race in one specific urban context we hoped that we could go beyond the rather generalised and abstract attempts to deal with the ways in which ideas about race and ethnicity gain specific meanings in the context of particular national and local political cultures, and provide an account which took seriously the complexities of racialised processes on the ground (Goldberg, 1993; Keith, 1993). Additionally, we sought to take up some of the questions raised by debates about the emergence of complex and ambiguous forms of racial/ethnic identities in the present political environment. The key questions that interested us then, as now, were: How do racial and ethnic identities interact with wider processes of racialisation and social change? Are there localised political processes that help to shape the development of racialised identities?

Before moving on to these issues, however, it is important to say something about how we conceptualise the interrelationship between race and social and political change. There are two general points that are worth making at this stage. The first is that if we conceive of racialisation as a process, we need to understand the complex ways in which racial relations are likely to be affected by the underlying processes of social, economic and cultural change in advanced capitalist societies. This is a point that has been emphasised in the work of radical geographers, who have begun to explore the ways in which the restructuring of labour markets and regional economic spaces reproduces new forms of incorporation and division along racial and gender-specific lines (Smith, 1989; Soja, 1989; Harvey, 1989).

On a broader plane other research has argued that the transformation of social and cultural relations in contemporary Britain and other capitalist societies has helped to produce a new politics of race and ethnicity. This politics is characterised by ambiguity and uncertainty, in the sense that the fixed identities developed in earlier times have broken down and been replaced by fluidity and change (Rutherford, 1990; Hall, 1991b). It involves a process of questioning the fixed boundaries established by the political discourses about race during the 1970s and 1980s. From this perspective the post-modern condition has had an important impact on the ways in which ideas about racial and ethnic identity are being articulated in advanced capitalist societies.

The second point to make is that in the present environment of fundamental restructuring of economic, social and political relations, racial and national symbols can take on specific forms within particular spatial and historical contexts. The wholesale reorganisation of regions, localities and nations has, if anything, helped to strengthen mythological claims about the national culture and the threats it faces. It is not surprising in this overall environment that the quest for definite boundaries for the nation coincides with fears about 'threats' to national identity from within and without (Keith and Pile, 1993). David Goldberg encapsulates the importance of space and time in the formation of racial symbols when he argues:

> Race has fashioned and continues to mould personal and social identity, the bounds of who one is and can be, of where one chooses to be or is placed, what

> social and private spaces one can and dare not enter or penetrate. Race inscribes and circumscribes the experiences of space and time, of geography and history, just as race itself acquires its specificity in terms of space–time correlates.
>
> (Goldberg, 1993: 206)

From this perspective, race and ethnicity are experienced and negotiated in specific spatial/historical contexts and it is difficult to generalise that there is one common perspective which characterises all societies or all localities and regions in a particular society. Ideas about race and the meanings attached to it can enter particular social contexts in complex forms, and this makes it impossible to conceptualise discourses about race and identity as monolithic and unchangeable.

This line of analysis has also been pursued in his recent work by Paul Gilroy (Gilroy, 1993a, 1993b). Whilst the specific objects of Gilroy's analysis are somewhat different from our own concerns, ranging from the social history of what he calls the 'Black Atlantic' to the changing morphologies of black cultures in contemporary Britain, his account of the dynamics of racialised ideas and languages has the merit of emphasising the flexible and constantly changing character of black political identities. Rather than assuming that there are fixed and historically unchanging cultural and political meanings which can be derived from notions of race and ethnicity, he argues that we can only understand how meanings are actually constructed if we focus on specific socio-historical situations. Gilroy argues forcefully that we have to see the modern history of race and racism as the product of the complex historical processes involving contact with and theorising about the 'other' which have been at work from the very beginnings of modernity (Gilroy, 1993a: 313–323).

There is much of value in the argument that we have to highlight the spatial and contextual boundaries within which particular ideas about race and ethnicity develop and take on social meaning. When faced with the need to analyse how ideas about race are worked through in political discourses and in political mobilisation, however, it is clear that there are major analytical problems in applying such a conceptual framework to the analysis of racism as it appears within specific socio-historical situations. George Mosse's analysis of the history of European racism illustrates some of the problems in an instructive fashion. Mosse's work can be seen in its broadest terms as a historical narrative of the complex variety of processes of identity construction that have helped to shape racism over the past two centuries (Mosse, 1985). Taking as his starting point the origins of racial thought from the eighteenth century onwards, he shows, in a masterful survey of European societies, that there has always been a linkage between racial ideas and politics and the wider social and economic transformations of modern industrial societies. For Mosse a key aspect of racist thought was a reaction 'against social, economic, and political conditions' combined with a refusal 'to use these conditions to explain the world' (Mosse, 1985: xxvii). In a very real sense, therefore, the 'power' of racism as a mobilising force can best be understood in the context of social and economic transformation, and the political and ideological uncertainty about how to respond to the challenges posed by the formation of new patterns of social and economic organisation. Moreover:

> Racist myths not only explained the past and brought hope for the future, but through their emphasis on stereotypes rendered the abstract concrete.
>
> (1985: 233)

It follows from this line of argument that at least part of the reason for the growth of racist ideologies is that they are able to offer a clear and simple explanation for the problems of the modern world and that they articulate fears of change through a rejection of existing social and economic relations in favour of types of social and political organisation which emphasise the need to protect the interests of the 'nation' and 'people' against other interests. Mosse's own work provides a powerful reminder of the ways in which Nazi theories of race and culture were able to utilise such ideas as 'racial purity' and 'national origin' as symbols of a political movement and later as the ideological underpinnings for the construction of a racial state.

Although it is unwise to draw direct comparisons with more recent trends, it seems clear that along with the transformation of social and economic relations that is characteristic of contemporary capitalist societies, we are seeing the emergence of new processes of racialisation in a number of European societies (Wrench and Solomos, 1993). Many of the racist and nationalist movements that have begun to have some impact on the political culture of countries such as France, Germany and Belgium have shown how powerful myths of race and nation are in the present environment of political uncertainty and social change. These processes have taken different forms within the specific national political traditions of countries such as France and Germany. But it is clear at the same time that in each national context there are a variety of socio-political and economic factors that have helped to shape a new politics of racism.

Michel Wieviorka, writing about the situation in France, sees the development of social movements which articulate openly xenophobic political arguments and engage in direct action against migrants and refugees as but one example of a much wider process that is evident in a number of societies. He argues that the growth of such movements is partly explained by (i) the decline of the traditional working-class movement as a key social actor, and (ii) the transformation of class relations more generally in advanced capitalist societies as a result of economic and social change (Wieviorka, 1993). How these changes are experienced is of course determined partly by economic and social relations in particular regions and localities. More importantly from the perspective of writers such as Wieviorka, the rise of new racist movements is influenced to a large extent by the decline of traditional working-class culture and the institutions that it helped to engender.

Studies of the situation in other European societies have highlighted similar trends. This is particularly the case in Germany, where the social and economic costs of reunification provide the immediate backdrop against which the resurgence of racist and nationalist movements is often seen. No doubt there are other factors that have led to the resurgence of racism as a political force, but it is important to bear in mind the role of social and economic changes in shaping current debates about race and ethnicity.

## IDENTITY, POLITICS AND CULTURE

Another important issue that has been widely discussed in recent years is the role that race and ethnicity play in the context of the global politics of culture and identity (Hall, 1991a). We have seen, for example, a growing concern with the status of cultural forms and a return to an analysis of the nature of ethnicity in metropolitan settings. The political naivety of the early work on ethnicity meant that for much of the 1980s the analysis of cultural processes and forms was rejected in favour of a focus on the politics of racism. The rejection of 'culture' was tied up with the notion that the culturalist perspective of the 1970s did little more than blame the victims of racism (Lawrence, 1982). However, the questions of cultural production and the politics of identity are fast becoming important areas for contemporary debate. New perspectives are being developed which examine the ways in which cultural forms are being made and remade, producing complex social phenomena (Hall, 1988; Hewitt, 1991). These new syncretic cultures are being plotted within the global networks of the African and South Asian diaspora (Gilroy, 1987, 1993a; Bhachu, 1991).

The process of reclaiming culture in critical debate has simultaneously involved a re-examination of how racism is conceptualised. These contributions engage in one way or another with the arguments of post-structuralism and post-modernism and they point to the need to avoid uniform and homogeneous conceptualisations of racism. Although not yet part of the agenda of mainstream research on race relations, a range of studies of racialised discourses in the mass media, literature, art and other cultural forms has begun to be produced. Reacting against what they see as the lack of an account of cultural forms of racial discourse, a number of writers have sought to develop a more rounded picture of contemporary racial imagery by looking at the role of literature, the popular media and other cultural forms in representing changing images of race and ethnicity (Gates, 1986, 1992; Dyson, 1993).

As David Goldberg has pointed out, the presumption of a single monolithic racism is being displaced by a mapping of the multifarious historical formulations of racism (Goldberg, 1990, 1993). In this context it is perhaps not surprising that a key concern of many recent texts in this field is to explore the interconnections between race and nationhood, patriotism and nationalism rather than analyse ideas about biological inferiority. The ascendancy of the political right in Britain during the 1980s prompted commentators to identify a new period in the history of English racism. The 'new racism', or what Fanon (1967) referred to as 'cultural racism', has its origins in the social and political crisis afflicting Britain (Barker, 1981; Gilroy, 1993b). Its focus is the defence of the mythic 'British/English way of life' in the face of attack from enemies both outside ('Argies', 'Frogs', 'Krauts', 'Iraqis') and within ('black communities', 'Muslim fundamentalists'). Gilroy points to an alarming consequence of the new racism where blackness and Englishness are reproduced as mutually exclusive categories (Gilroy, 1987: 55–56).

The emphasis on the new cultural racism points to the urgency of comprehending racism and notions of race as changing and historically situated within particular spatial contexts. This is exemplified by Goldberg's argument that it is necessary to define race conceptually by looking at what this term signifies at different times (Goldberg, 1992, 1993). From this perspective the question of whether race is an ontologically valid concept or otherwise is too limiting a way of looking at this issue, since what is necessary is a critical interrogation of the ideological quality of racialised subjectivities. The writings on new racism shows how contemporary manifestations of race are coded in a language which aims to circumvent accusations of racism. In the case of 'new racism' it is quite common for race to be coded as culture. However, the central feature of these processes is that the qualities of social groups are fixed, made natural, confined within a pseudo-biologically defined culturalism (Barker, 1981; Balibar, 1991). What is clear from these writings is that a range of discourses on social differentiation may have a metonymic relationship to racism. The semantics of race are produced by a complex set of interdiscursive processes where the language of culture and nation invokes a hidden racial narrative. The defining feature of this process is the way in which it naturalises social formations in terms of a racial/cultural logic of belonging.

With the widening of theoretical concerns has come a literature which looks at the aesthetic elements of the culture of racism. This is an area which has been neglected within the discussions of race and social theory in the field of race relations. Equally, with a number of notable exceptions (Cohen, 1988a, 1988b, 1991; Cohen and Bains, 1988) the emerging discipline of cultural studies has also been curiously silent on the issue of how to understand the cultural dynamics of racism. There is an important intellectual and theoretical project in interrogating the historical, cultural, literary and philosophical roots of ideologies of race (Gilroy, 1993a).

In recent years it has been widely recognised that questions of cultural production and change must be integrated within contemporary conceptualisations of racism. In our own work we have suggested that these theoretical debates need to be contextualised within a shifting political context (Solomos and Back, 1995). The certainties of the critique of the race relations problematic are no longer tenable. What seems to characterise the contemporary period is, on the one hand, a complex spectrum of racisms and, on the other, the fragmentation of the definition blackness as a political identity in favour of a resurgence of ethnicism and cultural differentiation. At the same time, and perhaps paradoxically, new cultures and ethnicities are emerging in the context of dialogue and producing a kaleidoscope of cultural syncretisms.

The importance of hybridity and social change in shaping racialised identities in the United States has been shown by the findings of a number of researchers in recent years. According to Cornel West, for example, the history of race in the US exemplifies the fact that 'blackness is a political and ethical construct' (West, 1993: 26). West's own analysis of the politics of race in contemporary American society is instructive for the way it shows that key aspects of social and political life have been inextricably racialised. Using the examples of debates about poverty and social policy, crime and policing and of affirmative action, he shows how in many urban localities 'race', or various coded references to it, has become a way of explaining complex social issues as well as a defining aspect of public policy.

What arguments such as this point to is the need for racist discourses and practices to be rigorously contextualised. This means that racisms need to be situated within specific social and economic situations. The effect of a particular racist discourse needs to be placed in the context of the conditions surrounding the moment of its enunciation. This means irrevocably crossing the analysis of racism with other social relations surrounding gender and sexuality or the culture of institutional politics. The meanings of race and racism need to be located within particular fields of discourse and articulated to the social relations found within that context. It is then necessary to see what kinds of racialised identities are being formed within these contexts.

We are suggesting a model for conceptualising racisms that is (i) sensitive to local and contextual manifestations of racist discourse, and (ii) able to connect local manifestations with wider or national public discourses. As yet, the theoretical work on racism has produced accounts of racism that derive contemporary forms of racism from public political discourse. This evidence is then used to generalise about broad trends within British society. Such an approach has produced some interesting studies, but it does not provide a rounded framework for the analysis of the changing dynamics of racism. The analysis of contemporary racisms needs to be situated within particular discursive contexts. Racism cannot be reduced to class relations, but neither can it be seen as completely autonomous from wider social relations such as gender and sexuality. There is a need, as we shall argue in the substantive chapters of this volume, for a rigorous analysis of the semantics of race and the elaboration of racisms.

## CLASS, RACE AND ETHNICITY

As we pointed out above, a recurring theme in much radical writing in this field is the interplay between race and class. Whilst in recent years there has been much criticism of class reductionism and economic determinism, this has not resolved the complex question of what, if any, relationship can be established between racial inequalities and wider patterns of class inequality. For some, the answer to this question is relatively straightforward. Miles, for example, as we saw above, argues forcefully that 'the influence of racism and exclusionary practices is always a component part of a wider structure of class disadvantage and exclusion' (Miles, 1989: 9). But even writers who have been at the forefront of attempts to produce a more rounded and complex analysis of racialised politics have found this a difficult question to deal with. Gilroy expresses some of this uncertainty when he argues:

> Discussion of racial domination cannot therefore be falsely separated from wider considerations of social sovereignty such as the conflict between men and women, the antagonism between capital and labour, or the manner in which modes of production develop and combine.
>
> (Gilroy, 1990: 264)

Similar analytical arguments can be found in the works of many writers who have been attempting in recent years to develop a critical theoretical framework for the analysis of patterns of racial domination in a variety of socio-historical settings. What is important to note, however, is that little attempt has been made to use such concepts to provide a grounded empirical analysis of specific social and political processes. This is part of the problem we faced in embarking on the research that we discuss in this book. Whilst we found an abundance of theoretical reflections on the issue of the politics of race and ethnicity, we found little guidance when we embarked on our empirical research in Birmingham.

Similar lacunae can be found in the extensive literature on the changing politics of race in the United States. Omi and Winant, in their analysis of the politics of race in the period since the end of slavery in the USA, have argued that processes of racial formation are intrinsically tied to wider patterns of social, economic and political change. Taking as their point of departure the historical and contemporary significance of race in American politics and in the key social and economic institutions, they argue:

> The state is inherently racial. Far from intervening in racial conflicts, the state is itself increasingly the pre-eminent site of racial conflict . . . . Every state institution is a racial institution, but not every institution operates in the same way. In fact, the various state institutions do not serve one co-ordinated racial objective; they may work at cross-purposes. Therefore, race must be understood as occupying varying degrees of centrality in different state institutions and at different historical moments.
>
> (Omi and Winant, 1986: 76–77)

Such arguments have been made in a number of other theoretical contributions to the analysis of the politics of racism. The key implication of these accounts is that the history of racialised relations in the United States has to be contextualised against the background of the development of specific social and political ideas about race, the development of political institutions and the emergence of forms of resistance to racism. This is the main concern that underlies the wealth of accounts that look at the changing morphology of racial and ethnic politics in the United States in the period since the 1960s.

Whatever the merit of theoretical propositions such as these, the difficulty has been that they have not been used systematically to inform historical and empirical analysis of particular racial situations. There have been some *ad hoc* attempts to do this, but they have been both partial and based on limited research on the dynamics of racism across historical and spatial boundaries. Whilst not diminishing the importance of these studies, the relative absence of empirical analysis has left a major gap in existing writings on this subject. Without analysing the interaction between racist structures and other social structures in capitalist societies it becomes difficult to explain how certain types of racialised ideologies and inequalities develop and help to shape the fundamental institutions of a society.

In his account of the interplay between racism and other social relations in capitalist societies, Stuart Hall argues:

> At the economic level, it is clear that race must be given its distinctive and 'relatively autonomous' effectivity, as a distinctive feature. This does not mean that the economic is sufficient to found an explanation of how these relations concretely function. One needs to know how different racial and ethnic groups were inserted historically, and the relations which have tended to erode and transform, or to preserve these distinctions through time – not simply as residues and traces of previous modes, but as active structuring principles of the present society. Racial categories alone will not provide or explain these.
>
> (Hall, 1980: 339)

Hall's approach runs counter to those approaches which assume that there is a harmonious articulation between racism and capitalist social relations. His emphasis on the ways in which racial and ethnic groups are incorporated historically in different societies, and how their position changes over time suggests that the relation between racism and wider social relations should be seen as historically and spatially variable and contradictory.

But such broad generalisations need to be tested out and analysed in accounts of processes of racialisation in particular historical situations. In order to develop a dynamic framework which can help us understand the historical and contemporary intersection between racism and politics in specific societies there is a need for an analytical framework that focuses attention on the processes that lead to the politicisation of racial and ethnic issues. Yet there is no attempt in Hall's work to go beyond general theoretical propositions by analysing the development of racism in particular situations. This failure to integrate theory with detailed historical and political analysis is to be found in much of the literature on racism.

This separation between theoretical analysis and political analysis needs to be overcome if we are to understand the history and present forms of racialised politics in British society. There is a need to move away from a notion of racialisation that is uniform across different historical formations or even particular societies. The paradox of attempts to construct a uniform conception of racism is that they seem to lose the ability to explain the dynamics of change and conflict. In so doing they fail to analyse the processes which lead to the racialisation of social relations in particular societies. This is a point made in an interesting manner by Hall in his exposition of the 'new ethnicities' thesis and its implications for how we analyse the transformative nature of racialised social relations. According to Hall:

> The central issues of race always appear historically in articulation, in a formation, with other categories and divisions and are constantly crossed and recrossed by the categories of class, of gender, and ethnicity.
>
> (Hall, 1988: 28)

On its own, however, this type of argument means little. It may be heuristically useful in thinking through some of the issues we have touched upon above, but the question of how social relations of class, gender and ethnicity interact in everyday social processes and in institutions cannot be adequately analysed without a detailed account of everyday processes both nationally and locally.

## LOCALITIES AND RACIAL POLITICS

One of the issues we have already touched on is the variety of ways in which discourses about race are contextualised and situated within specific localities. This is also a point which is at the heart of much recent writing on the role of race in the construction of images of cities and localities. For example Goldberg argues with some prescience that:

> Racisms become institutionally normalised in and through spatial configuration, just as social space is made to seem natural, a given, by being conceived and defined in racial terms.
>
> (Goldberg, 1993: 185)

In other words, notions of race and ethnicity intertwine with myths of territory, locality, neighbourhood and identity to produce mythologies about the role of spatially defined 'others'. Examples of how such processes work themselves out in particular historical contexts abound (Keith and Pile, 1993). The situation in contemporary urban America is a case in point. In this context 'race' is perhaps the key symbol through which questions about a wide array of issues, ranging from crime and drugs to the 'underclass', are discussed in both popular and official discourses. Another interesting example is the ways in which fascist ideologies in the earlier part of this century utilised notions of territory and space to define the 'otherness' of the Jews in relation to the *Volk*, and to argue that in the context of the 'crisis of modernity' there was a need to assert the importance of 'rootedness' and 'belonging'.

Part of our main concern here is to use our detailed study of the formation of racialised politics in Birmingham as a means of exploring in greater depth what role local political cultures and traditions play in the processes which shape the everyday understandings of race and ethnicity with which political actors work. This is a question which in some ways can only be addressed if we use a rigorously contextual approach, as we have attempted to do in our own research, but our findings address questions which are of direct relevance within a broader national and international context. By concentrating much of our discussion on an account of political debates and processes in Birmingham, we hope to gain the depth which many accounts of contemporary racial politics lack, without losing sight of wider processes and trends. Our picture of the situation in Birmingham may or may not be applicable to other cities and towns, but we believe that recent trends in a variety of localities highlight the ways in which, as social dislocation and political uncertainty take root in contemporary Britain, 'race is a privileged metaphor through which the confused text of the city is rendered comprehensible' (Keith and Cross, 1993: 9).

The furore which has arisen over the impact of neo-fascist movements in the local politics of parts of the East End of London and elsewhere is perhaps the most public example of the ways in which race can become an important variable in local political cultures. Yet it is also clear that the politicisation of race goes much deeper than the activities of openly racist political parties and movements. The impact of the election of Derek Beackon as a local councillor for the British National Party in the Millwall ward in Tower Hamlets in September 1993 is a case in point. The media response to his election tended to focus on the rise of support for the BNP and on the everyday experience of racial attacks in the locality. If one looked somewhat deeper into the history of political discourses about race in the area, however, it was clear that all the main political parties had become involved in one way or another in the complex politics of 'race' and 'place' for some time before the intervention of the BNP (Keith, 1994).

Such phenomena are important, and have a practical impact on the everyday lives of communities living in such localities, but we should not lose sight of the other equally important forms of social and political mobilisations which go into constructing relations of political participation and representation in the urban environment. This particularly important in the case of race and ethnicity, since it is in terms of space–time correlates that race acquires its specificity

This is well illustrated by the changing contours of contemporary racial politics in Britain. These have been shaped not simply by national political agendas and policies, but by how questions about race and ethnicity have been constructed and reconstructed in specific urban localities. In this context it is not at all surprising that one commentator describes contemporary London as a place 'where, by virtue of local factors like the informality of racial segregation, the configuration of class relations and the contingency of linguistic convergences, global phenomena such as anti-colonial and emancipationist political formations are still being sustained, reproduced and amplified' (Gilroy, 1991: 15–16). It is within this context of complex, and changing, sets of social relations that we need to locate and analyse the dynamics of racial politics.

## SUMMARY AND CONCLUSION

We have tried in this chapter to discuss some of the complexities we face in analysing the interrelationship between race, politics and social change. We have sought to show that many of the crucial features of contemporary racial and class politics cannot be fully understood without reference to the local and spatial context. Studies in both Britain and the United States have emphasised the massive impact of changes in the political economies, populations and spatial organisation of urban localities. What is notable about this literature, however, from the perspective of this book is that, in Britain at least, we have seen few detailed studies of the everyday politics of racialisation and the formation of new racialised political identities. There are signs that the increasing awareness of gender and other non-class-specific forms of social categorisation is resulting in an increasing interest in the local processes of racial categorisation and exclusion. But these developments are still at a relatively early stage, and it is true to say that the study of racist practices and ideas as they impact on specific spatial and local contexts remains sadly neglected.

This is why in the rest of this study our own focus will be on the political and social trends which have fashioned political debates and mobilisations around the meaning of race and ethnicity. Drawing on archival and ethnographic research we provide both an analytical framework that seeks to go beyond the limits of existing theoretical approaches and a detailed account of the changing racialised political discourses and practices that have emerged in the present conjuncture.

# 3 Power, racism and political mobilisation

In the first two chapters we have examined some of the key conceptual and analytical questions that lie at the heart of this study. We now want to move on in this chapter to the historical background and context of the politics of race and social change in Birmingham. In particular we want to deal with two sets of questions: What were the dynamics of political mobilisation and processes of racial formation during the early stages of migration and settlement? How have processes of racialisation intertwined with actual historical processes in shaping everyday political processes? These questions take us back to the theoretical and conceptual dilemmas that we touched upon in Chapters 1 and 2, but in the context of this chapter we want to move on and explore the ways in which processes of racialisation operated in the context of the specific political and cultural situation to be found in Birmingham during the period from the 1950s onwards. This will in turn link up with the analysis of more contemporary trends in subsequent chapters.

In dealing with these questions it will not be possible, of course, to leave out wider national dynamics and processes. In this sense, although our focus will be on Birmingham we shall at certain points have to broaden our frame of reference in order to situate the processes we are looking at within the broader framework of the changing dynamics of race and racism in British society as a whole. It needs to be said, however, that developments in Birmingham and its surrounding areas played a key role in the politics of race from a very early stage. Birmingham is, after all, the largest local government unit in the country, serving a population in excess of one million, and it was a centre of migrant settlement from the earliest stages of post-war migration from the colonies. It is no exaggeration to say that throughout the post-1945 period Birmingham has played a key role in political debates about race relations issues.

## POLITICS, IMMIGRATION AND RACE

Throughout the 1960s and 1970s the very mention of 'Birmingham' came to symbolise the changing politics of immigration and race in British society. But how did this situation come about? What were the central issues that led to the politicisation of questions about race and immigration during the period from the

1960s onwards? It is to these issues that we now turn. From the very earliest stages of post-1945 immigration to Britain a clear picture emerges of a complex intermeshing between local and national processes in the racialisation of political debates and conflicts. In other words, immigration and race became controversial issues within both the national and local political systems.

Seen from this perspective the situation in Birmingham was thus part of a much broader process. 'Immigration', the 'colour problem' and 'race' were never political issues that were played out at the national level, since from the very beginning they became questions of public debate within local political institutions and resulted in wide-ranging debates about the changing 'character' of particular localities and the impact of immigration on housing, employment, education and social services. Bearing in mind the arguments outlined in Chapter 2, it is important to emphasise that debates about 'immigration' and 'race' did not take place in a vacuum. In cities such as Birmingham the period after 1945 it was a situation of important social change in areas such as housing, education and welfare. Political institutions at both local and central government levels played an important role in the shaping of policy agendas about these issues, and in the articulation of programmes of reform and reorganisation. And it was into this broader context that debates about immigration and race were introduced in the aftermath of the arrival of sizeable migrant communities from the colonies or ex-colonies in the period after 1945.

Recent research on the period of the 1940s and 1950s has highlighted the complexity of political debates about immigration and race within British society in the post-war conjuncture (Harris, 1991; James and Harris, 1993). According to earlier common-sense perceptions this was a period in which there was little official or public debate about immigration and racial issues. It is argued that it was only later, from the late 1950s onwards, that these issues became increasingly politicised and led to controversy about such issues as immigration policy and race relations policy. Yet, it has become more evident as a result of recent research that successive national governments saw immigration from the ex-colonies as problematic from a political and social perspective, however welcome it may have been from an economic point of view. Indeed, it is clear that successive governments were seriously considering measures to either regulate or to stop immigration from the colonies from the early 1950s onwards. Such measures were not necessarily articulated on the basis of controlling 'coloured' or 'black' immigration, though despite the use of coded language the sources of fears about the social and cultural consequences of immigration were intrinsically about the issue of 'race'.

If one shifts focus to the situation in the key urban conurbations in which migrants settled it is clear that immigration became an issue that preoccupied not only the local press but local Labour and Conservative Parties, voluntary organisations, the churches and other bodies. In urban localities up and down the country 'immigration' and 'race' became issues of public concern from the earliest stages of the migration process. The situation in Birmingham and its environs is a case in point. Reports on key aspects of what was variously called the 'colour problem' or the 'race problem' can be found in the local press and in local political documents dating back to the early 1950s. The consequences of this concern were complex, and led to a number of proposals about what measures were necessary in order to respond to the growing number of immigrants arriving in Birmingham during this period. Some of these proposals were concerned with specific social issues, such as housing and employment, while others were about the broader issue of how to ensure the 'integration' of migrants into the mainstream of society. For example, as early as 1950 the Archdeacon of Birmingham, the Venerable S. Harvie Clark, helped to set up the Birmingham Co-ordinating Committee for Coloured People, consisting of representatives from religious organisations, voluntary organisations, the Colonial Office and concerned individuals. The Committee played an active role in various measures which were aimed at considering 'what action could be taken to help the coloured people in the City in dealing with their problems' (BCC, General Purposes Committee, 15 June 1954).

The Committee continued to exist under a variety of names for almost two decades, and it served as a forum for public debate as well as a means of responding to the changing political debates about race and immigration. It functioned as a special kind of what Ira Katznelson refers to as a 'buffer organisation' between migrant communities and political institutions (1976: 175). Its philosophy represented a combination of paternalistic attitudes towards minorities and a commitment to the provision of welfare services for them. In general it sought to (i) increase awareness of the specific needs of migrant communities, and (ii) educate the majority of white communities about the cultures and values of the 'new arrivals'.

The local authority itself was drawn into a more interventionist position in the mid-1950s. The Archdeacon of Birmingham recommended in February 1953 that Birmingham City Council appoint a welfare officer with responsibility for 'the welfare of the coloured population in Birmingham'. He argued that there was a need to accept the fact that the newly arrived immigrants were likely to 'be here for the foreseeable future'. Describing the situation in the city the Archdeacon bemoaned the failure of the Colonial Office to take responsibility for the welfare of 'coloured immigrants':

> Coloured people here find themselves in an alien atmosphere. Yet most of them are British citizens, free to come to this country, and the Colonial Office has specifically refused to accept responsibility. They maintain that as British citizens they are the responsibility of the Local Authority while resident in this country.
>
> (BCC, Memorandum by S. Harvie Clark, February 1953)

Partly as a result of pressure from the Co-ordinating Committee and the increasing politicisation of immigration the Council decided in 1954 to set up a post for a Liaison Officer for Coloured People in the Town Clerk's Department. The person initially appointed was William Davies, a former officer in the Colonial Service, but he was replaced in 1956 by Alan Gibbs, who had served previously as an Inspector of Police in Kenya (*Birmingham Mail*, 6 November 1954; *Sunday Mercury*, 5 February 1956). Throughout the 1950s and until the mid-1960s this was the key post within the City Council that addressed the question of what kind of initiatives were needed in response to growing black immigration into Birmingham. In this sense the creation of the post can be seen as an administrative response to the changing politics of immigration and race, and one which was to help to shape the local political climate for two decades.

Throughout the late 1950s and the early 1960s the Liaison Officer played a crucial role in mediating political debates about race and immigration in Birmingham. One of the first reports produced by William Davies put the choices which had to be confronted by cities such as Birmingham in the following terms:

> It is generally accepted that 'integration not segregation' is the slogan for the breaking down of the colour prejudice, but like most slogans it is easier to say than to carry out. Integration or assimilation is possible when there is no housing shortage, but Birmingham like other towns in the UK has its housing problems irrespective of the coloured communities, and until this problem has been solved there is no short cut to integration on a large scale. The Corporation can however attempt to assimilate coloured peoples into the social structure by advocating at the highest national level controlled immigration.
>
> (BCC, Report of the Liaison Officer, 15 October 1954)

This perception of a link between controls on immigration and social integration was part of a wider political discourse which constructed 'coloured immigration' into Britain as a problem. It was after all in the mid-1950s that political discourses in favour of immigration controls were first articulated in a sustained manner. It is interesting to note that the reports of the Liaison Officer throughout this period contain increasing references to the need for controls on the numbers of immigrants coming to cities such as Birmingham.

At the same time the situation in Birmingham highlights the centrality of everyday social issues such as housing and employment in the racialisation of political debates and policy agendas. The meanings which were attached to the role of 'race' and 'immigration' in everyday discourses about such social problems have to be seen against the background of social and economic change that was taking place in localities up and down the country. They also have to be seen in the context of the growing politicisation of 'coloured' immigration and the ongoing debate about how best to respond to pressures to regulate immigration from the colonies. In this process local pressures and mobilisations played an important role in helping to lay the ground for the move towards controls on immigration by constructing a close linkage between numbers of immigrants and 'social problems' in relation to housing and related social consumption goods.

It was already clear by the late 1950s, however, that the issue was not simply one of developing a policy about immigration. There was a shift in the content of policy discourses and public debate towards the longer-term issue of policies to deal with the 'integration' of minority communities. In a report to the local authority's General Purposes Committee in July 1957 the Liaison Officer noted the following trend:

> The pressure of work in the Liaison Office continues but a change has been noted in the type of assistance requested, the emphasis now being on problems associated with integration. On average some forty personal callers are being dealt with daily and there is also a marked increase in the numbers of requests for advice from the Courts, Tribunals and other official officers as well as from firms and private individuals. In the absence of any appropriate office in the Midlands the Liaison Office has been called upon to assist the Colonial Office in the repatriation of medically unfit and certain other people. There is not a great deal of administrative work involved in such repatriations rather do they call for a person who has knowledge of the countries and procedures involved who is centrally situated and in direct contact with the hospital authorities and medical practitioners etc. . . . yet who is also capable of advising the repatriates themselves.
>
> (BCC, General Purposes Committee, 20 June 1957)

This reflected a broader transformation in public debate about race and immigration. Common-sense images in the press presented areas of Birmingham as a kind of 'British Harlem' or a city with a growing 'race problem'. Part of the implication of these images was that the city was being transformed by immigration into a place where racial conflict and discrimination was an everyday reality. One newspaper report warned that there was a danger that a 'coloured quarter' would develop in the city which would eventually restrict the possibility of integration (*Evening Despatch*, 16 May 1959). At the time a particular area of concern was Balsall Heath, a locality with a reputation then as now for prostitution, drugs and 'vice'. This locality was also an important centre for some of the early migrants and it was not long before their arrival was seen as part of the explanation for the state of the area.

As we have tried to show in Chapter 2, however, the cityscape is more than a physical formation; it is also a discursive formation with identifiable regimes of representation. From the late 1940s the local and national media constructed Birmingham's geography through a racialised prism, resulting in the human attributes of its citizens being refracted and represented as spatially situated forms of pseudo-cultural difference. In the 1950s the areas of Sparkbrook and Balsall Heath in the south of the city became a focus of minority settlement. This was later to be overtaken by the northern district of Handsworth. What is interesting is that all these localities became the subject of repeated media scrutiny during this period.

In the mid-1950s, for example, there was a whole series of newspaper articles about the lifestyles of newly settled migrants in Balsall Heath and Sparkbrook. Some of these articles reported racial harmony. For example, the *Daily Herald* proclaimed: 'It's live and let live in Birmingham's Harlem' (4 November 1955). It was estimated that there were approximately 11,000 – mostly male – New Commonwealth citizens living in Birmingham. On the lack of crime Birmingham's superintendent of CID Sidney Richards commented, 'Birmingham works hard during the day and goes to bed at night. You might put it that we just don't cater for lawlessness here.'

However, the reporting of the black presence was also organised around themes of moral and social crisis. The *News Chronicle* on 1 March 1954 commented:

> Suddenly the coloured men became a problem. . . . How many coloured men are there in Birmingham? About 10,000! Why? How did they get here? This might affect our pay packets. Where will it end? Marrying white girls? Is Birmingham going to become a coffee-coloured town?

In April 1956 the *News Chronicle* ran another story developing the idea that the presence of black people in the city posed a serious social crisis: the headline announced 'Evils of Birmingham: Problems of good-time girls and coloured men in overcrowded lodgings'. It was authored by Councillor Joan Tomlinson. The article listed a catalogue of moral and social ills to be found within Balsall Heath (dubbed 'Little India'). What is striking is that these draw almost exclusively on images of young black men and white women. Here the notion of black male criminality is counterpoised by the idea of the 'kept woman'. This notion could be applied to any white woman who was in a relationship with a black man.

> There is a steady growth of drug-taking and something akin to, but legally different from prostitution – the 'kept woman'. . . . White girls live with coloured men. Many don't marry them and change to another man when they get bored.

She goes on:

> In Balsall Heath there are Indians, Pakistanis, Malays, Syrians, Irish labourers, unskilled workers from Lancashire and Yorkshire all huddled together. And there is the growth of the drug habit. The West Indians began it with the importation of marijuana, or Indian hemp, or 'hashish'. . . . Smoking marijuana cigarettes – 'reefers' – confers temporarily a feeling of great physical strength and well-being and a strong sexual appetite.

There is some irony in that, physiologically speaking, this connection between marijuana and sexual appetite could not be further from the truth. However, the key theme in this is the relationship between sexuality and miscegenation or 'race mixing':

> Too many white women of a certain type between 20 and 30 prefer coloured men. But the effects of inter-breeding are reflected in the ever increasing numbers of half-caste children. It seems almost insoluble.
>
> (*News Chronicle*, 15 April 1956)

There were a whole series of articles on the theme of interracial marriage during this period signalling an incredible preoccupation with the fear of Birmingham becoming a 'coffee-coloured town'. In this way, simply uttering the name Balsall Heath became associated with a whole range of racialised meanings. This resulted in particular districts being metonymically associated with racialised notions of place and identity as shown in the diagram opposite.

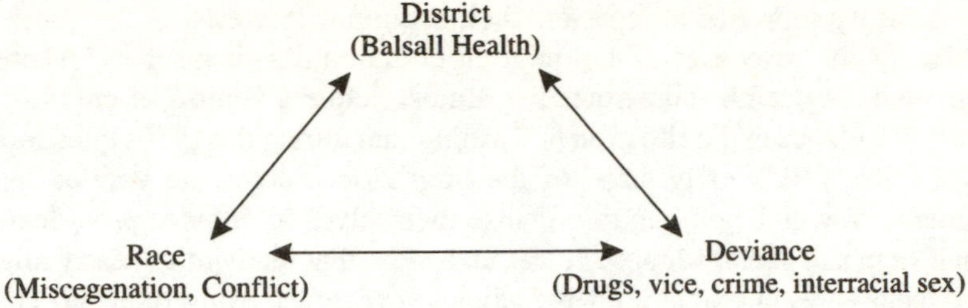


Our point here is that it is precisely through such racialised imagery that particular localities of the city were visualised. Within this discursive realm place names acted, and continue to act, as triggers which connect notions of race with a moral crisis concerning criminal behaviour and cultural corruption. This discourse is gendered in such a way that black men are seen to be an alien presence that will corrupt white women. In the logic of this moral panic women become the embodiment of the city and the nation. Thus the condemnation of the 'kept woman' is closely tied to a concern over maintaining racial purity. Similar processes of racialisation were also at work in relation to other areas of the city, such as Handsworth.

By the late 1950s a new theme emerged in popular discourse, namely the issue of racialised geographical segregation. The *Evening Despatch* ran an article entitled 'Little Jamaica can be a danger'. Under the headline 'Immigrant total 35,000' it reported: 'immigrants are living in tight pockets, turning inward on themselves' (16 May 1959). In 1961 *The Times* printed an article on Handsworth claiming 'Race prejudice grows in a suburb'. The story quoted one white person as saying: 'I fear that the immigrants are coming to hate us and we are beginning to feel the same way about them' (15 May 1961). What is interesting about this particular article is the way in which the blame for 'race prejudice' is pushed squarely back onto 'the immigrant'. The logic is that black people stay too close together, do not become integrated and consequently grow resentful and bitter.

Although housing and neighbourhood was at the heart of many of the early debates about immigration, issues of employment were also crucial. An interesting example of the response of the labour movement to immigration arose in 1954 when the Transport and General Workers' Union branch attempted to defend its policy of banning black workers from working on the buses. The branch defended this decision by saying that white conductresses disliked working with black workers (*Observer*, 21 February 1954). This led to a vigorous debate within the local council and in the local press about this stance, and indeed it is important to emphasise that there was noticeable opposition to the idea of having a 'colour bar' on the buses (*News Chronicle*, 1 March 1954). What is clear, however, is that throughout the 1950s and 1960s the position of the trade unions on the question of race was at best ambiguous and at times openly racist. Apart from the attempt to enforce a 'colour bar' on the buses there were numerous other examples of conflict between migrant workers and the trade unions which were in theory supposed to represent their economic interests.

What of the responses of the migrant communities themselves? There is a danger that they can be constructed as almost helpless victims of circumstance. Yet a quick glance at the situation in Birmingham during the 1950s questions this image. Even at this early stage of the migration process the various migrant communities were beginning to organise themselves in order to provide a basis for self-help and social support. It was also clear that many of the early migrants found themselves in a situation where they felt excluded from equal participation in society. One West Indian migrant was quoted as saying: 'In America I should be accepted as a coloured American in ten years. If I stay in England for 40 years I shall still be a foreigner' (*Birmingham Post and Gazette*, 14 December 1958). This feeling of not being fully accepted, even in the longer term, has to be seen in the context of two interlinked processes. First, the ways in which hostility towards immigrants was being expressed in everyday situations and interactions. As we have noted above, this hostility was by no means universal and there was also clear opposition to racism and support for migrants. But by the late 1950s there was also mounting hostility and opposition to immigration. This was reflected in the second process that influenced the situation in Birmingham as elsewhere, namely the growing support for controls on immigration. It is to this issue that we now turn.

## IMMIGRATION CONTROLS AND INTEGRATION

By the late 1950s there was a noticeable increase in political pressures in favour of controls on immigration. This was partly through the activities of local anti-immigration groups, which became active in Birmingham during the late 1950s and which helped to ensure that immigration achieved a higher profile on the local political agenda. Although these groups were relatively small in size they were a symptom of the changing terms of political discourse about immigration. It was clear that sections of the Conservative Party, both locally and nationally, were rapidly moving towards opposition to immigration. Such opposition was often legitimised at the local level by reference to such issues as pressures on housing, welfare provision and the cultural 'differences' which were likely to hinder the integration of migrants. There was also some movement in this direction within the Labour Party. Denis Howell, a local Labour MP, argued forcefully that measures to deal with employment and housing problems needed to be linked with a policy on immigration (*Evening Despatch*, 4 September 1958).

This duality in policy debates was one that was to continue to influence policy debates for some time. For example, a report produced in 1962 by the Conservative Party on *Helping the Immigrants* reflected some of the common-sense views about the social and cultural impact of immigration on urban localities when it argued that there was a need for a national policy on the assimilation of migrant communities:

> There are areas of Birmingham (and no doubt other cities) where a virtual breakdown in our accepted standards has taken place. Many requirements of our highly-developed civil code are disregarded. The authorities do not have the means or organisation to regularise the situation. It cannot be right or in the interests of the country as a whole that this state of affairs should continue. Without prejudice or discrimination we must concentrate on maintaining the standards established in this country. The reception areas must be assisted in their task of bringing immigrants up to these standards.
>
> (Conservative Political Centre, 1962: 14)

This helps to illustrate the way in which the experience of immigration at the local level acted as an important mechanism for the reproduction of ideas about 'immigrants' and about the social and cultural values that were seen as under threat from too much immigration. In this sense the articulation of many of the common-sense images about immigration which have dominated our political culture ever since can be seen as the products of what were quite often localised processes up and down the country.

At the local level there was by no means a consistent set of policies in response to immigration. Rex and Moore's classic study on *Race, Community and Conflict* (1967) contains the following interesting account of the way in which the Liaison Officer perceived his role both in relation to the local political system and to the immigrant communities:

> The Liaison Officer defined his task as the integration of the immigrants, by which he explained that he meant seeing that they got their rights and that they conformed. He had helped many immigrants to get lodgings, but had found that they preferred their own people. He had also helped to increase opportunities for employment. Again we must record that very few of our respondents had received these services and those who had complained about their inadequacy. But in any case, these services were no longer in operation. Emphasis was now on the second stage of getting the immigrants to conform. Housing standards and eating habits were among the most important issues, in the Liaison Officer's opinion.
>
> (Rex and Moore, 1967: 161)

This emphasis on strategies for the assimilation and integration of immigrants symbolised the complex manner in which political discourses about immigration involved images of the social and cultural differences represented by migrants in the context of British society. The idea that migrants needed to 'conform' to some wider standard carried with it certain notions about their social and cultural background which continued to influence both national and local policy debates for some time. It also symbolised the still commonplace paternalism to be found at all levels of political debate at this time (Robert Moore, interview, November 1991).

In a sense the very role of the Liaison Officer in the period from the 1950s to the 1960s symbolised the neo-colonial imagery that was still a key means by which politicians at both the local and national levels made sense of the changing politics of immigration and race in conurbations such as Birmingham. The reports produced by the Liaison Officer are saturated with neo-colonial paternalist language, often articulated in terms of images of immigrants needing to receive help to either integrate into British society or to return home. It is interesting to note in this regard that towards the end of his tenure as Liaison Officer Alan Gibbs set up a project near Birmingham to train immigrants in modern farming methods. He argued:

> You see, I'm trying to prove something to the people of this country. I want to make them see that they have this marvellous opportunity to train people who will go back home and use – and know *how* to use – modern British equipment . . . I've done my own survey among 4000 immigrants, and 60 per cent said they wanted to go home one day, most of the Indians and Pakistanis to join family farms.
>
> (*The Times*, 25 August 1967)

Yet despite his enthusiasm for this project Alan Gibbs was less sanguine about the future of race relations in Birmingham after twelve years in office. He saw integration as a difficult objective:

> Integration anywhere is a difficult thing. Look at white and coloured workers during the day. They labour side-by-side and visit each other if one goes to hospital. Yet when the factory whistle blows, the Indian says cheerio and trots off home to Little India – in Balsall Heath or Sparkbrook. That this still happens is the fault of both coloured and white people.
>
> (*Birmingham Mail*, 10 October 1967)

What is interesting about this example is the way Gibbs manages to use an array of images to highlight the idea that the existence of 'Little India' is a sign of the limits of integration. Yet at the same time he articulates the need for programmes to train immigrants so that they can be better prepared to return to their countries of origin. There is a tension between these arguments, but it is clearly not one that was evident to Gibbs or others involved in the administration of race relations policies at the time.

To summarise the argument so far, we have tried to show that in the political climate of the 1950s and early 1960s the question of immigration was becoming an issue of some political importance through a mixture of local and national processes. While much of the focus of recent research about the racialisation of British politics has been on the national picture, it is important to understand the role that localised processes played in shaping the politics of race and immigration during this crucial period. Additionally, we have argued that policy aims were by no means fixed and unchanging throughout this period. There was, for example, a mixture of paternalism and common-sense racist stereotypes in the formulation of political discourses about the social impact of immigration in localities such as Birmingham. At the same time calls for controls on immigration were made alongside demands for measures to promote 'integration' and deal with discrimination.

## SMETHWICK, RACE AND ELECTORAL POLITICS

By the early 1960s debates about immigration and race in Birmingham and surrounding localities were becoming more noticeably politicised. Local newspapers began to reflect aspects of this politicisation in their news coverage, editorials and correspondence columns. At the same time local institutions and political parties became increasingly involved in debates about what should be done about immigration and the impact of migrants on housing, employment and education. Rex and Moore (1967) capture some key aspects of the situation in the early 1960s in the following description:

> The visitor to Birmingham in the early 1960s could not but be struck by the way in which racial problems dominated public discussion. It was hard to imagine, as one scanned the columns of the *Post*, the *Mail and Dispatch*, the *Sunday Mercury*, and the *Planet*, that this was a city long famous for its radical and egalitarian tradition. Often the sentiments expressed by those who wrote to these newspapers or those who were reported in them, smacked more of the Deep South in the United States or of settler Africa than of the City of Reform.
>
> (Rex and Moore, 1967: 19)

Other accounts of this period are full of examples of the variety of ways in which questions about race and immigration fed into broader debates about economic and social agendas. Perhaps more importantly, however, they also highlight their growing impact on political agendas and electoral politics.

Perhaps the most clear example of this process was provided by the situation in Smethwick, a small industrial town a few miles west of Birmingham, in the period leading up to the General Election of October 1964. The history of post-1945 immigration into Smethwick was in many ways similar to the experience of other localities in the region, with immigration becoming a noticeable feature of the local situation in the mid-1950s. Migrants had come to seek work in the local manufacturing industries, which provided the backbone of the local economy. Much of the debate in the local press about immigration focused on the question of housing, an issue which had long been a problem in the locality. But it was not until the early 1960s that immigration began to come to the fore in local politics, with the formation of a branch of the Birmingham Immigration Control Association and pressure to exclude black people from local authority housing.

It was during this period that Peter Griffiths rose to prominence within the local Conservative Party. He took an active interest in immigration and related issues and succeeded in placing them firmly on the agenda of local party politics. In the period leading up to the General Election of October 1964 Griffiths made the question of immigration the core of his campaign as the Conservative candidate for the constituency. He issued a document entitled 'Ten Points on Colour' which advocated a five-year ban on unskilled immigration along with assisted passages to countries of origin for unemployed migrants, deportation for criminals and other related schemes. This was by no means as radical a programme of action as that advocated by Enoch Powell towards the end of the decade, but his interventions created controversy beyond the borders of Smethwick. This was partly because the success of Griffiths's populist campaign against immigration was seen as heralding a more substantive racialisation of political debate across the whole country. But it was also because it highlighted the possibility of using an anti-immigration platform to undermine support for the Labour Party.

Throughout the campaign in Smethwick there was an interesting play on ideas of place and community in the debates between Griffiths and the Labour candidate, Patrick Gordon Walker. Perhaps the most powerful of these debates was the controversy aroused by one of the slogans circulating in Smethwick, namely the infamous 'If you want a nigger neighbour, vote Labour'. When asked about this slogan Griffiths responded by saying: 'I would not condemn anyone who said that. I regard it as a manifestation of popular feeling' (*The Times*, 9 March 1964). This response symbolised the way in which Griffiths self-consciously constructed himself as somebody who was close to the feelings of the 'local people', as a politician who understood the fears of the white residents in a situation of uncertainty and change. This mode of political discourse was one which was later to be taken up by Enoch Powell and later by Margaret Thatcher.

Griffiths captured Smethwick for the Conservative Party, even though the national trend was towards the Labour Party. Although he was to hold on to it only for two years, the symbolic impact of his victory should not be underestimated. The events in Smethwick neatly encapsulated the role that 'immigration' and 'race' came to play in specific localities as well as nationally. In many ways 'race' came to symbolise not only the politicisation of debates about immigration but also the variety of ways in which wider social and economic concerns were an integral aspect of this process. Given the extent of national debate about the politicisation of racial issues in Smethwick and surrounding areas it is not surprising that one of the local papers in Birmingham bemoaned the fact that 'Birmingham has lately become almost a dirty word in some circles' (*Mail and Dispatch*, 15 September 1964).

All of the Birmingham MPs who fought the 1964 General Election made a prior agreement not to campaign on the issue of immigration. This included Conservative figures such as Anthony Beaumont Dark and Sir Edward Boyle. Boyle, in particular, had a reputation for being liberal on the question of immigration and represented a section of the party which found the events in Smethwick alarming. However, there was a little-reported exception to this cross-party consensus. On the eve of poll the Conservative candidate for Perry Barr decided to bring immigration into his campaign, albeit in a more coded way than his counterpart in Smethwick. Perry Barr at this time was a marginal seat and Labour had won it in 1959 with a majority of just 185 votes. One of his workers, a Conservative councillor who owned a printing works, produced a leaflet which portrayed a map of Birmingham with Handsworth shaded in, invoking the racial geographies which we have already mentioned. Handsworth had previously been a stronghold of the Conservative party but it had become less so in part due to demographic changes and the large-scale support of the Labour Party by recently settled Caribbean migrants. A Labour activist involved in the campaign remembers:

> The leaflet was in the form of a cartoon, really. It showed Handsworth coloured in, which was the adjacent constituency to Perry Barr, and what it said was: 'Are we next'! It was cleverly done but everyone knew what it meant and it worked. The printer used his own workers to deliver the leaflet and they flooded the place with it up until the early hours of the night before election day. We went out 'knocking up' on election day, we went in to some of our strongest areas of support with white working-class people and it was just no dice. They didn't want to know and as a result we lost the election by 364 votes.
>
> (Interview, May 1990)

Smethwick, and to a lesser extent Perry Barr, demonstrated the potency of popular racism in the electoral domain during this period. In both cases 'immigration' had enabled Conservative candidates to be returned in an election where there was a national swing of opinion towards Labour.

## RESHAPING THE POLITICAL AGENDA

Events such as the ones in Smethwick and Perry Barr did not of course take place in a vacuum. It seems clear that during this period similar developments were occurring up and down the country and that these in turn interacted with changing political priorities at the national level. By the mid-1960s an important shift in political debates about race and immigration began to emerge, both at a national and local level. This was symbolised at the national level by the agreement of both the Conservative and Labour Parties that there was a need for (i) strong controls on immigration, and (ii) measures to deal with the social impact of immigration and with racial discrimination. At the local level there was also a marked shift away from a preoccupation with immigration as such. The key areas of concern became social issues such as the relationship between immigration and housing, education, employment and welfare services.

This is not to say that there was just one view of the relationship between race and social change. There were a number of often contradictory discourses at work. Robert Moore, looking back to his research in the Sparkbrook area of Birmingham in the early 1960s, describes the general climate of opinion in these terms:

> Race had a very high profile. . . . There were all sorts of stories about the decline of Sparkbrook and some people said the black people had caused it; other people said that everybody there was a victim, it didn't matter whether you were black or white.
>
> (Robert Moore, interview: November 1991)

In this sense the situation can best be understood as one in which there were contrasting ideological perspectives about the relationship between immigration and social problems. It was only through a process of debate and conflict throughout this period in localities such as Birmingham, Smethwick and elsewhere that the common-sense association between the 'decline' of certain areas and immigration was established.

At a broader level other 'problems' commonly associated with 'Birmingham's coloured people' were the pressures on the school system and on the housing market. These issues became major areas of concern during the 1960s, and both local and national political figures saw Birmingham as an important test case for the future of race relations in British society. Education represented a particularly difficult issue, since it encapsulated the shifting terms of concern from the issue of immigration as such to the question of the future of the children of migrants and their social position in British society. Throughout this period there was an ongoing debate about how best to respond to the position of migrant children within the school system, whether to control the number of migrant children in particular schools, and a whole set of related issues. In this sense the area of education represented one of the key arenas in which the debate about the 'integration' of migrants was played out.

But increasingly other issues forced themselves onto the local political agenda. From the late 1960s the issues of black youth and policing became key concerns in local press reports and in political debates (Solomos, 1988). The fear that the second generation of young black people would become a socially marginalised group and drift into conflict with the police and society generally became an important theme of political discourses during this time. It was signalled by press reports which warned that 'race riots' were on the agenda in Birmingham if local and national political leaders did not take action to deal with the problems faced by young blacks in areas of the city such as Handsworth (*Birmingham Evening Mail*, 2 March 1968). Yet other reports began to talk of the process by which young West Indians in Birmingham were 'turning into hardened criminals' and alienated from the rest of society (*Birmingham Evening Mail*, 12 August 1969).

A conference organised by the local council in July 1968, at the height of national political debate about immigration, reflected in a clear manner the growing impact of debates about the social consequences of immigration on the local political agenda. Given the concern with the integration of immigrants into the mainstream society and culture, a growing preoccupation in this period was the fear that black minorities would develop their own enclaves in the inner cities and resist integration. Elements of this fear are clearly expressed in the following quotation from a report to this conference:

> Immigrants tend to settle in specific localities forming their own communities which reacts against integration with the general population. It would seem that immigrant communities are formed because of circumstances (e.g. relatives, suitable surroundings) and the advantages to be gained by collective settlement in a manner not dissimilar to the selection by individuals of the established population of neighbourhoods in which to live. Some services tend to be overburdened by this concentration of immigrants in specific localities because of the above normal demands which they make.
>
> (BCC, General Purposes Committee, 16 July 1968)

This signalled the convergence of concerns about immigration and about the problems faced in particular areas of the city. It was as a result of this process that policy debates about urban decline became an important element in the politicisation of race. An important point to emphasise in this regard is that developments in Birmingham, and the West Midlands generally, were not purely of local significance. The developments we have looked at in Birmingham during this period played an important role in national debates about race and immigration and helped to focus the attention of the Government and of the national press on this area. Developments in Birmingham thus played a key role in the racialisation of national political discourses.

## INSTITUTIONAL CONTEXTS AND POLITICAL ACTION

Whatever the impact of the processes we have analysed above on the political agenda it is clear that by the early 1970s the racialisation of political debate in Birmingham had been firmly established. But what impact did the processes we have analysed above have on political action and on the key institutions of political life? This is something that we shall explore in more detail in the following chapter, but here we want to touch on some of the historical background.

One measure of the changing politics of race during this period is its growing impact of race on public political debate. This took the form partly of the growing debate about race and immigration in the context of political party competition. But it was also evident in the ongoing coverage of race and immigration issues in the local press and the ways in which this connected with political concerns. Although as we have mentioned earlier there was some awareness that in the longer term minority votes were likely to become significant in some constituencies, the main concern at the time was with maintaining the support of white voters. This was particularly the case in the aftermath of Smethwick and the impact of Powell on the public debate about race and immigration.

During the 1960s minorities remained largely outside of the main political parties. They certainly seemed to exercise little or no influence within political party structures. The situation in the Labour Party at this time, at both national and local level, was a case in point. Although the Party took a public stance against racism and was in favour of measures to deal with racial discrimination there were entrenched means of excluding minorities from key institutions of the labour movement. This included clubs and societies which were run under the auspices of the Party or by the trades unions. These exclusions were not universally accepted within the labour movement. Indeed, there were constant protests against them and this issue was often a site of conflict. The operation of a 'colour bar' by working men's clubs continued to be a subject of public debate well into the 1970s.

The issue of the impact of minorities on political institutions was not as yet widely discussed. There was some recognition that migrant communities could exercise some influence on electoral politics in the future, but this was by no means widely recognised at the time. During the 1964 General Election, for example, the *Birmingham Planet* argued under the headline 'Can Birmingham Ignore the Immigrant Vote?' that it was likely that minority communities would seek in the near future to use their potential to influence electoral politics in order to pressurise the main political parties to take their concerns more seriously (23 January 1964). But this was not a view which gained wide currency at the time, and there was little sign that either the Labour or Conservative Parties were taking measures to incorporate minority communities within their institutions.

The question of the absence of black local councillors from the political scene was not one which could be easily ignored. Minority members of the Labour Party were themselves beginning to see their own party as in effect operating a 'colour bar' in the selection of local councillors. One example of this process was the case of Dr Dhani Prem. He was a prominent local figure who had represented Perry Barr as a Labour councillor in 1945–1950, been an active member of the Advisory Council for Commonwealth Immigrants and taken an active stance against the views of Peter Griffiths in Smethwick (Griffiths, 1966: 121–123; Prem, 1966). Yet in 1968 he argued:

> It is quite true that I would not now be adopted by the Labour Party. I tried on two or three occasions to get on their panel of candidates after leaving the Council, but I was never selected. . . . One reason why they do not want immigrant candidates is that it is difficult enough for them to hold seats, and for them to put up a coloured candidate they feel would be even worse. They do not seem to be interested in capturing the immigrant vote or support.
>
> (*Birmingham Post*, 19 July 1968)

Although Dr Prem was in some ways an exceptional figure, his views about the Labour Party's perception of minority candidates reflected a much broader scepticism about its ability to incorporate the political mobilisations of minorities within its institutions.

The story of his political involvement in many ways serves as a metaphor for the state of racial politics in the 1950s and 1960s. Born in Aligarh, 60 miles from Delhi, in 1904, his father and mother died when he was very young and as a result he was raised by his uncle. As a teenager he was a member of Mahatma Gandhi's Congress Party and a supporter of anti-colonial politics. He was imprisoned twice for his political activity, once at the age of twelve for a day and again at fourteen for a year. Prem was self-educated and graduated from the National Medical School in Bombay. He first came to Britain in the 1930s, attaining a medical degree from Edinburgh University. After returning to India to edit a literary magazine, Dr Prem came back to Britain and settled in Birmingham, practising as a doctor in the working-class district of Aston, where he also joined the Labour Party and Socialist Clubs.

Lauded in the local press as the 'architect of race relations' in the city, Dr Prem had a mixed relationship with both the Labour Party and the emerging political figures within black voluntary sector politics. His position regarding the political agenda for migrants was clearly assimilationist. Reflecting on his political career in 1978 he commented:

> The immigrant's duty was to learn English, to aquaint himself with British law and to become as British as possible. You must throw in your lot with the people you have chosen to live with in order to be accepted.
>
> (*Medical News*, 20 July 1978)

In 1968 his politics was out of step with the anger of black activists. After exchanges at the annual general meeting he was forced to resign from his position of Vice-Chairman of the Birmingham Advisory Council for Commonwealth Immigrants. Mihir Gupta, organiser of the Birmingham Indian Association, was reported to have said during this turbulent meeting:

> Dr Prem lives in an Ivory Tower. He is not in touch with the grassroots of the immigrants' problems and his ideas on how to tackle them are obsolete.
>
> (*Birmingham Post*, 2 July 1968)

Gupta went on to claim that the Birmingham Corporation had appointed 'safe' representatives to the Advisory Council from within the minority communities without proper consultation. The Advisory Council was chaired by an alderman and constituted a 'buffer institution' (Katznelson, 1976). This is not to say that figures like Dr Prem were uncomplicatedly conservative. As we shall argue later, black politicians can be both accommodated by the political system while at other moments remaining its fierce critics.

Dr Prem was a sustained opponent of Enoch Powell and on a number of occasions in 1968 challenged him to an open debate on race and immigration. In 1974 he stood unsuccessfully as a Liberal candidate in the General Election in Coventry South East. Four years later he died in a car crash in India at the age of 75. The significance of Dr Prem's political career is that he symbolises the first step in the emergence of black politicians in the electoral sphere. Equally, the fact that Prem was not selected as a local candidate for Labour during these torrid years, points to the Party's unwillingness to confront racism within the ranks of its supporters. It would take more than ten years for the political climate to shift and for the next black councillor to be elected.

## RACISM AND ANTI-RACISM

Perhaps the most important aspect of the impact of immigration and race issues on the political agenda was the prominence of racialised political debates at both a local and national level. The late 1960s and early 1970s represent a key turning point in the sense that we saw a noticeable racialisation of political debate within the mainstream political parties and in the influence of extreme right-wing movements with an explicitly racist political stance.

The most important development in this regard was the rise of Powellism. It is perhaps the most interesting example of the intertwining between local and national discourses about race. Enoch Powell had in fact begun to make interventions in debates about immigration from the mid-1960s, but his influence was at its height during the period of the late 1960s and early 1970s. He achieved this most notably through numerous public speeches and by his participation in parliamentary debates. Powell was an MP for neighbouring Wolverhampton but he had strong connections with Birmingham and indeed made perhaps his most famous speech at the city's Midland Hotel, namely his so-called 'Rivers of Blood' speech in April 1968. This speech with its imagery of the white British majority 'made strangers in their own country by the inflow of immigrants' and 'their homes and neighbourhoods changed beyond recognition' (*Observer*, 21 April 1968) was quite clearly addressing the situation in cities and towns such as Birmingham.

Moreover, it was also in areas such as Birmingham that Powell's speeches had the most effect. Indeed, in a number of his speeches Powell chose to use figures about Birmingham's 'coloured population' in order to give support to his arguments about the future size of the migrant communities. For Powell, as with other politicians at the time, the situation in Birmingham was symptomatic of the situation in the whole country. In this sense it is of some importance to note that at the centre of his various interventions was a concern not just with the number of immigrants as such but with the social and political consequences that the growth of minority communities was likely to have in the future. This was perhaps the theme that was at the heart of attempts by the Conservative leadership of Birmingham City Council in 1968 to propose restrictions on the number of migrants settling in the city. As a leading Conservative politician commented at the time:

> If the immigrants are to enjoy a full and equal life that we all want them to enjoy, we must restrict the numbers. If we allow a flood of immigrants, we shall not be able to provide them with the jobs and social services that they will need to enjoy a full life. This statement is a report of facts. If the citizens are to have equal enjoyment of the facilities there must be some restriction of the numbers.
>
> (*Birmingham Post*, 17 July 1968)

Though these arguments did not by any means go as far as Powell's own pronouncements it was also clear that it was the climate of opinion created by the public debate about his intervention that allowed such views to be articulated as almost a common-sense response to the situation. It is worth noting that in the aftermath of his speech there was a widespread campaign in some local factories under the slogan 'I am backing Enoch'. A local white Conservative politician who was active at the time remembers the situation as one in which 'the ordinary people in the street in the main believed him'. There is clear evidence that some local Conservatives supported this strategy and during the local elections of 1968 some Conservative candidates fought their campaigns on an openly Powellite agenda. The City Council, at the time controlled by the Conservatives, made representations to the Government urging tight immigration control. Beyond this, Alderman Beaumont Dark, later to become a Conservative Member of Parliament, urged the diversion of black people away from Birmingham on the grounds that it was claimed to be 'full up' (*Birmingham Post*, 15 May 1968). This provoked opposition from the then Leader of the Labour Group, Frank Price:

> They [the Conservatives] have been at some pains to say that this is not a colour bar.
>
> I challenge this, since some Conservative Council members campaigned on colour and an 'I back Enoch' ticket in last week's election. If this latest move is not a colour bar it means that everyone, be they from Tamworth, Tonypandy, Tipperary or Tannochbrae, will be vetted at the city boundaries . . . . This is the most stupid suggestion I have ever heard. It is making Birmingham look completely ridiculous.
>
> (*Birmingham Evening Mail* 15 May 1968)

This Conservative initiative was little more than a coded attempt to limit the growth of Birmingham's black population. However, Price could be less sanguine about the degree to which Powell had struck a sympathetic chord within the ranks of the labour movement and its supporters. It is interesting, however, that in interviews with local politicians which we carried out in the early 1990s the symbolic value of Powell's speech was widely mentioned by Conservative politicians. Powell had a strong impact on Birmingham's political culture and his legacy has had enduring effects on the local politics of race (see Chapter 5).

Another feature of the political scene during the early and mid-1970s involved the activities of the National Front and other extreme right-wing organisations. Such groups saw the possibility to use race as a means of political mobilisation and they were very active in Birmingham throughout this period because they perceived the area as one in which they could attempt to attract support on the basis of their anti-immigration platform. Although such groups did not manage to achieve an electoral breakthrough they did succeed in having some impact on the local political scene through their interventions in both local and national elections. During 1976 and 1977 the National Front managed to gain at least respectable support in the Stetchford and Ladywood by-elections, as well as in local elections. But beyond that it was also able to gain widespread publicity for its views on race and its calls for the repatriation of immigrants. This success allowed it to maintain an active profile in the area during what in many ways was the high point of its national influence.

An interesting example of this process was the controversy surrounding the case of Robert Relf, who acquired both local and national notoriety when he put up a sign outside his house in Leamington Spa which said: 'Viewing. To avoid animosity all round positively no coloureds.' He later changed the sign to say: 'For sale to an English Family' (*Sunday Times*, 4 July 1976). When he refused to take down the signs he was jailed for contempt of court. He then went on a 'hunger strike', which eventually led to his release on health grounds. His case became a *cause célèbre* for the extreme right and he was used as an example by the National Front of the kind of 'honest Englishman' who was made to suffer by the race relations bureaucracy. His case became a significant political issue in Birmingham and the surrounding area and demonstrations and counter-demonstrations were organised in response to his jail sentence. At the same time the Relf case symbolised the increasingly volatile and conflictual terms of political debate on racial issues during this period.

## PROTEST AND COMMUNITY POLITICS

One of the main lacunae in many accounts of the politics of race and ethnicity during this period is the neglect of the role of community associations and political groups functioning within minority communities themselves. This absence tends to give credence to notions of ethnic minorities as helpless victims. Yet what is clear from numerous studies of the experience of diverse countries is that minority communities tend to develop a wide range of organisations and forums which aim to provide support and protection in an often hostile environment. Comparative studies of migrant groups have shown that a key feature of the migration process involves the setting up of community-based organisations which seek to provide social and cultural support in the countries of settlement. Such organisations can have specific concerns, such as maintaining religious and cultural identities. They can also espouse broader political and ideological values concerned both with the situation in countries of origin and in the new environment.

The British experience in the period since 1945 provides clear examples of this process. Throughout the 1960s and 1970s a key dimension of the racialisation of politics involved the development of various kinds of community and protest politics. Community mobilisation and self-organisation are known to have been strongly established features of the local scene from the very earliest stages of the arrival of migrant communities in Birmingham. It is a feature that Rex and Moore highlighted throughout their account of race and community in Sparkbrook, where they provide a detailed account of the development and role of various kinds of associations which were set up by specific communities or political groups (Rex and Moore, 1967). Such organisations were not necessarily organised by the minority communities themselves, but they played an important mediating role between them and wider social and political institutions.

The findings of Rex and Moore from the early 1960s were supported by later research in Birmingham and elsewhere. Indeed, one of the interesting features of the situation in Birmingham was the great variety of organisations and groups which emerged from within the migrant communities and the active role they played in shaping political debate and policy agendas.

From the very earliest stages of post-1945 migration to Birmingham there is evidence of the existence and impact of community organisations. But they began to grow in numbers and to become more formally organised from the early 1960s onwards. One indication of this is the growing pressure for minority organisations to be represented in forums such as the Birmingham Liaison Committee for Commonwealth Immigrants. By the mid-1960s there was significant representation on the Liaison Committee from a wide range of West Indian, Pakistani and Indian groups. Some of these community organisations were organised partly on the basis of ethnic, religious or other bases of identity. Others, however, were defined by a concern with particular social issues or espoused the general objective of defending the political interests of minorities and promoting racial justice.

Whilst many of the community organisations were relatively small and concerned with social issues, others developed a broader political and ideological stance. There were a number of attempts, with varied degrees of success, to construct an alliance between minority organisations and other sympathetic political groups to campaign for measures against racism and racial discrimination. One of the most important of these was the Co-ordinating Committee Against Racial Discrimination (CCARD). This was formed in Birmingham in 1961 with the support of the Indian Workers' Associations and various West Indian and Pakistani organisations. At a general level CCARD saw itself as promoting collaboration in the fight against 'racial intolerance' and as helping to promote 'racial harmony'. This allowed it initially to attract support on a relatively broad basis.

Throughout the 1960s and 1970s community organisations continued to be formed, reformed, disappear and quite often reappear under different names. But increasingly such bodies were not organised autonomously by minority communities themselves. As central and local government began to intervene more and more to deal with various aspects of racial relations there was a noticeable attempt to develop networks of minority organisations and community leaders to 'represent' the interests of minorities within political institutions. The National Committee for Commonwealth Immigrants (NCCI) and later the Community Relations Commission (CRC) saw a clear need to involve minority organisations in order to help with the overall objective of 'integration'. In Birmingham a ready-made vehicle existed for this through the Liaison Committee, although it faced pressure to increase the level of representation that it gave to minorities. In October 1966 Nadine Peppard, the General Secretary of the NCCI, wrote to the City Council approving a grant to help the work of the Liaison Committee. In doing so, however, she added:

> My committee welcomes the appointment of two West Indian representatives and hopes that the Lord Mayor will also agree to the extension of representation to two members each of the Indian and Pakistani communities.
>
> (BCC, Letter from Nadine Peppard, 7 October 1966)

Such moves to institutionalise channels of representation for community leaders were part of a broader trend in public policy in this field. This trend in essence involved a move in the direction of integrating minority organisations and influential leaders in the mainstream of politics. The money awarded by the NCCI was used to create a post for a Secretary of the Liaison Committee, and it is of some interest to quote the description of the objectives of this appointment:

> The officer appointed will be required to promote good relations between members of different communities, nationalities and races in the City of Birmingham and to assist in the integration of Commonwealth Immigrants within the local community. . . . It will be necessary for him to ascertain what organisations interested in promoting good community relations already exist

> in the City and how they are assisting the integration of the immigrant population: to formulate proposals for the co-ordination of this work and for the establishment of new organisations where necessary.
>
> (BCC, Birmingham Liaison Committee for Commonwealth Immigrants, 1966)

This appointment reflected a new stage in the articulation between the local council and black community organisations in the city. It signalled the growing links between the local political system and voluntary and community organisations.

By the mid-1970s there were a variety of local organisations that were in one way or another attempting to deal with key aspects of race in the increasingly complex environment of Birmingham. These can be characterised in the following terms:

- associations which claimed to represent particular communities on the basis of religious, ethnic or cultural origin;
- churches, temples, mosques and other places of religious worship;
- local community organisations which were concerned with particular social issues or the provision of services for minorities;
- the Community Relations Council, which provided a quasi-official forum for dealing with racial and ethnic issues in Birmingham.

This is by no means a complete list of the range of organisations which in one way or another represented part of the local political scene in relation to race. Rather it is meant to highlight the increasingly complex situation which was emerging in cities such as Birmingham and the diverse nature of forms of organisation that were involved in the making of policies in this field.

Such community organisations were playing an increasingly active role in introducing new issues on the political agenda. For example, an emerging area of debate, which prefigured developments in the 1980s and 1990s, concerned the question of the demands of religious and community groups for recognition of their specific needs by local and central government. The building of mosques, community centres and other communally based developments became a focal point of negotiations between community groups and the local council. Throughout the 1970s the development of mosques by sections of the Muslim communities became a focus of public debate, and led to intense debates in the local council and in the press.

## POLITICAL PARTICIPATION AND EXCLUSION

A noticeable feature of the 1970s was that despite the growing impact of political mobilisation among minority communities, black political activists were not as yet widely represented within mainstream political parties. There were, however, some clear signs that at least some black political activists saw the mainstream political parties as an important channel of political representation – one that they needed to use if they were to achieve a significant impact on the political agenda. Whilst participation through community organisations and bodies such as the Community Relations Council allowed access to some political influence, there was a noticeable absence of minority representatives on the local council and within political parties.

This was not a sign of a lack of political consciousness or activism within minority communities, since the 1970s saw a flowering of political mobilisation and protest groups within minority communities. This mobilisation did not, however, have a direct impact in terms of increased minority representation within the main political parties. Indeed, a number of community activists who were later to join the Labour Party and gain positions of influence within it during the 1980s were still at this stage suspicious of mainstream political parties. Two contrasting examples of this phenomenon were James Hunte and Raghib Ahsan who stood against the Labour candidate in the 1977 Ladywood by-election, with moderate success.

During this period there was a noticeable increase in public debate about the politics of race and the role of minorities in the context of the political system. During the two General Elections of 1974 there was widespread debate for the first time about the likely impact of the growing black voting power in many inner city constituencies. At the same time the pressure for the main political parties to select black candidates for local elections and as candidates for parliamentary seats began to grow. There was still a marked reluctance on the part of the Labour and Conservative Parties to respond to this pressure in a positive manner. Kenneth Newton commented in his study of Birmingham's political culture conducted during the late 1960s and early 1970s:

> Interviews with council members revealed a fairly widespread ignorance about the basic facts of the city's coloured population mixed, in a large minority of cases, with an unmistakable degree of racism and bigotry.
>
> (Newton, 1976: 208)

He concluded:

> Race relations offers an example of the politics of the powerless. None of the major institutions of local government and politics seems well adapted to dealing with race and, on the contrary, the issue has been gently shunted onto a political siding where it has been left for powerless and harmless bureaucrats to handle. Race relations in Birmingham has been half a political issue because only half the case has been put – the case of coloured immigrants has yet to see the light of day as a force in local affairs.
>
> (Newton, 1976: 222)

As we shall see in Chapter 4 it was not long before this situation was partially transformed under the weight of important changes at both the local and national levels.

## SUMMARY AND CONCLUSION

This account of the emergence of racialised politics in Birmingham during the period from the 1950s to the 1970s has illustrated the processes of racial formation that helped to shape both the local and the national political culture in ways which are still of some importance today. What we hope we have shown is that it is only through a detailed analysis of the social and political context that we can begin to make sense of the meanings which are attached to 'race' and 'immigration' in specific situations and in relation to policy choices. It should also be clear from our analysis that the processes of racialisation in practice took various forms, both as a result of institutional processes and because of the actions of political actors and community organisations. Far from following a linear or predetermined path, the developments we have explored in this chapter can be seen as the product of often contradictory political and social relations which led to the construction of a politics of race in Birmingham. This construction was partly shaped by national processes, but developments in Birmingham played a central role in the emergence of new forms of political mobilisation around the issue of race.

Having explored this history we are now in a position to analyse the ways in which the contemporary politics of race have moved in new directions over the past two decades. The next five chapters take up what we see as the major components of this transformation and explore both their impact on the local political culture and their broader implications for the question of how we can adequately conceptualise the role and impact of a politics of race in the present environment. These chapters are particularly concerned with the emergence of new forms of racialised political participation and representation, the articulation of political discourses about race and the impact of these transformations on political agendas. In turn, this approach will allow us to address the thorny problem of how to conceptualise the role of racial politics in the present environment and also to consider possible routes of change in the future.

# 4 Parties, black participation and political change

Having analysed some of the key processes that shaped the racialisation of politics in Birmingham during the 1960s and 1970s, we now turn to the question of the impact of growing participation by black communities in mainstream politics during the 1980s and 1990s. It was during this period that the black political presence became a major feature of Birmingham's political culture, as indeed it did in other urban localities. Yet we still know relatively little about why this transformation took place at this time and what the consequences are likely to be for the racialisation of social and political relations in British society. This is why we are exploring key dimensions of this process in the rest of this chapter.

We begin by examining the circumstances under which black people entered the local political system and the reasons for the emergence of black politicians as significant actors. This allows us to examine the interaction between the new black politics and established patterns of political involvement. We then move on to analyse the two issues that dominated the political agenda during much of the 1980s, namely urban unrest and the debate about black sections in the Labour Party. In September 1985 serious urban unrest and civil disorder broke out in Birmingham's Lozells district, and this event was to exercise a major influence on the political system. Large-scale conflict between young black people and the police marked a crisis within the city's social fabric and exposed the stark inequalities that had emerged in the aftermath of de-industrialisation. It also signified an important failure on the part of the political system to satisfy the aspirations of large sections of the city's youth. We will discuss the impact these rebellions had on black politics and the labour movement, and attempt to account for the rapid growth in the number of black elected representatives that took place in their wake. Finally, we explore the terms of the debate about black sections that took place in the Labour Party during the 1980s and the ways it helped to shape the new politics of race. Before going on to discuss these issues we want to situate the conditions and circumstances in which black politicians entered the local political system.

## UNEXPECTED BEGINNINGS: BLACK COMMUNITIES AND POLITICAL PARTICIPATION

Until the mid-1970s both major political parties had done very little to recruit support from Birmingham's established black communities. Labour had benefited from their support electorally whilst offering little in return. This situation changed dramatically during the 1980s. The impulses behind the opening up of the political machinery were complex and often more to do with the ideological battles going on within the parties themselves. What is clear is that by the beginning of the 1980s both the major political parties realised that their electoral fortunes in many urban localities were increasingly dependent on the black vote. This sometimes had bizarre effects.

In a desperate attempt to gain credibility with minority communities, Douglas Osburn, the Conservative candidate for Sparkbrook in the 1983 General Election, canvassed while dressed in a kilt. He explained the rationale behind this in the local press: 'We are all part of some minority or other and you should not make any judgement on race. We are all British' (*Birmingham Evening Mail*, 3 June 1983). However, his new-found ethnic consciousness did not stop him from supporting legislation to maintain strong controls on immigration. More seriously, this election also saw an Indian-born woman, Pamila Le Hunte, stand as the parliamentary candidate for the Ladywood constituency. While Pamila Le Hunte increased the absolute numbers of people voting Conservative in Ladywood, her overall share of the vote fell by 3.2 per cent (*Observer*, 19 June 1983). Ironically, the candidacy of Le Hunte, a clear supporter of immigration control, was contrasted by the independent candidate, Baba Bakjtaura, who fought the election under threat of deportation. Through an anomaly in the law Bakjtaura was allowed to stand for Parliament under the banner of 'Stop Deportations of Black People Now' while not being legally entitled to stay in the country.

Whilst acknowledging a degree of activity within the Conservative Party, the labour movement initially provided the main context within which black people became involved in the political process. Throughout the 1960s and early 1970s inner city Labour Parties had done little to engender political participation from black communities. Indeed many of the inner city Labour Party branches had very small memberships.

It is also relevant that during the late 1970s Birmingham's political system was in large part controlled by right-wing Labour politicians like Brian Walden who represented Ladywood, Denis Howell in Small Heath, Roy Hattersley in Sparkbrook and Roy Jenkins in Stetchford. During this same period, however, at the national level the Labour Party's internal politics were undergoing some important changes. The most notable of these was the emergence of the left as a political force both nationally and at constituency level. A senior official in the labour movement outlines the implications this had for the relationship between the Labour Party and black communities in cities and towns all over the country:

> When the party was going through its changes in the seventies and the left was emerging as a political force, some of the right-wing chose to recruit people

> from the ethnic community as a way of sustaining their position. I think if you were a moderate councillor in 1977 in a ward like Soho what you would do is talk to a couple of 'community leaders' and say that you were under threat and the community leader would recruit thirty people from within the community.
> (Interview, December 1991)

In this sense, part of the impulse to recruit black people to the Party during this period was the need to ensure that the white Labour right retained control in a situation when challenges were being made from the left. We do not want to suggest that these shifts were merely a form of conspiratorial politics concerned with holding on to political power. Equally, as we demonstrate in later chapters, black activists entered politics with a range of commitments. The point that we want to stress is that the growth of black political participation was produced by a complex range of factors. However, the ideological shifts occurring within the Labour Party need to be foregrounded when assessing the political impact of these changes. This scenario was first played out in Birmingham in the then Ladywood and Handsworth constituencies.

The politics of Birmingham's Ladywood constituency were absolutely central in the development of Birmingham's inner city political culture. In 1977 Brian Walden retired as MP for Ladywood to take up a career in broadcasting. Walden, it is said, had by this time established strong links with key people in the local black community. Walden's retirement resulted in a by-election, and he was replaced by the moderate John Sever. The by-election was important for a number of reasons. First, it provided an opportunity for neo-fascist political organisations to mobilise around the election. On 15 August 1977 clashes took place between the Socialist Workers Party and other anti-fascist groups and the National Front outside a political meeting. Three days later Labour held the Ladywood seat with a reduced majority. During the campaign controversy ensued after it was discovered that John Sever's initial agent, inherited from Walden – Peter Marriner – had a long-standing involvement in neo-fascist politics, including the British Movement, National Socialist Movement and British National Youth Movement (*Searchlight*, September 1977). This further discredited Sever and was later to become a crucial factor in the internal politics of the constituency.

The Ladywood by-election also saw two black candidates contesting the seat. Raghib Ahsan, standing as the Socialist Unity candidate, polled 534 votes, whilst the West Indian James Hunte, known for his exposure of the pyramid selling scandal during the mid-1970s, received 336 votes. Both men were later to become councillors, with Ahsan serving on Birmingham City Council and Hunte on West Midlands County Council. The important point here is that charismatic leaders were emerging from within black communities. Hunte, for example, had received widespread attention through his campaign against financial racketeering affecting black people and initially built his political reputation upon this. Saeed Abdi, also later to become a councillor, was involved in the pyramid selling campaign and worked closely with Hunte. The most significant event in Ladywood during this period was not affected, however, by these emerging black politicians.

Sever had attempted to consolidate his position by recruiting key members of the local minority communities. Under the recently changed selection procedure, however, Sever's position was successfully challenged by the then left-winger and Secretary of the District Labour Party, Albert Bore. The deselection of Sever sent a shock wave through the labour movement; this had simply never happened before and suddenly the position of other right-wing MPs could be challenged. Labour activist David Spilsbury wrote in the letters page of the *Guardian* on 1 June 1981 that Sever 'only in the last few months discovered that there are Mosques, Gurdwaras and Temples within the con- stituency'. This was followed by a testimonial letter from a number of local religious leaders (*Guardian*, 6 June 1981) but it was by this time too late. Other MPs in the city were to learn from these events.

During the later part of the 1970s left-wing activists also gained a stronghold in the Handsworth constituency. This resulted in the displacement of black party members who were deemed not left-wing enough. A white activist remembers:

> In the late seventies a handful of militants got control of Handsworth CLP and managed to replace all the black delegates on the General Management Committee. The result was that a white member organised a centre-right take-over and sacked all the militants. This involved mass recruiting through a couple of black party members.

In the ensuing struggle the left were indeed defeated by the white right, with help from the black supporters of people like James Hunte and Saeed Abdi. James Hunte became chairman of the branch and his wife Sharon Hunte became membership secretary. Hunte was eventually elected as a county councillor in 1980, but Handsworth's politics were dogged by allegations of membership irregularities.

Hunte continued to be a controversial yet charismatic figure. There were repeated rumours that as Vice-Chairman of West Midlands County Council's Race Relations Committee his allocation of small grants was irregular – even discretionary. Hunte was also the National Director of the Midland Community Growth and Support Association that organised the prestigious Mohammed Ali Community Centre, which was opened by the former world champion himself. The importance of Hunte to the right-wing Labour leadership was demonstrated in May 1980 when Clive Wilkinson, leader of the City Council, wrote to Tom King, then Minister for Local Government, urging him to approve an extra payment of £150,000 to the Centre. Howard Sharron, writing in the *New Statesman*, commented:

> There is nothing improper in any of this. Rather it is a testament to the influential position James Hunte now holds in Birmingham's Labour Party decisions. As the white working-class vote becomes increasingly volatile, the support of black voters is going to become increasingly decisive.
>
> (*New Statesman*, 4 March 1983)

A black councillor was less sanguine about the legacy of James Hunte's political practices:

> James was on the County Council until it was disbanded. James was involved in all kinds of dubious deals; basically he was put in charge of a small grants committee and he was accused of giving money to his friends. There was no doubt about it. This was true and many church-going West Indians were absolutely appalled by this. But James Hunte always ensured that there was a trickle down in terms of black communities getting some money. I obviously didn't like the fact that he was acting as some kind of patron giving out money according to people he liked. James Hunte was corrupt – no doubt about it – but he was actually the Labour Party's creation. The Labour Party had effectively created him and he was used on lots of occasions as the easy person for the Party to deal with.
>
> (Interview, May 1991)

Politicians like James Hunte provided easy fodder for the local popular press whom they could caricature through predictable racial stereotypes. In January 1983 the *Birmingham Evening Mail* ran a full-page story on the allocations of funds to black projects proclaiming to its readership: 'Where your money goes'. Under a cloud of allegations James Hunte and his wife returned to Barbados in the late 1980s amidst rumours that they had been 'paid off' in order to ensure minimum scandal.

During the early 1980s Rudy Narayan, the Guyana-born barrister and black activist, made an attempt to be nominated as Handsworth's parliamentary candidate. The selection was subject to an enquiry after it was alleged that Narayan had made anti-Semitic comments in his book *Black England* (1977). Equally, it was suggested that his supporters had offered a free lunch to volunteers prepared to visit 200 party members in Handsworth seeking their backing for the Narayan nomination. After the enquiry the Labour executive ordered the selection to be re-run, with the clear implication that Narayan should not be put forward. Shortly afterwards Narayan left the Labour Party, vowing to stand as an independent candidate and encourage other black politicians to do likewise. He accused the Labour Party of racism and antipathy to the emergence of black parliamentary representatives (*Birmingham Evening Mail*, 24 November 1981). The *Birmingham Post* ran an editorial that would establish a pattern of reaction to autonomous black political organisations to be replayed later in the decade. It warned:

> The only way in which black candidates can expect to become MPs is for them to work within the present party system and to be selected on merit. An all-black party, however loosely formulated, would almost inevitably lead to black voters voting for black candidates and white voters voting for whites. Any racially-partial party can only be a backward step in the struggle for harmony.
>
> (*Birmingham Post*, 30 November 1981)

Clare Short, a local anti-racist activist, was to get the nomination, and under the boundary changes Handsworth and Ladywood constituencies were amalgamated. In the ensuing selection battle with Albert Bore, Short emerged as the victor.

The significance of these events can be summarised as follows: first, the deselection of a sitting MP meant that it was possible that others would come under similar challenges; second, black people were being brought into the Party largely to bolster support for the established local leadership; third, that these forms of recruitment did not necessarily result in unthinking compliance, and by the early 1980s the issue of the relationship between race and political representation was already being hotly debated both inside and outside the Labour Party. These shifts need to be seen within the overall context of a decline in political activity within Labour branches. A long-time Labour activist remembers:

> In the 1950s the level of membership was much more than it is today and generally I think the fall in participation has been a disaster. We used to have membership drives bringing hundreds of people into the party. I remember my ward in 1952–53 had over 800 members. In the sixties the Party had five full-time agents and Birmingham was noted for having one of the wealthiest local organisations in the country.
>
> (Interview, May 1990)

By the mid-1970s this situation had shifted dramatically. Along with the demise of the city's industrial base there was a sharp fall-off in popular interest in political participation in the Labour Party. Nowhere was this more acute than in the inner city districts. Strangely, some activists have claimed that in some circumstances small memberships were actually fostered. A white Labour Party activist recalls:

> In general, Labour Parties in those days were very small and the inner-city ones unbelievably small. Sparkbrook had a very small membership. It met on a Sunday morning in the old Sparkbrook Labour club and there wasn't a proper meeting but they would just count the first ten Labour Party members to come in for a drink and that would be it – 'Yes, we can go with the meeting now'. That would have been about 1976. . . . In 1982 when I joined the Small Heath party – and they'd had this system for years – they used to have their own membership application forms so that they could limit who became a member of the Party. Unless you'd filled in one of these forms you couldn't join Small Heath Labour Party. If they kept a limit on the distribution of the forms then they could limit the membership.
>
> (Interview, December 1993)

In the context of the potential threat posed by the emergence of the left, retaining a small local membership could be an effective way of keeping political control, as well as pre-empting the possibility of an attempt to deselect the Member of Parliament. Constituency Labour Parties such as Small Heath and Stetchford were nationally notorious for having a small party membership.

In the interviews that we have conducted with party activists – both black and white – a common assertion was that the recruitment of sections of the black community in the late 1970s and early 1980s was the means by which established factions within inner city constituencies managed a growth in membership that did not threaten the local balance of political control. In these accounts a common assertion is that this resulted in a crude form of 'patronage politics'. A white Labour activist suggested:

> I think that MPs looked to groups that they knew they could offer patronage to in return for votes. I think it was a simple as that. Particularly when MPs had the power to intervene in deportations. I remember when neighbours of mine had relatives who were being deported, you could phone up Roy Hattersley, or any other MP, and have the deportation stopped. The MPs also had power over everyday matters like housing. If you get a direct line to the MP and you can get things done then you can owe that person a favour. It was cynically set up in places like Sparkbrook and Small Heath where people were discouraged from going to see their MP directly but went to see someone who was a community leader, who would speak to the MP on your behalf.
>
> (Interview, December 1993)

We shall return to this question in Chapters 5 and 6, but it suffices to say here that in these cases the growth of black political participation did not necessarily ensure a significant growth in political influence. Beyond this it was almost exclusively established men who were becoming active and recruiting members for the Labour Party. A Muslim woman commented:

> It is difficult for them [community leaders] to see a woman as having an equal say or having any views at all because it is always the men who make the decisions and have the final say. In politics women have no chance.
>
> (Interview, July 1991)

This has clear political implications for the degree to which such increased political participation reflected the age, gender and other constituencies within minority communities. A white Labour activist comments:

> It wasn't as if the Labour Party went out on the streets with stalls saying – 'Come and join the Labour Party, we are the party that fights racism'. It wasn't that kind of open recruiting. It was very closed recruiting. I am sure that MPs picked certain people within the community who made it clear what would be expected in return for their patronage. Two meetings a year would be crucial, the AGM and the councillor selection; these were the moments when the favours were called in.
>
> (Interview, December 1993)

In this context the participation of black members in the political machinery of the Labour Party was in practice extremely limited. Community leaders effectively acted as vote brokers who delivered the vote and courted patronage and influence over the everyday matters that affected black communities in their neighbourhoods such as housing, refuse collection and immigration cases.

What emerged was an instrumental form of political mobilisation: white right-wing MPs received bolstered support, and black power brokers – or 'Kingmakers' as they are referred to in the political vernacular – could make fast and effective representations to the MPs, who had the means to achieve results. We are using the notion of 'instrumental politics' as a way of describing the form of political exchange that was established. In many ways, local black communities were willing to submit to this politics, despite its neo-colonial connotation, because it was an effective way of achieving tangible results. It could be the difference between having a powerful advocate who could stop a relative from being deported or have new windows installed, and being confronted with a state bureaucracy that was at best indifferent to the needs of black communities and at worst openly racist.

Roy Hattersley, MP for Sparkbrook since the 1960s, alluded to this new politics in an endpiece article published in the *Guardian* newspaper in March 1982. After a long discussion of the relationship between the city's economy and imperial exploits he comments: 'So after a 100 years of Birmingham going out to the Empire, the Empire began to come to Birmingham.' Invoking the memory of Joseph Chamberlain, who was in large part the chief architect of Birmingham's civic structure, he continued:

> I hope that Joseph Chamberlain would have been proud. If he were still a central Birmingham MP he would certainly be required to take the old empire and new Commonwealth very seriously.
>
> He would have to go to the mosque barefooted and to the temples with head covered. He would argue with the Home Office about the rights of relations anxious to make brief visits . . . . And, if he had either sense or sensitivity, he would rejoice at what he saw all around him – Aston Villa fans who wear the bracelets and badges of a pious Sikh; Muslims who play bar billiards but will not drink alcohol; girls in jeans who want their husbands to be chosen by their fathers.
>
> (*The Guardian*, 6 March 1982)

This quotation barely conceals reference to the kind of politics that we have discussed. It also highlights the patron–client relationships that characterised the local political culture.

Initially, black members were not elected to the executive of the local constituency parties. This changed later, but in the early stages of black participation local political institutions were divided along stark racial lines. The workings of important meetings, such as those concerned with the selection of candidates, were often influenced by racialised divisions. A white activist who was involved in such meetings remembers:

> The officers would generally remain white and they only wanted to get through the business. Very little politics was actually discussed; usually the balloting system was very complicated. So you would have this explained for perhaps five minutes in English by the Chair, then he would ask for a translation in Urdu. But usually the translation was 'vote for . . .', then a list of people. It was as crude as that. Then you would get Asian members saying that

> this wasn't a translation and that people should be left to make up their own minds and arguments would break out.
>
> (Interview, December 1993)

The racial divisions in the political vernacular of these meetings reflected the contradictions within this kind of politics. He continues:

> People weren't even known by their own names. The white officers called them Khan 1, Khan 2 and things like that. I always remember an Asian member – who is a councillor now – complaining: 'Can't you at least learn our names?'. It was amazing the white officers would never meet with the members. The thing that always sticks in my mind is that the white officers acted as if the Khan 1, Khan 2 business was some mutually agreed friendly nickname when it obviously wasn't, and more than that it was deeply patronising and offensive.
>
> (Interview, December 1993)

The everyday political process was affected to such a degree that political campaigns – particularly in the context of elections – in inner city wards would be conducted along *de facto* segregated lines. A white activist here describes the situation in the Nechells ward of the Small Heath constituency in the early 1980s:

> Even the election organisation in Nechells was divided on ethnic lines, in that where I live on the big council estates it was completely white, or almost completely white helpers. Whereas in Saltley the party workers were mainly Asian but there was never a coming together of the two. After the election when we used to go back for a bit of a celebration there were only white people.
>
> (Interview, December 1993)

The situation was to change as more and more black activists were elected onto the general management committees of constituencies. The fact that black activists emerged is perhaps not the crucial issue; it is the conditions in which they emerged that are of paramount importance. This is not to say that black activists were simply co-opted in some crude conspiratorial way. There are many cases where local activists came into the Labour Party under the conditions we have described and later became critical of the local political culture. In this sense these forms of local political mobilisation were unstable and open to change. A Labour Party official summarised the more dynamic situation that was emerging by the 1980s:

> In the seventies that was the pattern – white politicians securing their position by recruiting support from within the ethnic community – but by the eighties I think that people within the community started to realise that they could be players themselves.
>
> (Interview, December 1991)

It is precisely these shifts and the possible potential of a loosening of the relations of patronage in local politics that we want to examine.

In many ways the situation in each of the inner city constituencies where large-scale recruitment of black party members occurred had unique local qualities. However, they all demonstrate the emergence of an instrumental model of political mobilisation. We will discuss this more fully in the following section, but two points need to be summarised here:

- The crisis that inner city MPs faced with regard to defending their position in the late 1970s is an important factor in understanding the increase in black participation in the Labour Party.
- An instrumental form of politics emerged that can be characterised by a form of exchange, where MPs secured their position while an elite group of black activists could influence the distribution of local resources, services and representation to state bureaucracies.

The end result was an elite negotiation within the local machinery of the labour movement. This local political culture was to have an enduring, although not determining effect on the struggles for political representation that were to emerge later in the decade. Alongside these instrumental forms of politics other more ideologically inspired challenges were also taking place. In addition to this, as the ranks of the local Labour Parties started to swell, complex, often competing factions emerged producing a volatile political terrain where lines of alliance and support proved dynamic and open to revision.

## 'SENSIBLE SOCIALISM': RACE, THE LOCAL POLITICAL AGENDA AND THE EMERGENCE OF BLACK POLITICIANS

In 1979 the first post-war black councillors were elected. Egbert Carliss, born in the West Indies, became councillor for the inner city ward of Aston, and Prem Singh Kalsi was elected in All Saints. In the fifteen years that followed the number of black councillors representing the city grew dramatically. In 1994 33 per cent of the ruling Labour Group, some twenty councillors, were from Birmingham's black communities. Of these politicians 95 per cent represent inner city wards where the black population is at least 40 per cent of the total. These dramatic changes have not resulted in a marked change of political direction on the part of the local Labour leadership. However, these changes took place at incredible speed.

In 1979 the local authority was controlled by a Conservative administration. Labour then took control for two consecutive years, only to be replaced by the Conservatives in 1982–1983. During this time the number of black councillors increased to five. There was also quite intense activity by black activists within Birmingham's Labour rank and file to get the issue of race and racial equality taken seriously. In February 1982 an Ethnic Minority Liaison Committee was set up within Birmingham's Labour Party. The committee consisted of representatives from ethnic minority communities and the group was committed to ensuring that the party fought the election in 1983 on a commitment to racial equality and greater representation for black people within the party's decision-making machinery. The Committee constructed a detailed report outlining key policy initiatives that should be placed on the political agenda. It was passed by Conference but not included within the Party's manifesto for that year.

What seems striking is that although clear policy statements were passed throughout this period by the District Labour Party, when it came to presenting these suggestions to the electorate, the dominant faction within the Labour Group diluted these resolutions so as not to threaten the Party's traditional base of white working-class support. During the mid-1980s, however, an important shift took place and the policies that had been formulated within the District Party over a five-year period formed an integral part of the 1984 manifesto.

In 1984, a new Labour administration with a policy commitment to set up a political infrastructure to address issues of racial equality replaced the Conservatives. A Race Relations and Equal Opportunity Committee was added to the Committee structure of the Council, and a number of initiatives seemed to indicate that the issue of race had at last arrived on the local political agenda. In addition to this the new Labour administration also saw a rise in black politicians amongst their ranks. The number of black Labour politicians grew gradually in the early years of the Labour administration from eight in 1984, to nine in 1985.

In reality, however, the new policies led to conflicts and tensions. This resulted in 1987 in the dissolution of the Race Relations and Equal Opportunity Committee, along with the Women's Committee, into a Personnel and Equal Opportunities Committee. The move was a response to what the leadership perceived to be policies that were unpopular and therefore an electoral liability. Councillor Phillip Murphy, a leading black political figure, who was removed as Vice-Chair of the Committee in November 1986, commented at the time:

> Clearly, they (the Leadership) felt that getting rid of the Race Relations Committee and the Women's Committee would be popular with the traditional skilled and white collar working class vote. It was a totally wrong perception. But this is the reason why they got rid of the committee.
>
> (Quoted from *AFFOR Quarterly Newsletter*, July 1987)

The pattern that developed during this period shows a clear division between the policy commitments passed within the District Labour Party and the resistance of the controlling members within the Labour Group elected to the City Council.

During this period the number of black politicians in the Labour Group grew rapidly. In 1987 the number increased from eight to fourteen. With a few notable exceptions, the black councillors supported the leadership's stance and the shift of emphasis to play down the Party's commitment to tackling racial inequality. This is explained in part by the association of the District Labour Party with the left. The Labour leadership was determined during this period to avoid any association between Birmingham and local authority anti-racism as practised by the Greater London Council. The support of moderate black councillors was important in steering Birmingham away from the left. Opposition by these councillors to the formation of black sections within the Labour Party was another issue that was fully exploited by the Birmingham Labour Group.

The then council leader, Dick Knowles, presented Birmingham as a moderate right-wing council, interested in achieving results rather than 'championing slogans'. Throughout this period the Personnel and Equal Opportunities Committee, headed by a white male, enjoyed some successes. This was particularly the case in relation to employment within council departments, as well as in relation to service delivery. Dick Knowles summed up the situation in this way:

> I think we have been successful without having the high profile which some of the London Boroughs have had. I do basically what is possible to do with the £1,350 million worth of expenditure that is what the city spends in a year.
>
> (Interview, March 1990)

In contrast to left-wing local authorities in London, Birmingham presented a modest policy package on racial equality and equal opportunities. In this sense a not so new 'new realism' (Sewell, 1990) – or what some Labour politicians prefer to call pragmatism – was being operated within Birmingham from the mid-1980s onwards. It is ironic that this should coincide with the heyday of local authority anti-racism in London and elsewhere. This approach was characterised by what Dick Knowles referred to as 'sensible socialism'.

The symbolism of black political participation – in particular the emergence of black elected representatives – was used by some to signify the Labour Group's commitment to racial equality. In 1987, during a debate that centred around immigration, a Conservative member accused the Labour party of 'humbug and hypocrisy'. The charge was met by the Chair of the Race Relations Committee with the following riposte: 'Look at the benches opposite. Show me your black members. You have not got any and you do not know anything about race relations' (*Birmingham Evening Mail*, 8 April 1987). This is an interesting example of the rhetorical use of black political representation as a way of deflecting criticism. In this sense the existence of black representatives became a means whereby Labour's purchase on the politics of race was legitimised. The fact that a relatively sizeable number of black politicians have been elected to the Council has been used as proof of the commitment within the Labour Group to racial equality. As the then Leader of the Council argued:

> I look at my Colleagues down in London and I say . . . well my argument is when they say look at racist Birmingham, I say, 'How many councillors have you got on your local authority, how many members have you got in your party who are black?'
>
> (Interview, March 1990)

However, as we have argued, there are interesting and important questions to raise about the terms on which black politicians entered the political arena and the relationships that put them there. By the late 1980s there were seventeen black councillors, all representing the Labour Party. If they could have acted as a cohesive caucus they could have held the balance of power between right and left and set an agenda of their own. However, as we shall see in Chapter 6, this did not happen. As we shall argue later this needs to be explained in terms of the way these politicians were situated within Labour's ideological divisions and political networks. Equally, the position of black politicians is affected by the dynamics of ward and constituency Labour Party branches.

The situation in local Labour Party branches was changing rapidly throughout the 1980s. Local black political figures were emerging under the patronage of local MPs. In addition to having important powers to represent constituents, local MPs could also play a key and important role in influencing the selection of councillors. This was not conspiratorial or underhand, but purely worked by the fact that the MP was an important local figure and he or she could influence local activists by simply sponsoring a candidate. Those people who wanted to retain the patronage of the MP would obviously listen to and comply with such requests. Equally, what was also happening during this period was that rival factions within local communities were emerging.

The whole process of vote brokering also often involved the mobilisation of kin and clan relations. Somctimcs issues of caste were crucial in establishing common lines of support and mobilisation. These divisions were determined by a Birmingham variant of the Rajput caste system. In particular, two high castes were significant in the south of the city: a landowning caste called Chaudhury and a military caste called Raja. As a Muslim woman comments here on the significance of caste divisions:

> It is not just a matter of one particular caste supporting this or that faction. It is also that the other lower castes will be loyal to that person. The village that my father in law is from was mostly made up of Chaudhurys so in his village working people from lower castes have loyalty to them; and certain people in the village will have to the Rajas in a neighbouring village. It was fading but it has all come back.
>
> (Interview, July 1991)

Caste plays a significant role in defining lines of support and recruitment. For example, we noted that a number of minority Labour candidates used caste names when fighting elections. This was the mechanism by which supporters could not only be recruited but also persuaded to support particular candidates. This system was particularly significant in the south of the city, within Pakistani and Kashmiri communities. In the Muslim community caste endures despite the fact that it is prohibited by Islam. These divisions themselves have their origin in Hinduism and crossed into Muslim communities during the sixteenth century. Some political activists we interviewed were critical of the continued significance of caste divisions, often arguing that this was discouraging young people from getting involved in the political arena. Others we interviewed claimed that the new forms of patronage politics had revived and exacerbated caste divisions in inner city constituencies:

> No one mentioned caste names ten years ago. Now people use them in politics

all the time. It is the old-colonial trick of divide and rule but this is actually being made worse by our own community. I came to Britain to get away from things like that.

(Interview, July 1991)

In the context of political struggles and rivalries, caste is utilised either to court support or discredit an opponent from a 'lower' caste. As a result caste identities are a crucial feature of the local political culture, and they encourage key forms of internal division. In addition to this other social identities that have their origin in Kashmiri village politics are being adapted and transformed within the Birmingham context. An example of this is the fictive kin notion of bradthery (literally meaning brother) which is used to describe trans-kin relations, sometimes relating to a shared village origin. These divisions have become more important in the context of the instrumental politics we have described because they provide a social mechanism for delivering support and ultimately votes.

The types of exacerbated internal divisions are not confined to Kashmiri and Pakistani communities. Similar processes were also in operation in the north of the city, amongst African-Caribbean and Indian communities. In this situation there could be intense rivalry between factions, particularly over the selection of a councillor. However, there was not necessarily a clear fit between the mobilisation of a particular community or faction and the selection of a councillor from within that faction. In one case we encountered in our research, two factions from within the Pakistani Muslim community were competing over the selection of a councillor. Rather than accept the Muslim candidate from the rival faction the numerically superior group opted for an Indian Sikh.

The importance of these developments is that they signalled a shift in the control that was formerly exercised by the traditional white working-class leadership. MPs now had to negotiate with minority vote brokers who were beginning to realise that they could revoke their support. However, it is equally important to stress that the growing number of ethnic minority councillors were in large part the product of the political mobilisations that were taking place in the 1980s. Indeed, some of our informants suggested that the emergence of black councillors was in part a strategy on the part of MPs to manage or pre-empt any political challenge.

We shall return to the full significance of these changes in later chapters but for now it is important to stress that both the developments we have discussed – the growth of black membership and the increase in the number of black political representatives – did not necessarily challenge the established local political leaders. On the contrary, they could actually serve to bolster their influence and retain control. This political situation was not ideologically inspired, rather it was the result of an instrumental and pragmatic approach to politics. In short, black vote brokers and activists were motivated by a desire to access the local political system via the patronage of white politicians without challenging their position. It would be inaccurate to present the changes that took place during this period as merely forms of political accommodation. Alongside and sometimes inside the trends we have discussed important arguments were taking place about the position of black politicians within the local system and the prominence of the issue of racial equality on the local agenda. This is why the crucial issues of the mid-1980s became the political empowerment of black communities and the efficacy of the local state in facilitating an open and multiracial democracy. In the following section we want to shift our emphasis and explore the way these issues became focused on struggles for organisational change within the Labour Party and the outbreak of civil unrest within Birmingham.

## URBAN UNREST AND THE BLACK SECTIONS CONTROVERSY

Two key events in the mid-1980s became focal points for the discussion of the position of black communities *vis à vis* the political system. These were (i) the outbreaks of urban unrest in major urban conurbations, and (ii) the furore over the attempt to create black sections within the Labour Party. Both of these events helped to shape the pace of change in relation to black political participation in Birmingham. The outbreak of urban unrest can be seen as a spur to change because of the political meanings attached to the appearance of violence on the streets. More directly the controversy over black sections in the Labour Party put the question of the role of black politicians firmly on the political agenda. The black sections issue came to dominate the debate about the political representation of black people in the Labour Party throughout the 1980s. In many ways the suggestion that black sections were necessary to engender equality of access to Labour Party institutions raised serious questions about the ways in which black people had previously entered the Labour Party. We shall return to these issues later. But first we want to look at how the outbreak of unparalleled urban conflict influenced political debates and conflicts.

### Urban unrest and political change

In 1981 widespread civil unrest was experienced throughout Britain's major cities. In the Midlands young people clashed with the police in Smethwick, Sandwell and Birmingham. Civil conflict in Birmingham was fairly limited, particularly when compared with London or Liverpool. Four years later, however, this situation was to change dramatically. On 9 and 10 September 1985 large-scale conflict broke out on the Lozells Road, culminating in the tragic murder of two Asian shopkeepers who were trapped in their burning shop during the disturbances. No one really knows what happened. The point here is that the event itself became a symbol to be claimed. The national and local press all covered the story. The dominant newspaper image was a picture of a young black man carrying a lit petrol bomb. The picture, taken by a Canadian photographer, documented a skirmish that took place in the aftermath of a visit to Birmingham by the Home Secretary, Douglas Hurd. The *Daily Express*, the *Mirror*, the *Sun*, the *Observer* and the *Daily Mail* all used the photograph. The papers announced the arrival of the latest racial insurgent:

> He walks with a chilling swagger, a petrol bomb in hand and hate burning in his heart.
>
> (*Daily Telegraph*, 11 September 1985)

> A black thug stalks a Birmingham street with hate in his eyes and a petrol bomb in his hand. The prowling West Indian was one of the hoodlums who brought new race terror to the city's riot-torn Handsworth district yesterday. . . . Two Asian brothers screamed in agony as West Indian rioters beat them – and then left them to burn alive in the petrol-bombed sub-post office.
>
> (*Sun*, 11 September 1985)

The dominant theme of the reporting of these events suggested that a 'race riot' had taken place and that the death of the Moledina brothers was the result of tension between the African-Caribbean and Asian communities. This was despite factual details such as the presence of large numbers of whites and Asians on the streets who were arrested during this incident, and the fact that the person charged for the Moledina murders was in fact white. Mark Andrew Barratt was charged with the crime on 23 September 1985 (*Express and Star*, 23 September 1985).

This event marked a definite shift in the way in which black male youths were represented. In Chapter 3 we discussed how black criminality had been one of the key themes in the ways in which the black presence in Birmingham had been described. At one level the reporting of the events of September 1985 was merely an elaboration from one form of racialised criminality (mugging) to another (rioting). The 'black mugger' was surpassed by a new folk demon, the 'black bomber'. This shift not only associated black youth with crimes against the person but also with crimes against society.

While these events were dubbed, by local and national media alike, the 'Handsworth riots' they did not take place in Handsworth at all. Rather, they happened on the Lozells Road, in the neighbouring district of Lozells. How can it be that events that took place in one part of the city can be shifted and represented as happening somewhere else? This can be partly explained in terms of the imagined racial geography of Birmingham we discussed in the previous chapter. The regimes of representation that metonymically connected the district of Handsworth with black criminality were able to map these events within the context of antecedent racialised meanings. To invoke the name 'Lozells' did not communicate the racially coded information that we described in Chapter 3. 'Handsworth', in contrast, could be used to signify the full legacy of racist images that had been used to represent Birmingham's black communities.

The historical weight of these constructs was symbolised in a cartoon that appeared in the *Daily Telegraph* on 12 September. It featured Douglas Hurd, the then Home Secretary, looking at a police line-up of five young black male figures. Hurd's 'fact-finding' visit to Lozells in the aftermath of unrest on the night of 9 September had provoked controversy. It was widely reported that he was jostled and forced to leave the area prematurely (*Birmingham Evening Mail*, 11 September 1985; *Daily Mail*, 11 September 1985). In the aftermath of this visit further civil unrest occurred and it was at this point that the pictures of black youths holding petrol bombs were taken. Each figure presented in the cartoon had written across their chests an emblem of urban malaise: unemployment, drugs, crime, poor housing, racial tension. These figures were illuminated by a spotlight covering the line up. The cartoon can be read as a metaphor. The figures are represented as symptomatic of how Handsworth is socially constituted: made visible by a white light.

This, we feel, sums up how whiteness as a discourse is manifest within urban environments, acting as an illuminating presence that we cannot see, while determining what is made visible. bell hooks has commented that racism constructs black people as being unable to 'view' white people and that they can only be looked upon. Her book entitled *Black Looks* (hooks, 1992) is an attempt to undermine and expose this syndrome. From this perspective the riots that took place during this period constitute an elaborate series of 'white looks'. This had little to do with the pigment of the image and news-makers' skin. Rather it reflected the colour of their imaginations. Importantly, these images have a historical depth and they connect with the legacy of what we referred to in Chapter 3 as a racialised imagined geography. It is only here that we can begin to understand how the events on the Lozells Road in 1985 came to be called the 'Handsworth riots'.

These 'white looks' have consequences. In the aftermath of the disturbances the news photographs provided a crucial resource in pursuing criminal cases. In particular there was a great deal of reporting in the local media over the issue of the identity of the 'bomber' (*Express and Star*, 13 September 1985). Within days the name of James Hazell was released in connection with the image by the police. Hazell was eventually brought to trial and prosecuted in 1986, although there has been some doubt surrounding the conviction. The trial itself took on a bizarre quality because of claims on the part of the prosecution that Hazell had changed his physical appearance.

The events of 1985 constituted a crisis of legitimacy within the local political culture. Equally, they exposed divisions within the emerging black political elite. Within the ranks of the City Council both major political parties established a bipartisan consensus on these civil conflicts. They were almost uniformly condemned by politicians regardless of political affiliation. Indeed, the primary concern of some influential politicians was how to repair the city's public image in view of a bid to host the 1992 Olympic Games. For example, Denis Howell went to the length of pointing out at a presentation to the members of the International Olympic Committee (IOC) in Spain that the proposed Olympic sites in Birmingham were 'vastly different' from the Lozells Road (*Sunday Times*, 15 September 1985). This was taking place at a time when large numbers of the city's young people were facing public order charges and a broad-based Defence Campaign was being organised in Handsworth. One local black activist viewed the response of the City Council as a telling statement on their priorities:

> It was crazy. You had MPs and practically every politician in the city worried about the Olympic bid, the image of Birmingham, and others just scoring political points, while we were trying to get people out of custody and getting

> legal representation for droves of young people who were being pulled off the street. It was crazy – as if the politicians didn't care as long as they could blame the 'drug dealers' which really mean black youth.
>
> (Interview, February 1994)

The leaders of the Labour Group maintained a strong line of condemning the violence. This included the majority of the nine black Labour councillors. However, in a well-publicised public dispute, James Hunte stated that while he regretted the loss of life he refused to unreservedly condemn those involved in the conflicts. This was brought to a head in September during a meeting of Birmingham's Community Relations Council. A number of Asian members, including the then Chair of Birmingham City Council's Race Relations and Equal Opportunities Committee, Sardul Marwa, threatened to resign. The controversy continued for a number of weeks and there were calls from within Labour's Ethnic Minority Liaison Committee for Marwa in particular to resign because he was making divisive remarks.

The construction of the events of 1985 as a 'race riot' was partly explained in the media in terms of the logic of African-Asian antipathy. Such images were at best simplified versions of quite complex social processes. We are not suggesting that these divisions are merely projected onto the city's minority communities. We have found in our research a popular racial discourse that mirrors these media formulations. The point that we want to make here is that simplistic images of Afro-Asian antipathy have little value in explaining political conflicts. An example of this was when the new ruling Labour Group attempted to construct a forum for ethnic minority voluntary sector groups. The conference was held in Digbeth in 1984. During the proceedings an all 'Asian' executive was elected; as a result African-Caribbean delegates walked out of the conference and boycotted the forum. These kinds of assertions are political constructions that need to be critically evaluated within the context of racialised politics. We do not want to deny that these ideas have a political validity, yet we want to make it clear that there are severe problems in reifying these constructions of identity and giving them explanatory power.

The then Leader of the Council, Dick Knowles, caused controversy in 1985 when he spoke publicly of 'black and brown youth'. Black activists argued repeatedly and forcefully in the local and national media that these divisions were spurious. Beanie Brown, long time black activist, maintained that the 'idea that this riot had anything to do with a West Indian/Asian situation is completely untrue' (*Guardian*, 12 September 1985). Equally, evidence that important cultural dialogues were taking place between young Asians and African-Caribbeans was also presented to counter claims of intercommunal strife. David Rose wrote in the *Guardian*:

> Young Asians in Lozells Road Asian Resource Centre said that young Asians and blacks shared the experience of unemployment and harassment by the police . . . Narinder, aged 21, said that he often went to West Indian blues parties and went to African clubs.
>
> (12 September 1985)

The existence of these dialogues was to be borne out by the emergence of transracial Afro-Asian youth cultures in the late 1980s, highlighting the crudity of the racial discourses that were used to explain intercommunal relationships in Handsworth. Despite the frequency of dismissive comments from politicians and ample evidence of youthful dialogue, the notion of Afro-Asian antipathy is a resilient discourse. We shall examine this in detail in Chapter 6.

The conflicts that happened on the Lozells Road in 1985 had a range of important implications for Birmingham's politics. In one sense they were an enigma, a series of events that needed to be explained or possessed. There were, for example, no fewer than three inquiries into the events. This first was headed by Geoffrey Dear, the Chief Constable of West Midlands Police (Dear, 1985), another was conducted by Julius Silverman for the City Council (Silverman, 1986) and a third conducted by black intellectuals and key figures such as Herman Ouseley, Reena Bhavnani, Stuart Hall and Paul Gilroy for the West Midlands County Council (Ohri and Phillips, 1986). All three inquiries came up with rather different accounts. At a broader level the mass media had to give an explanation of these events. We have argued that this led to a further elaboration of racist constructions of the city's citizens and its internal geography.

The sheer scale of the civil unrest sent clear messages to the city's political leaders that the local political system was failing young people in the inner-ring areas of the city. This also affected the emerging black political representatives involved in the Community Relations Council and the Labour Party, who needed to show loyalty to their political patrons while placating the desires and fears of the communities with which they were associated. In addition to civil unrest on an unparalleled scale, the Labour Party also faced new demands for equal political access and representation by black members within its ranks.

## Black sections in Birmingham

The debate on the political representation of black people within the Labour Party during this period revolved primarily around the issue of constructing black sections within the party's organisational structure. The influx of black activists into the Party on a national level was triggered during the 1970s by the hope that greater democracy within the Party would provide a space for the organisation of black interests (Wainwright, 1987; Shukra, 1990a). As we explained in the early parts of this chapter, the situation in Birmingham needs to be seen in the context of the way in which black members were often recruited to support threatened right-wing white politicians. In this situation the black sections controversy must necessarily be viewed in the context of the pre-existence of these instrumental forms of minority political mobilisation. The venom which surrounded the debate in Birmingham is in part a result of the fact that by raising the issue of minority interests and representation the movement for black sections threatened the lines of political patronage that had been established by the mid-1980s.

The first attempt in the West Midlands to set up a black section was in

Ladywood in the summer of 1984. The MP for the constituency, Clare Short, was openly supportive of the initiative. She commented:

> In a city like Birmingham where we have a big black membership there is not a representative proportion of black people in influential positions.
>
> (*Birmingham Evening Mail*, 25 July 1984)

The majority of the key political figures involved in black sections were from London and had developed support in left-wing constituencies in the capital. In many ways Short, on the left of the party, subscribed to some of the political agendas being formulated in London. The same, however, cannot be said of the rest of the parliamentary constituencies.

In Roy Hattersley's Sparkbrook constituency the proposal to allow a proposal to form a black section was defeated narrowly by the casting vote of the chairman. Jeff Rooker, the MP for Perry Barr, joined in the opposition to black sections by claiming that they would be tantamount to importing 'apartheid' (*Birmingham Post*, 30 June 1984). However, the opposition to black sections was not merely from those members of the Party on the white right. Councillor Sardul Marwa, at the time leading the city's race relations structure, echoed Rooker's warning. He was quoted in the local press as saying:

> It is segregation, it is apartheid. . . . We have got nine coloured councillors in Birmingham who have all gone through the system that exists now.
>
> (*Birmingham Evening Mail*, 3 August 1984)

Despite this, the first national conference of Labour Party black sections was held in Birmingham on 9 June 1984. Roy Hattersley was invited to speak to the conference but he declined the offer, commenting that the movement was a 'retrograde step' (*Birmingham Post*, 30 May 1984; *The Times*, 11 June 1984). Over 300 delegates attended the conference at Digbeth Civic Hall, and messages of support were received by prominent left-wing figures such as Ken Livingstone, the then leader of the Greater London Council and Tony Benn, MP. The conference poster set the tone and sent out a clear challenge: 'Labour Party we love you, do you love us?'

The conference was attended by such black local political figures as James Hunte and Phillip Murphy, who was to become a prominent black councillor on the City Council. Vidya Anand, Chair of the Community Liaison Sub-Committee of the Greater London Labour Party, sent a clear warning from the conference floor:

> Up until now we seem to have been taken for granted. It has been thought sufficient to have a few Uncle Toms and Godfathers to perform the same role on behalf of our people. That is to deliver our votes at election time by keeping them ignorant and outside the mainstream of the party. Those days are now over.
>
> (*Observer*, 10 June 1984)

James Hunte warned Hattersley, the Deputy Leader of the Labour Party at the time, that:

> There is no turning back. We are faced with a situation where our Leader and Deputy Leader think there is no accommodation for us. They will have a hell of a fight on their hands. We should surround his [Hattersley's] surgery in our hundreds to seek redress for the statement he has made.
>
> (*Observer*, 10 June 1984)

Roy Hattersley's Sparkbrook constituency became a focal point of the debate on black sections in the West Midlands. As became clear, however, this was more to do with local political practices than any political move to establish support for black sections.

On 26 September 1985 Channel 4's black current affairs programme *Bandung File* screened an investigation into the relationship between black people and the Labour Party in the Sparkbrook constituency. The programme's title, 'Till Death Do Us Part', was drawn from a statement by Roy Hattersley. He proclaimed at the beginning of the film that he would represent Sparkbrook until death or retirement parted them. Significantly, Hattersley also said that he did not approve of the deselection of 'good sitting MPs'. This unfortunate, but prophetic, quote provided the foreground for a discussion of the recruitment practices within the local Pakistani community. This centred in particular on the activities of a local West Midlands county councillor and supporter of Hattersley, Mohammed Rafique. Kevin Scally, the Membership Secretary for the constituency's Sparkhill ward, appeared on the programme presenting clear proof that from the end of 1983 a mass recruitment drive was being operated in the constituency. Kevin Scally received 140 applications for the Sparkhill ward whose overall membership at the time was 200. The programme presented footage of people who had been recruited against their will. Kevin Scally was shown visiting 'members' whose addresses were no longer current, and even in one case where the house stipulated on the form had been demolished. It also claimed that the signatures on some of these membership forms had been forged. At this point about one-third of the General Management Committee was drawn from the local minority communities. Rafique appeared on the film boasting that he had been able to recruit members, to get elected to the constituency's GMC and make himself indispensable to the MP. This, Rafique claimed, meant that Roy Hattersley would pay special attention to his requests, particularly with regard to the immigration cases he presented to him.

Kevin Scally claimed that the recruitment drive was organised because the

> [R]ight-wing of the party were making a concerted effort to oust active, mostly left-wing, members from the branch and the right were becoming paranoid about safeguarding Roy Hattersley's position. His re-selection was due just after the applications were received.
>
> (quoted in *Birmingham Labour Briefing*, no. 17, December 1985: 2)

Hattersley himself was viewed locally as a popular MP, respected within the local black communities. So much so that his supporters nick-named him 'Hatter-ji', the south Asian suffix meaning a mark of deference for an honoured man. Scally claimed in the programme that there was no conspiracy by the left to deselect Hattersley.

On 22 September a local black councillor called Amir Khan, who appeared briefly in the *Bandung File* programme, organised a meeting to discuss the issue of black representation and to launch a constituency black section. The black section was the thirty-sixth in the country and the second in Birmingham. Amir Khan's intention was to challenge the local patronage system and to campaign for positions of influence and for black interests to be represented within the local Labour Party. Within days of the programme and the black sections meeting, Amir Khan and Kevin Scally were called to a meeting of the constituency Executive Committee, who recommended their expulsion from the Party. The reasons given by the local party were that Scally had released internal Labour Party documents to the press, and that Khan had shown disregard for the Party Constitution, and failed to disclose that he had stood as a Socialist Unity candidate in 1978. Scally and Khan appealed and their appeal was heard before Ken Cure, a trade unionist member of the Labour Party's national executive. He prepared a report to the NEC that recommended the rejection of the appeal. The expulsions of Kevin Scally and Amir Khan were endorsed in June 1986 by a vote of thirteen to twelve.

Ironically, Rafique was also expelled after accusing Roy Hattersley of racism. Rafique claimed that his expulsion, in December 1985, was because he stood against a local white councillor for nomination for the City Council elections. Rafique briefly joined the black sections movement and he claimed: 'My expulsion will split the party as I have enormous support in the community.' He was also later to join the Conservatives. Demonstrations followed and there were widespread warnings that a 'witch hunt' was being conducted of left-wing members. Khan and Scally threatened to take their cases to the High Court (*Birmingham Post*, 28 August 1986). Meanwhile, the Labour Group of city councillors unanimously decided that Amir Khan should continue to serve Sparkhill as a councillor (*Labour Weekly*, 10 January 1986). Over the following six months a national campaign gathered pace against the Sparkbrook expulsions. As the campaign mushroomed and numerous fund-raising demonstrations were staged, the controversy threatened to create a serious embarrassment for the Deputy Leader and the Party. At the 1986 Labour Party Conference thirty-five constituency parties called on Conference to reinstate them and the campaign had the support of several trade unions, including the Transport and General Workers' Union.

In September 1986, Birmingham Labour Party members set up a city-wide black section. The new group elected Amir Khan as Chairperson. With national pressure for the three men to be reinstated and the realisation that, because of procedural mistakes, a High Court challenge could be successful, the Sparkbrook Constituency Labour Party voted unanimously to reinstate Khan, Scally and Rafique on 25 November 1986. In the context of the continued refusal of the Labour Party nationally to recognise black sections, the reinstatement of Khan and Scally was a significant victory. However, this did not signal a significant change in the attitude of Birmingham's influential right-wing political leaders.

In April 1987 a meeting was planned by Birmingham's black sections to raise the profile of the organisation. It invited prominent figures such as Bernie Grant and Linda Bellos from London to come and speak at the Summerfield Centre, a place associated with Birmingham's left-wing faction. In a joint letter local Labour MPs such as Roy Hattersley, Jeff Rooker, Terry Davis and Robin Corbett publicly stated:

> As Labour MPs in Birmingham fully committed to racial equality and ending discrimination, we want to make it clear that neither the Birmingham District Labour Party not the city council needs any advice from you or the Haringey and Lambeth councils.
>
> (*Guardian*, 7 April 1987)

Despite this and other warnings the meeting went ahead on 7 April, with speeches from Black Sections activists such as Linda Bellos and Sharon Atkin. Amir Khan, the Chair of the Birmingham black section, did not chair the meeting and stated publicly that it was a mistake given that a general election was imminent (*Guardian*, 8 April 1987). The meeting was fraught and tense, with members of the audience questioning the usefulness of participating in the Labour Party.

By coincidence this meeting had been scheduled on the same day as the monthly city council meeting. The prominent black councillor Phil Murphy left the council meeting at 6.30 pm, a few hours early, in order to attend and speak at the Summerfield black sections rally. After the council meeting a special meeting of the Labour Group was called. This meeting decided to suspend Phil Murphy from the Labour Group and to advise the National Executive that he should be expelled. No action was taken against the thirteen other councillors who were not present at the council meeting. Murphy was subsequently suspended from the Labour Group for an entire year. He had formerly been a Vice-Chairman of the Race Relations and Equal Opportunities Committee. However, in the aftermath of a clash with the then Chairman, Bill Gray, he was replaced. During the period of his suspension he also faced reselection. The Sandwell Ward that he represented decided that he should continue to be their candidate. He was returned as councillor for Sandwell in May 1988 with a large majority. Before the election he was reinstated after reaffirming his loyalty to the Labour Party. Reflecting on the incident he comments:

> Looking back on those events I realised I established something quite important. I established that it's possible to be suspended from the Labour Party and still win an election . . . one of the things which inhibited a lot of Labour councillors from being radical was the threat that they'd have the whip withdrawn from them and that they'd stop being councillors.
>
> (Interview, June 1990)

Others who attended the Summerfield meeting did not endure the scrutiny of the Labour establishment so well. Sharon Atkin, for example, was quoted as saying: 'I don't give a damn about Neil Kinnock and a racist Labour Party' and 'I don't want a parliamentary seat if I can't represent black people' (Jeffers, 1991: 80).

This was to cost her the prospective parliamentary candidacy for Nottingham East. The National Executive Committee took the decision to replace Sharon Atkin as the Party's candidate in Nottingham East because of the remarks she made at the meeting. A defence campaign for Atkin and Murphy was initiated and chaired by the Birmingham MP Clare Short. It was, however, in Sharon Atkin's case to be unsuccessful.

The importance of these events lies in the degree to which the debates around black sections challenged the forms of patronage politics that were being operated between prominent Labour politicians and politicians from the black communities. In this sense the black sections movement contrasted with the instrumental forms of politics that we outlined in the early sections of this chapter. Black sections posed an important challenge to leading figures in the Labour Party, and it is perhaps for this reason that local politicians were so venomous in their opposition. In this respect the black sections movement constituted an emblem for all of the uncertainties and instabilities that were afflicting right-wing politicians in inner city areas.

A range of critiques were levelled at black sections from positions other than the centre right. Some on the left accused black sections of merely being a vehicle for a relatively small group of ambitious black middle-class politicians. This, however, seems an ironic critique, given the almost complete refusal of the Labour Party, particularly in the West Midlands, to accept their legitimacy. If black middle-class activists were using black sections cynically they had made a poor and strategically limited choice. Beyond this the membership of Birmingham's black sections movement was not uniformly middle class.

In the second half of the 1980s black sections dominated the debate on political representation and race. By the end of the 1980s an accommodation had been reached with the Party, resulting in the setting up of a Black Socialist Society initiated by the black leader of the Transport and General Workers' Union, Bill Morris. Black sections continued to exercise some influence, although severely depleted in numbers and divided over the compromise that had been offered to them by the labour movement. Despite the quite vindictive treatment meted out to black sections activists, many of them returned to the Labour Party, signing pledges of loyalty and being careful about their public statements. It is worth noting, however, that the black section in Birmingham was always small compared to the overall numbers of black people holding party cards in the city and connected to the networks of political patronage. The failure of black sections to become a mass movement needs to be explained, in part, by the pre-existence of mass recruiting in black communities and the instrumental mobilisations that were initiated in the early 1980s. But the situation in Birmingham cannot be solely understood in these terms. The fact that the left in Birmingham was weak was clearly a factor in the inability of politicians supporting black sections to develop numerically strong alliances within the local Labour Party. In addition, local black sections leaders were often fighting merely to stay in the Labour Party. In the context of expulsions and continued attacks, it was difficult to establish a local base of support within black communities themselves. As a result, black sections appeared to many to be a political import from London with little local relevance.

In addition, the pressure was on to define the political identity of black activists in terms of the primacy of the Labour Party. This was an enduring feature of the attacks on black sections (Shukra, 1990a, 1990b). Moderate black political activists concurred with this position. During the debates on this issue at Labour Party Conferences a number of black Birmingham activists spoke against resolutions promoting black sections. It is equally telling that of the twenty-three black councillors that we interviewed for the research only 20 per cent supported the idea of black sections. This is all the more surprising when compared with the 33 per cent of white Labour councillors who supported the formation of black sections. All the white councillors who supported black sections situated themselves on the left of the Labour Group.

The preoccupation of right-wing members of the party with black sections can be seen as largely defensive, but it also emanated from an attachment to a particular view of Labour politics. The chief concern of many of the white politicians whom we interviewed was to define class as the primary factor in developing political consciousness. This is significant because it indicates the limits of this agenda in relation to racial equality. As we shall see in Chapter 7 one result of this approach is that the politics of race is confined to the economics of discrimination within employment and the equal distribution of resources in service provision. Thus, the orbit of racism is defined in a highly economistic way, which effectively excludes the sphere of electoral politics. The result is that racial equality is organised into such areas as employment, in the form of equal opportunity procedures and ethnic monitoring, but is organised out of the internal institutions of the Labour Party. This makes configurations of popular racism within the Labour Party invisible and beyond discussion.

## SUMMARY AND CONCLUSION

The 1980s and 1990s saw a noticeable growth in black political participation and mobilisation. We have argued that these mobilisations ostensibly took two forms. Instrumental forms of political mobilisation were orchestrated through key political actors within minority communities. In large part this form of politics connected with established networks of political patronage and did little more than reinforce the dominant white leadership. In contrast, more ideologically inspired political mobilisations took place, such as the black sections movement, which sought to challenge the fundamental tenets of the local political culture. It was, however, a testimony to the enduring nature of the instrumental mobilisations that the black sections movement never achieved mass support.

In the midst of these conflicts the number of black politicians grew steadily, although as we shall argue later they did not act as a coherent political group. Indeed, it is interesting to note that black councillors continued to support the Labour Group even when it was revoking its commitment to policy initiatives addressing racial equality. However, by the end of the 1980s there were signs of change. The lines of political support and patronage were fast becoming more volatile. Factionalism within inner city wards produced complex forms of conflict, alliance and negotiation. In some areas these divisions were organised along caste, kin or clan lines whilst in other parts of the city they relied on establishing political coalitions. A feature of these factional disputes was that the selection of Labour local council candidates became hotly contested. On a number of occasions rival black candidates were involved in deselecting other black councillors, producing acrimony, division and deep resentment. In this context the expectation on black politicians to produce results was high and disappointment led to challenges, while in other cases these machinations were little more than the result of local struggles over controlling the membership and ultimately the ward or constituency. The point we want to stress here is that the lines of patronage and influence that we have described in this chapter were rapidly being modified. A more complex and volatile political situation emerged in which black activists and politicians played an absolutely central role in deciding who controlled Labour politics in Birmingham.

It is also important to note that by the early 1990s the Labour Party no longer held a monopoly over black political participation. The phenomenon of black Conservatives – both as candidates and activists – had become an important feature of inner city politics, particularly in areas where local people had become dissatisfied with Labour's commitment to political equality. On a much smaller scale the Liberal Democrats also showed interest in establishing links with minority communities. In the next two chapters we will attempt to describe some of the important features of the shifts and changes occurring within mainstream politics during the 1990s. In particular we will examine the way white politicians constructed these new circumstances and the emergence of new forms of black political involvement.

# 5 Political discourses and race

One of the most important features of the processes that we have looked at in the previous two chapters is the emergence of new forms of racialised political discourse. These discourses relate both to the general issue of increased political participation by minorities as well as the role of black and ethnic minority politicians. In the following chapters we want to explore the distinct discursive forms emerging within electoral politics in the past decade that deal with these phenomena. These forms of racial discourse are not simple or unitary, reflecting as they do diverse views within both the Labour and Conservative Parties. It is also clear that there are in practice a complex set of political discourses articulated by black and ethnic minority politicians.

We have already documented some aspects of the new forms of racialised politics and black and ethnic minority political participation that emerged in Birmingham during the period from the 1960s to the 1990s. In this and the following chapter we want to examine the variety of ways in which political discourses and mobilisations around the issue of race have been articulated in the period since the 1980s. This chapter specifically explores the ways in which white politicians have responded to the growing political participation of black communities. Our starting point is that it is essential to appreciate how white politicians deal with these issues because they have traditionally controlled the local political system.

Our analysis focuses on the main two political parties but we also conducted a limited amount of interviews with Liberal Democrat councillors. In large part the Liberal Democrats have not attempted to establish links with minority communities in Birmingham. The City Council has a small group of white Liberal Democrat councillors who represent largely suburban wards in the south of the city. Formerly they had some electoral success in the inner city areas. But they then abandoned these areas and targeted predominantly white outer city wards. The leader of the Liberal Democrats, Paul Schofield, put it in these terms:

> Outside of Tower Hamlets, Leyton, Rochdale and in the past the Crownhills ward of Leicester, we have little or no contact with New Commonwealth populations in our major urban areas. . . . My own views are that there are a number of reasons for this. . . . For reasons of security and self-interest many

> Asian communities tend to identify with the group that was in power. On almost all occasions this is the Labour Party and it is only a Labour Council, for example, that could deliver the services that these communities felt they deserved. [Another reason] in my view is one of mutual misunderstanding. The nature of Liberal Democrats in this country is not that which would feel comfortable with such a morally conservative, in some cases religiously extreme and in many cases male orientated social structure. It is also a society that tends to deal with politicians through intermediaries, headmen, community representatives who would deal with the various political parties on behalf of these communities and then be expected to deliver votes in return.
>
> (Personal communication: October 1991)

This account demonstrates a clear set of ideas about the nature of minority communities and their social and political structure. These constructions provide the means through which minority communities are comprehended. The Liberal Democrats quite consciously opted to forsake areas where black communities constitute a significant proportion of the electorate. The question we want to pose in this chapter is: How far do these racialised forms of political common sense affect the position of black communities within the political process? It is with this in mind that we want to explore the ways in which local white politicians within Birmingham speak through the language of race. We look first at the views of various sections of the dominant Labour Group and then at those of the minority Conservative Group.

## RACE AND LABOUR POLITICIANS

The composition of the Birmingham Labour Group is diverse. It has been controlled for most of the period since 1984 by – in Labour Party terms – a right-wing, moderate leadership. In this sense the Group saw itself as very different from the left-wing councils in London, Sheffield and Liverpool which received so much attention during the 1980s. Whilst members of the Labour Group can be characterised in a number of ways, we want to identify two crude but important groupings. The first is composed of the right-wing leadership that dominated Labour politics for most of the 1980s and early 1990s. Much of the rhetoric of the leadership reflects the relationship between Birmingham's labour movement and the industrial heritage of the city. There are a number of white working-class men within the Group who consciously articulate their politics in reference to the concerns of the 'hourly paid'. Thus a kind of 'shop-floor rhetoric' is prevalent within accounts offered by right-wing Labour members. Outside of the controlling right-wing group there exists a diverse collection of councillors that are labelled the 'intellectuals' because of their professional status, i.e. as lecturers, social workers, teachers. This group of 'intellectual' councillors is at the core of a left-wing faction, and their political concerns are wider than the rhetoric of the 'hourly paid' and incorporate issues like gender and racial equality. These divisions are significant because they have implications for the ways in which the political agendas of these groupings connect with understandings of race and the orbit of racism.

During the late 1980s and early 1990s the hegemony of the first group was subject to challenge. Indeed, it is interesting to note, as we shall see in the next chapter, that the control of the Labour Group by this faction was in large part facilitated by the support given to them by black councillors. However, during the late 1980s there was continued talk of the possibility of the right-wing faction losing control and the emergence of a new alliance between black and white councillors on the left. The political transformations outlined in the previous chapter were also the subject of concern for white Labour politicians regardless of their ideological positioning. The considerable growth in political participation within mainstream politics from black communities during the late 1970s and early 1980s posed an important challenge to the established leaders within the Labour Party. As we saw in Chapter 4, the initial impulse for white politicians to welcome black members was to consolidate their own position. However, once in the system there was always a possibility that this support could be revoked. Fear, or uncertainty, with regard to the consequences of greater political participation from members of black communities has underpinned the forms of racialised political discourses which have emerged.

## White politicians and racialised codes and discourse

The responses of white Labour politicians to the growth in black political participation are varied and complex. The majority of white councillors speak positively about the growth of black representation. Equally, signs of tension and ambivalence are also present in the accounts of this phenomenon given by white politicians. An established right-wing councillor put it this way:

> One thing I do worry about, and I say this sincerely, is that, em there could come a time, and I can't see it for the next decade or so, where the overwhelming proportion of the Labour members on the council, and by overwhelming . . . you know over 60 per cent, could be of ethnic minority background. Don't ask me whether I think this is a bad thing, but, you see, if the inner cities remain predominantly Labour and the inner cities remain predominantly represented by ethnic minorities – and I am not saying there is anything wrong with that . . . the Tories, as they will, will take the outer wards, em . . . because 60 per cent of the population in an area is of ethnic minority, I don't think we've got to have ethnic minorities to represent the ward. . . . I think that is almost as racist as some of the other things that are said.
>
> (Interview, February 1990)

The sub-text of this account is the issue of relinquishing power. This councillor is concerned that if the ethnic composition of his ward is linked to the kind of representative that should be preferred he will be placed in a vulnerable if not obsolete position. In a sense he is suggesting that the Labour Group is going to become 'swamped' with black representatives. In this sense the process of defining representation is intimately linked with social constructions of race and difference.

The question of what representation means was not always clearly stated in the interviews we conducted with local councillors. For some, particularly more left-wing members of the Group, the local politician should reflect the broad composition of the ward and have the right credentials to adequately represent all the constituents. Others maintain that the primary factor is the ability of the individual candidate, but at the same time they argue that the composition of the Group as a whole should reflect the population of Birmingham. Whatever the arguments are, however, it is also clear that in many of the urban localities traditionally represented by white Labour politicians the dramatic social and economic transformations of the past few decades have questioned some of the main institutional structures of the local political culture. White Labour politicians, who have previously drawn their electoral support from the white industrial working class, have found themselves representing localities which are increasingly multicultural. The industrial order and the institutions of organised labour have been severely diminished in recent years.

In this context the emergence of black politicians poses a serious challenge to the monopoly that these politicians have enjoyed within the Labour movement. It is not surprising, therefore, that a common refrain in the interviews we conducted with some white councillors is the argument that colour or race are unimportant, suggesting a deracialised political ground where their position and credentials are safe. This is a crucial rhetorical turn within the political culture because: (i) it makes it possible for white politicians to deflect the discussion away from the issue of the relationship between race and representation, and (ii) it can also provide an important way of disavowing accusations of racism and exclusion. The key importance of this claim is that it enables white politicians who are being challenged to be constructed as the victims. We shall return to this later, but for now we want to explore some of the key contradictions within the way that white Labour politicians talk about the relationship between race and representation.

Before going on to outline in detail some of the manifestations of these processes we want to define clearly what we mean by the notions of 'discourse' and 'code' and their relationship to racialisation. By discourse we mean the way in which social meanings are organised around principles and attributes. These provide the premises around which meaning can be organised. However, our notion of discourse is more than merely the establishment of patterns of meaning; it also incorporates the dimension of social action or operation. From this perspective the notion of racial discourse includes both the premises around which meanings are organised and the consequences that follow from its elaboration. The model we are using combines an examination of the content of particular formulations with an analysis of their effects. The central problem we are concerned with is the way in which discourses are racialised within Birmingham's political culture. By this we mean the ways in which the pattern and quality of political life within black communities are explained by invoking racial or pseudo-cultural attributes. The racialisation of political discourses in Birmingham needs to be conceptualised in terms of the particularities of local contexts whilst at the same time taking account of continuities between these forms and the currency of racial images and constructs at the national level.

Alongside the concept of racialised discourse we want to also develop the notion of racialised codes. In other words, we are concerned to understand the elements that make up particular discourses within the local political culture. Here we use the idea of 'code' to signify semantic elements which communicate racialised information in brief. These elements are pre-arranged signals and act as a shorthand, a kind of political vernacular which defines the character of inter-racial politics.

This way of talking about the racialisation of politics is best demonstrated by working through some of the key forms that we encountered in our research. There are, however, important methodological issues to consider. For example, when do we know that a particular discourse is being invoked? How do we separate racialised discourses from non-racialised ones? At one level the answer to these questions is simple. We can say, for example, that the key determinant that we use when defining racialised codes and discourses is the point at which an actor explains the nature of social relations by appealing to a sense of racial or cultural difference. But what is clear is that at the level of everyday political debate and conflict the answer is by no means simple.

While the political credentials of white politicians are often deracialised, effectively deflecting any discussion of their whiteness, black political activity is the subject of widespread racialisation. This exposes one of the core features of the culture of racism in political institutions: whiteness is constructed as the norm and rendered invisible while blackness or difference is defined as the problem. The point we want to make here is that the construction of difference through regimes of racial difference is one of the key features of how local political struggles are both understood and managed. In this way disputes over representation and political influence are viewed by white politicians through a racialised prism. This form of refraction within the political culture produces a whole spectrum of racialised codes that can be applied to all aspects of political life.

Within accounts given to us by white Labour activists and politicians it was often suggested that new and 'alien' political traditions have been imported into the inner city constituencies where black members predominate. One white male Labour activist put it this way:

> There are people from the subcontinent who have a very different view about politics from the way politics is in Britain. If you are in a political party in India you can get favours done for you. It's about having connections and money does change hands. I think what we are seeing in Birmingham – these are experiences of the subcontinent. What people expect here is that they will be able to command favours in the same way.
>
> (Interview, May 1991)

What does this type of argument tell us? At one level what we see here is the operation of a racialised discourse to explain shifts in Labour politics. The organising principle of this discourse is that quasi-corrupt political strategies have been imported from the Indian subcontinent. These principally relate to issues of political patronage and disputes over membership. He continues:

> Problems over membership disputes tend to happen in the inner city constituencies, these problems don't happen in the indigenous branches. A few years ago Northfield went to the left. It had been a right-wing constituency before and there was not one complaint about the change or challenges based on rule transgressions. You see the expectation of ethnic minority councillors is that it is all about power and the means justifies the ends.
>
> (Interview, May 1991)

In this case the notion of 'inner city' is used to connote racial difference. This is contrasted by a reference to 'indigenous branches' which are associated with normal political practice. Beyond this the referent 'indigenous' connotes a racialised code: it simply means white. Again we see here the traces of a racialised couplet of deviance and normality. These racialised discourses have the ability to focus on particular groups, as we shall see later, while they can be conflated and applied to all of Birmingham's diverse black communities. The account of this Labour activist starts with a reference to 'subcontinent' politics which would include references to India, Pakistan and Bangladesh. However, it ends with a generalisation about the predilections of 'ethnic minority' councillors. This kind of slippage is prevalent within discursive forms to which we are referring.

It is also interesting to note that these discourses can be articulated by political actors regardless of their ideological position within the Labour Party. Consider this account from a white woman who positions herself on the left of the Party:

> [Inner city politics] have operated exactly the same system that is operated in Pakistan which is they say the patronage system is just the norm. It is absolutely normal out there, they have a Godfather figure who comes along to meetings, who does all the dealings. In this sense one voice can control the opinions of 200, 300 and he will say to them this or that or the other person is fine, you go along and you vote. Now when I came in to this situation I thought this is really wrong, you shouldn't be doing this and what are you thinking of, we really ought to be informing people and let them make up their own mind, well that is a very very naive theory. After a period of time you begin to live with things that are way below your principles.
>
> (Interview, June 1991)

The interesting thing about this quotation is the way in which it uses the notion of 'Godfather' as a racialised code. Equally, white Labour politicians also talk about the existence of an 'Asian Mafia'. This triggers the discourse mentioned above and acts as the foreground for the discussion of political participation. We do not want to dispute that these forms of instrumental politics operate within Birmingham. There is widespread evidence that they do, as we shall discuss later. But we are suggesting that there is also a tendency to see these forms of politics as connected to racial attributes.

What is interesting, however, is that despite the racial imagery, it is quite clear that politicians on the left and right of the party are complicit in these forms of machine politics. As the politician quoted above argues:

> It is like Muslim women are not involved at all in politics, are not involved in any of this business, so as left-wingers we turn a blind eye, we are as bad as the right-wingers to the fact that we don't do any dealings through women and that we are doing nothing particularly to change the situation that Muslim women find themselves in. We have our people that we deal through who we depend on to go and speak to the other people within the group to continue our vote, where we are more moral is that we won't give up, we won't fiddle the people who vote for us, we won't openly slip in 10, 20, 30 votes.
>
> (Interview, May 1991)

The references to political morality betray the hierarchies that are being established within this account. The absence of Muslim women within the local political process is indisputable. What is significant here is that this assertion is being used to introduce an idea of political/moral superiority on behalf of the white left. This is elaborated in the following quotation:

> We don't want to deal in that way, we don't want particularly, we don't want at all to deal in the patronage way but we know it is our best bet for starting with a very slow process towards that on an individual basis, getting through and actually talking to people and actually getting some kind of commitment from people, but my personal opinion about is that most other Asians that I know are, by their nature, Tories. They are great believers in property ownership, in businesses. I would say that *I've yet to meet the Asian who is a natural socialist*, an ideological socialist, but even the Asians who support us really aren't in any way different from the Asians who support the Right. I think people are beginning to judge on their basis; people have been away from Pakistan for long enough to think this isn't a village, this isn't Pakistan, this is Britain, I can vote for whoever I want to vote for.
>
> (Interview, May 1991, our emphasis)

There are two points which emerge from this quotation. The political proclivities of 'Asian' communities are being defined in terms of a 'natural' leaning to conservative values. This is dependent upon a range of stereotypes which suppress the diverse political traditions of these communities through referring to racial attributes. Additionally, these discourses construct Asian politics as on a lower point in an evolutionary scale of political activity.

The other theme is the association of black politics with corruption. In the main this is associated with 'subcontinent' politics, but it is by no means exclusively applied to Asians. As we saw in Chapter 4, the political activity of African-Caribbean politicians has at times been subject to similar processes of criminalisation. In the following quote from a white former councillor we see how direct connections are often made between corruption and Asian politics:

> It's only relatively recently the Labour Party has been targeted in some cases for a complete take-over in inner areas by Asian groups. One can see the tensions there as well. That's the more worrying factor and the allegations are that it is tainted with corruption to an extent. That is worrying. Well, there seems to be an interest in becoming a councillor or persuading others to stand down in favour of others, one Asian against another Asian in which money has changed hands, and it's alleged that a candidate recently has been recompensed with something like £4,000, without making too many waves. I try to be even-handed, but there is this feeling that there are those who equate position with power with money. If they or their families or friends wanted to see the MP they'd get an introduction through one of their own senior members and the inference was that money changed hands, whereas the elected member in seeing that person wouldn't know that that individual had felt he had actually paid to see that in a sense of acceptable practices in India.
>
> (Interview, February 1991)

Again we see the association of corruption and criminality with Asian politics. The point that we want to emphasise is that the issue of whether particular allegations are true is not necessarily the key issue. This way of accounting for minority politics has become the dominant way of speaking about political struggles. In the above quote this particular white Labour politician starts by referring to 'Asian take-overs' but goes on to catalogue a whole range of quasi-criminal practices which are associated with particular communities. These formulations are discursive responses to local struggles over power and influence.

This way of narrating politics is also being echoed within the Labour Group itself. In particular, the Muslim councillors in the Group are being constructed as duplicitous and inscrutable. We will return to this issue later, but this kind of argument is captured in the following quotation from a white female Labour councillor who positions herself on the left of the Group:

> Now we have got the Muslims negotiating a great deal of things – we will do this, we will do that. If more of our candidates had won, that's to say the left candidates had won, we would have been in a very different position. . . . If you can show that you have got the power then the Muslims will throw in with you. They are holding everything to their chest at the moment because both sides are weakening. The right are losing their grip and we haven't shown that we have got it yet. So they [the Muslims] are not suddenly behind us and they haven't totally defected from the right. So the right gets their votes on some things and we get their votes on other things. They are playing a very clever game I suppose.
>
> (Interview, May 1991)

While racialised generalisations are abundant within the accounts of white Labour politicians, these are elaborated alongside comments about exceptional cases. This is an important rhetorical move for it allows racialised assertions to be made while pre-empting accusations of racism. The councillor mentioned above provides an example of this. We have changed the names of black councillors referred to in this following account:

> Councillor Ahmed to me is the hope for the Muslims and he is a man who is different from the others. I mean just a single gesture makes him different in that we went to this do, the Mayor's do, none of the Muslims never, never, ever bring their partners to these do's. Ahmed always brings his wife. I mean people will think it is a silly thing to justify it by. I'll tell you that is a huge. That says he is a different man from the others. This man is different from others in that he brings his partner with him. I have got a lot of time for Ahmed. Paul Johnson [an African-Caribbean councillor] is terrible as far as women's issues are concerned and I am always spouting off about black rights, he has a long way to go on women's issues.
>
> (Interview, May 1991)

The interesting thing about this account is that the idea of exceptionalism cannot work without a racialised discourse which fixes black political activity within the codes we have discussed. To make particular black allies exceptional cases is a common response on all sides of the party. In this sense particular black people can be incorporated while racialised discourses remain intact. The above quote also points to the uneasy relationship between black politics and sexual politics. We shall be exploring this in Chapter 6. Indeed, some of the most ardent critics of black politicians in the city are white women. This is complicated by the fact that racialised discourses are often used to legitimise claims about the gender politics of black men.

In summary, there is clear evidence that white Labour politicians are accounting for the emergence of black politicians through the construction of racialised codes and discourses. The crucial theme within these discourses is the association of black politics with patronage, criminality and corruption. This gives weight to the idea that these practices are being imported into Labour politics from outside, through what is sometimes called 'subcontinent politics'. Whilst often relating to particular racialised collectivities (including Asian, Muslim, Pakistani, Indian) such notions can also be used as a way of accounting for the political activity of black communities as a whole. It is also clear that a range of codes exist within the vernacular of local politics which trigger these discourses. These include notions like the 'Asian Mafia', 'godfathers', 'inner city corruption'. These codes serve as shorthand references to the criminalisation of black politics.

The point that we want to make is that these constructs take on a life of their own regardless of the truth or falsehood of particular allegations against black politicians. These discourses act as the cultural and political resources which white politicians use to understand black politics. In short, they plot the boundaries of what is believable. The pre-existence of these constructs means that allegations of corruption can be made against black politicians and taken seriously. These notions have important effects when situated within particular political struggles. These racialised discourses can be used to weaken and undermine black politicians who are challenging white politicians for positions of power. It is to this issue that we now turn.

## Local racisms: political struggles, rumours and racialisation

One of the key arenas in which the racialised discourses we have discussed above have played an important role is in the selection or non selection of black candidates within the Labour Party. As we saw in Chapter 4, the mass recruitment of black people into the Party during the 1970s and early 1980s was closely connected with an attempt to use support from minorities to retain the dominant role of the right-wing faction of the party. But this situation changed dramatically during the late 1980s and early 1990s. This was symbolised around struggles over the selection of candidates in key wards of the city. A white male councillor on the left summed this up:

> I think that very frequently the white old guard has sought to do all in their power to discourage the taking of it [access to the Party and ultimately to the position of councillor]. They are happy to have the members, certainly happy to have the votes if they go on the right side, but there are plenty of examples of certain councillors who have felt most aggrieved when their 70 per cent Asian ward has actually turned round and said we're sorry but we think Mohammed should represent us rather than you.
>
> (Interview, March 1990)

In this situation the question of representation, and specifically of claims to privileged access by minority politicians, became a key theme in everyday politics in the inner city wards. This issue became the subject of countless rumours and myths. Local political cultures are rife with rumour and folklore. This dimension of the political process is little explored but in many ways these informal circuits of knowledge provide the basis on which qualitative judgements are made. And it is clear that racialised meanings are being mapped onto these processes.

The impact of such racialised discourses on black political activists can be disastrous. The case of Mohammed Rashid Naz, who was selected to stand as a councillor for the Small Heath ward of Birmingham in 1986 is a case in point. After he was selected he was the subject of repeated rumours and in early 1987 pressure was placed on Rashid Naz to stand down and resign his nomination. A close friend and associate of Naz describes this as follows:

> He felt that they had decided they didn't want an Asian candidate and that [a prominent Labour politician] had 'phoned him up and said 'be a good chap won't you and stand down'. Naz didn't want to stand down and didn't see why he should stand down, and [there was] a preferred candidate at the time who was white. Now you have to look very carefully at what happened there because in the end the candidate they put in was Asian. But the campaign was about getting a white candidate in.
>
> (Interview, July 1991)

This incident was taking place during a period when Labour's electoral fortunes had slumped locally. In the May 1986 election Labour had lost a number of crucial seats in the marginal predominantly white areas of the middle ring. One explanation for this was that the Labour controlled City Council was becoming too strident on the issue of race policy and that white voters were unhappy with the growth of black political representation. In the midst of this it is alleged that controlling members of the Labour Group wanted to keep a firm grip on newly elected councillors:

> He wasn't the chosen candidate because he wasn't going to be under the thumb. What they had been looking for in a candidate was basically people that could be controlled . . . . Therefore they don't want honest, upright, thinking for themselves types of candidate because that is not at all what [the leadership] wants, [they] want people who will do what they're told. So those were the reasons why Naz wasn't wanted, the campaign to get rid of him was incredibly dirty.
>
> (Interview, July 1991)

A number of years previously Naz had been convicted of fraud. He had cashed a cheque through his personal bank account for a member of the community and it was claimed that he had not paid the person. Naz maintained that the case against him was unjust but unfortunately the only person who could prove his innocence was in India at the time of the trial and the affidavit which was sent from India was not admissible in the British courts. In the years following this case Naz had acted as Denis Howell's agent and treasurer of the constituency party. The fraud case was thus not seen as important enough to stop him taking up key positions within the local party. However, in the aftermath of his selection as a candidate and his unwillingness to give up the candidacy the fraud conviction was raised. Documents relating to the case were circulated within the local Asian community. This was coupled with other accusations of fraudulent behaviour. In the midst of this Naz found himself under incredible pressure from both the public forms of character defamation that were occurring and the action that was being taken against him by the Labour Party. It is impossible to calculate the degree to which the forms of racialised rumour-mongering that occurred around this case effected the death of this young man. However, a number of sources – both black and white – claim that Naz's death was a direct result of the public humiliation to which he had been subjected. Reflecting on the experience of Naz, his white associate concludes:

> Since that time I have learnt much more about just how corrupt Asian politics can be. Now I am saying Asian politics, the Asian people who came to this country, to this part to Birmingham, found a totally corrupt system here waiting to exploit them. These politicians have done this to the Asian community and it has become endemic, I don't know it is quite dreadful – they have set a norm for ways of carrying on that is now understood by hundreds of people across Birmingham. I am not condemning

> the Asian community for what was very much the product of a certain type of Labour politician.
>
> (Interview, July 1991)

From this perspective the prevalence of forms of political patronage among Asian politicians in Birmingham is the product of established patterns of political involvement and cannot be reduced to some essential ethnic characteristic or seen as a 'foreign import'.

In Labour Party circles a common use is made of the idea of an 'Asian Mafia' within the party. This notion is used to connote that there are various corrupt black members – perhaps significantly in areas where there is high membership – who manipulate the Asian vote. In a parliamentary selection in Perry Barr that took place during our research an extraordinary measure was introduced and aimed at the Muslim members of Handsworth ward. An additional form was sent out with postal vote applications. The form asked the applicant to swear an oath on the Koran that the vote they were submitting was theirs. This request needs to be contextualised within the racialisation of local politics. This move clearly related to fears about vote rigging and corrupt practices within the Handsworth ward. As a black councillor commented:

> You know it is as if they think that the moment their back is turned the Asians will change their support. It is as if they see us as like devious Arabs with political knives drawn ready to stab them in the back. This whole thing about oath on the Koran is so ridiculous as if this is something that the average Asian does all the time.
>
> (Interview, December 1990)

This micro-ideological process was clearly a response to the growing influence of black members and politicians. Nor was it confined to the constituencies; within the Labour Group itself there has been some ambivalence as to the potential that black councillors may have if they can act with one voice. As a prominent black councillor commented:

> This thing about the Asian Mafia, only comes out of fear. They know that if we at some point come together in a force, then we might be able to hold the balance. People are starting to do their sums you know.
>
> (Interview, August 1990)

These constructions are not simply pernicious symbols which circulate without effect. They can have an impact on political representation and in this sense constitute a response to a dynamic political landscape where black political participation is a growing force.

The struggle to replace white candidates in areas where there are high proportions of black people is of course not solely a local issue. In fact this same process has been going on for some time in parliamentary constituencies. Important racialised codes are operated around the question of the selection of parliamentary candidates. Perhaps the most clear example of this process is the debate that took place from 1989 to 1992 about who should succeed Denis Howell as the Labour candidate in the parliamentary constituency of Small Heath. When Howell announced his retirement in 1989 a furious struggle for succession ensued. We have documented elsewhere in some detail the nature of this selection and the politics of researching it (Back and Solomos, 1992; Back and Solomos, 1993). We shall be returning to this incident in Chapter 6, where we look at what it tells us about the position of black politicians in the Party. In this context we want to explore the part that racialised discourses played in this selection.

The controversy around the issue of who should represent Small Heath can be seen as an example of the tensions that began to emerge in the late 1980s between some minority politicians and the traditional leadership of the Labour Party. According to the 1981 Census 43 per cent of the constituency is from black and ethnic minority backgrounds, consisting mainly of people from Pakistan, and in particular Kashmir. However, current estimates suggest that black communities make up well over 50 per cent of the local population. Denis Howell was elected as Member of Parliament for Small Heath in 1961. Over thirty years he earned a reputation as being a hard-working constituency MP. In relation to the local Kashmiri population he was renowned for working hard on immigration cases and representing the interests of the community. Amongst his supporters within the community he was referred to as 'Baba', which literally means grandfather or an old and respected man. It is important to note that throughout the 1980s Denis Howell was not challenged at reselection times. The composition of the Labour Party membership in the area is primarily drawn from within the Kashmiri community. The growth of participation in Labour Party politics from this group is relatively recent. It is in the last ten years that the community has been mobilised and active within the Party.

Party activists in Small Heath have suggested that Howell's seemingly invulnerable position in the constituency was achieved by the operation of an elaborate form of political patronage within the community. In other words, Howell maintained support by developing links with key 'community leaders' who would then mobilise support in the community. The development of this process depended on the mobilisation of kin and clan networks which brought relatives and family associates into the Party. The implications of this are that these 'members' would often know little about the content of what was going on in the Party but simply turned up to important meetings to vote. This is made clear in the following comments from a member of the Small Heath party who is Kashmiri in origin:

> You see sometimes people at the meeting do not even understand what is going on. I remember talking to one person who I knew in a meeting and I asked him why he voted this way and he said to me 'I don't know I am here to give [the Community Leader's] vote it is not my vote'. What they do is just watch to see when the person who paid the fees puts his hand up and they do the same.
>
> (Interview, July 1991)

This kind of mass recruitment was endemic in constituencies such as Small Heath during the 1980s. But until the Small Heath selection contest this form of political mobilisation had worked in favour of right-wing politicians in the area. Some activists in fact claim that recruitment of this sort was encouraged by right-wing politicians in the city as a way of combating the emerging influence of the left during the 1970s and 1980s. The 'community leaders' in return gained access to the MP, who can exert influence on their behalf in dealing with problems such as immigration and welfare. The importance of having access to a Member of Parliament is hard to overemphasise, particularly in relation to immigration cases. Up until the late 1980s a Member of Parliament could stay deportation merely by making a telephone call to the appropriate immigration officer. This placed the representative in an extremely influential position *vis à vis* the community.

In the following quote from an interview with Denis Howell, conducted in August 1990, he makes his approach to the component parts of the community clear:

> With the West Indian community it's very difficult, because the West Indian community have no allegiance, but you can talk to them. There's a West Indian club . . . but you never find out who the leaders are, you only find out who runs that club. With the Asian community there's a noticeable difference. I know all the organisations, I know all the Mosques, I'm very welcome to go to any Mosque at any time and address them. It's totally different to anything we have. They would stop their religious service while I told them to vote Labour in the coming elections. I related the election issues as they affected their community and also trying to tell them whether their mothers and fathers can come here on visits, or whether their girl or boyfriends can come here to marry them.
>
> (Interview, August 1990)

The Asian community has been particularly susceptible to this kind of politics. However, this process of operating through political brokers was not just confined to the Asian community. Some local commentators suggest that similar processes have been operating within black and white migrant communities in the city.

Denis Howell maintains that this is the only way to ensure that consultation occurs with the community. He comments:

> Well, how else can you communicate with them? We're better at communicating in our constituency with the electorate than anybody else in Britain. We've got 30,000 homes, and we send 30,000 communications three times a year. . . . So there's nobody in my constituency who can ever say they don't know where to find me or to find any of the councillors . . . so apart from communicating with them individually and communicating through the leaders, and visiting schools . . . I don't know what else you can do.
>
> (Interview, August 1990)

This kind of politics became the norm in the area. There are important implications here with regard to the political participation of minority communities. Whilst some key actors exerted a degree of influence and some favoured members of the community became councillors, they were dependent on the renewed patronage of the MP. This meant that Denis Howell maintained his position and fostered a right of centre political philosophy in the constituency. Here responding to a question on immigration policy he makes clear his view of Asian party activists and his political emphasis:

> I never found any great disenchantment in my Asian people with the Labour government's policy [on immigration]. There was a lot of disenchantment with left-wing groups, but that was an entirely different matter. None of our immigrants are left-wing people, they're inclined to be very right wing and one of the things over the years I've had to do is to try to counsel them and talk to them about liberal/socialist values and what they mean in practice.
>
> (Interview, August 1990)

For some activists in Birmingham the situation in Small Heath, and other inner city constituencies, represented no more than a 'neo-colonial' form of politics where a white, powerful figure maintained his position through a network of black intermediaries. The result was that black people became integrated in the political system, but in a dependent position.

This is the context in which politics in Small Heath functioned until the late 1980s. The right-wing leadership in the constituency was kept in control through Asian brokers who mobilised support behind them. Whilst the left within the constituency, particularly in the Small Heath ward, on occasions challenged for positions in the local party, they were never able to challenge the right's control of the constituency. But the situation was to change once the issue of whether Denis Howell should be succeeded by an Asian candidate became a key concern.

There had been rumours during the late 1980s that Denis Howell would retire and that there would be an opening for a new candidate for Labour in Small Heath. This was finally announced on 2 February 1989, eight months before our research in Birmingham had begun and ten months before we started serious field-work. In our early interviews the selection in Small Heath was repeatedly brought up. Accusations that Denis Howell was manoeuvring into place a hand-picked successor, a white trade union official called Roger Godsiff, were prevalent. Initially, we did not pay much attention to this selection contest, but as the battle for the Small Heath candidacy progressed it became clear to us that this event was going to be extremely significant and formative in terms of the local politics of race in the city.

Whilst Godsiff was clearly Denis Howell's preferred candidate three Birmingham councillors were also fighting the selection, including two prominent Asian councillors. One of the Asian candidates had significant grassroots support within the constituency. Throughout the selection campaign accusations and counter-accusations were being bandied around. Some suggested that Roger Godsiff had personally manipulated the trade union vote within the electoral college so that his position was invulnerable. Others suggested that Muhammad Afzal had been mass recruiting members into the Party in order to support his selection campaign.

It was in this context that we decided to follow the campaign more closely and to see if we could piece together what was happening in Small Heath. In May 1990 we started to interview some of the key actors in Small Heath. It was at this point that we met a white lawyer, called Tony Rust, who was acting on behalf of the candidates opposing Roger Godsiff in the selection. Through contacts developed with the lawyer we were able to get access to some of the key people involved in the Small Heath selection battle. We interviewed all of the candidates and some of their supporters. While there was much conjecture about transgressions of the selection procedure there was no conclusive proof that any impropriety had taken place. A number of documents were available which pointed to some very strange procedures within the General and Municipal Boilermakers' Union but no conclusive proof was available to support the theories of union corruption or that the selection had been rigged for Roger Godsiff.

In January 1991 the National Executive of the Labour Party conducted an investigation into the allegations of trade union vote rigging. The NEC enquiry found against the allegations and on 2 February 1991 the votes for the selection were counted and Roger Godsiff prevailed and became the prospective parliamentary candidate for Small Heath. This was later ratified by the NEC and Godsiff's candidacy was endorsed. However, there was a crucial development in the summer of 1991.

On 17 May 1991 a series of documents were leaked from the West Midlands office of the General and Municipal Boilermakers' Union. These documents clearly implicated Roger Godsiff in fixing the GMB union delegation to the Small Heath constituency electoral college. It even indicated that Godsiff himself was paying the fees of some of the delegates. Tony Rust was supplying the local and national media with copies of these documents. On 10 June 1991 television journalists from the BBC's current affairs programme *Newsnight* came to Birmingham to interview key political activists. However, coverage of the documents was piecemeal and many of the newspapers held back on many of the issues raised in the leaked documents.

It was at this point that we decided to pull together the interview and press material that we had collected on the selection and write a paper which attempted to match the claims and counter-claims that were being made within the constituency against the documentary evidence we had been given by Tony Rust. On 13 September 1991 the *Newsnight* programme was eventually screened. The programme stimulated a second investigation by the Director of Organisation of the Labour Party, Joyce Gould. A few days later two campaign groups were launched in Small Heath to lobby against the selection of Roger Godsiff. This included a cross-party organisation called the Small Heath Voters Group (SHV) and a group of Labour Party members who opposed the Godsiff selection – Small Heath Affair Democratic Solutions Committee (SHADeS). We had been working closely with the people involved in these organisations and we were attending the meetings being held in the constituency. SHV organised several public screenings of the *Newsnight* programme to rally support.

At this point our paper on the Small Heath affair was in a draft form. We showed the draft to a number of key activists in SHV and SHADeS to check the accuracy of our account. We received feedback on our paper and made amendments. Throughout this period there was a great deal of excitement and a belief that the NEC was going to change its mind and re-run the selection. The Asian community in the area was split over the issue of the selection. On one side, there were a significant number of people who were supporting Godsiff and the old-style patronage politics that existed in the area. On the other, there was a group of people supporting the main Asian candidate, councillor Muhammad Afzal.

On 18 December 1991 Joyce Gould submitted a report to the NEC of the Labour Party suggesting that there was a prima-facie case for implementing Clause XV (5) of the Party Rules which states that a candidate can be investigated after endorsement if there is evidence of a breach in the rules of the Party. At this meeting three members of the NEC were directed to visit Roger Godsiff to discuss the allegations being made against him. The same evening BBC *Newsnight* screened a follow-up programme on Small Heath.

It was at this point that we decided that we should attempt to distribute a draft of our paper to a wider audience in order to stimulate debate about the events in Small Heath. Our paper was perhaps the only attempt to record the sequence of events leading up to the selection. Through our contacts within SHADeS and SHV we found out the names of the three NEC members who were going to be conducting the interviews with Roger Godsiff. We were also aware that the next NEC meeting was to be on 29 January 1992. We decided that we would update our paper and send it to all the key members of the NEC. We also decided to make it available to the sitting Member of Parliament and the prospective parliamentary candidate. The papers were sent out on 2 January 1992.

The first reply we received didn't arrive until 9 January 1992. John Evans, MP, one of the three NEC members asked to re-examine the Small Heath selection, replied. He chose completely to ignore the systematic reconstruction of the selection process and focused on one paragraph of the paper. In this paragraph we listed the allegations which were made against all of the candidates, including those made against the Asian candidates in the selection contest. John Evans ended his letter: 'When can I expect to receive your report on your investigation into allegations about the conduct of councillor Najma Hafeez?' What became clear to us was that the members of the NEC were choosing to read our paper in a highly selective way. Equally, they were trying to use us as an 'independent' source of information.

The next turn in this sequence of events shifted attention away from the constituency and directed it towards the internal dynamics of the NEC. Roughly a week before the NEC was due to meet we received a series of phone calls from a member of the NEC suggesting that it was imperative for us to answer the questions John Evans had asked. It was suggested to us that this could exert real influence on the selection processes. Rumours were being circulated amongst senior members of the Labour Party's Executive that Muhammad Afzal had been involved in quasi-criminal activity. We telephoned John Evans and stated that to our knowledge no impropriety had been perpetrated by councillor Afzal. He asked us to put our comments in writing. We immediately facsimiled a letter to Evans in the hope that this would shift the focus away from the candidates who according to the NEC's brief should not have been under investigation. We also suggested that we considered smear campaigns of this sort were connected with new political forms of racism.

At the meeting of the NEC on 29 January, the Small Heath affair was placed at the end of an agenda which dealt with a range of other selection controversies. We were told by a contact within the NEC that John Evans presented a short report on Small Heath. He did not mention any of the evidence we presented for the indiscretions on the part of Roger Godsiff. He chose to concentrate on the paragraph in our paper which stated that allegations had been made against all of the candidates. Then he read out our letter which stated that the accusations in relation to Muhammad Afzal were false and implicitly racist. Evans then complained that he had received 'a mountain of paper' on this issue. He stated that he was satisfied that there was some evidence that Roger Godsiff had 'made some mistakes'. However, our contact within the NEC reported: 'What John Evans told the NEC was tantamount to saying that Godsiff had been a "naughty boy" but this was not a hanging offence.' A motion was put to the meeting to approve the report and the motion was carried with three members of the NEC voting against.

It is interesting to note that allegations of misconduct against Asian politicians were rife in Small Heath at this time. Some of these were aimed specifically at the Asian candidates in the selection process. For example, the two most common claims made against Muhammad Afzal were (i) that he abused his position as Chairman of the Urban Renewal Committee of the City Council to offers favours and funds in return for political support, and (ii) that he orchestrated an improper campaign of recruitment into the Labour Party in Small Heath. In addition to these two accusations further rumours were in circulation within the city that Afzal was implicated in a property fraud. This rumour suggested that Afzal was assisting in a scheme where landlords were buying up housing stock under false names, then applying to Urban Renewal for renovation. A smear campaign was conducted against Afzal utilising the kinds of racialised discourses we mentioned in the previous section. Muhammad Afzal was also characterised by many as being part of a so called 'Asian Network' or 'Mafia'. His activities were heavily scrutinised both in terms of his position within the Birmingham City Council and locally in Small Heath. In November 1989 an official complaint was made against councillor Afzal for the incorrect management of improvement grants. These allegations were subject to an investigation carried out by a local ombudsman and he found no impropriety.

We have found little proof to suggest that these allegations were true. However, the existence of these elaborate racialised discourses had important consequences in this struggle over who should represent the constituency in Parliament. The pre-existence of these racialised codes played a vital role in the deliberations of the NEC of the Labour Party. The members of Labour's NEC believed that these accusations could be true and this was enough to affect their decision. The criminalisation of black politics can thus play a key part in struggles that are taking place over new forms of political representation. The point we want to emphasise is that the existence of these racialised discourses means that black political corruption does not have to be proved in order for it to be believed. The assumption is that black politics is by definition corrupt and that emerging black political figures have to prove otherwise.

The discourses that we have described need to be understood as local forms of racism that are being generated within the specific context of electoral politics. The prevalence of such discourses is hard to ascertain. We in no way want to suggest that these discourses were uniformly adhered to by all white Labour politicians and activists. Responding to the suggestion that 'subcontinent politics' have been imported into Birmingham's political culture a white male councillor on the left comments:

> I have heard this argument. It [black politics] is just what has happened in Pakistan, it is how politics are dealt with in India. I don't believe that anyway. But the idea is that the Asian members are to blame. I definitely put the blame on the MP and the white councillors. They brought into being the system, the divide and rule, the patronage and all the rest of it. Therefore the blame goes on them, not on Asian politics – Indian or Pakistani politics or anything like that.
>
> (Interview, December 1993)

Equally, a left-wing white female councillor claimed:

> It is hypocrisy all this stuff about the 'Asian Mafia', single-issue politicians, crooks and the rest of it. All it is, is a way of justifying and creating an excuse for the fact that Asians and black people are not willing to just say 'Yes sahib we will support you for ever'. I am sad to say that for some white people in the party that if black people are not your friends then they are automatically criminals.
>
> (Interview, January 1990)

However, as we demonstrated earlier these racialised discourses are also utilised by white politicians on the left. A working-class white councillor attempted to explain the presence of left-wing Labour racism in the following way:

> By and large councillors on the left in Birmingham don't live in the inner cities, they are quite middle class. I think it is because they don't actually meet with the rank and file Asian members that there is a lack of understanding. People can be political, people can want to fight for better urban renewal schemes or against racist violence or whatever, and yet still be pledged, when it comes to the Labour Party to vote in a particular way. So they don't see the kind of two aspects that people might have. Yes, they can take part in full political discussion but when it comes to the Labour Party – because of the systems that have been set up – their vote is pledged in a certain way. There is also – and this is often forgotten – that not all Asians or black people are part

> of this patronage system. There are many Asians who stand up honourably and argue against the things in the Labour Party that are wrong. What happens is that people on the right and the left justify what is going on by saying that every Asian member is a part of this patronage system and that it is their own fault.
>
> (Interview, December 1993)

Out of the twenty-one Labour councillors clearly on the left of the party, only five live within the inner-city area and could be classified as having working-class occupations.

It is interesting to note that whilst black politicians have been constructed through the regimes of racialised discourses, the racial identity of white politicians is rarely referred to. For example, it simply makes no sense within the culture we are describing to refer to a 'white Mafia', although one could clearly argue that the control of powerful positions in the political system is actively maintained by white politicians. There is, however, one case where the whiteness of politicians is invoked: when white politicians are seen as the victims of political insurgency. In the aftermath of the controversy over the selection of Roger Godsiff, for example, two white Small Heath councillors were deselected. Jim Eames, a former Lord Mayor of Birmingham, was replaced by a moderate black politician called Paul Haymeraj. Eames had served on the council for forty-three consecutive years. Mike Sharpe, a former member of the Liberal Party, was deselected in the Nechells ward by a respected and locally active Labour Party member, Abdul Malik. On 2 June 1992 a headline appeared in the *Birmingham Post*: 'Whites are victims of vote-fixers – Howell'. In this article Denis Howell claimed that white councillors were being deselected as a form of revenge in the aftermath of the parliamentary selection. This, it was argued, had occurred through illicit means and illegal forms of party recruitment. The irony here is that this form of machine politics had been in operation for a very long time. The significant change was that Asian members in particular were no longer supporting white patrons. In at least one of the cases it was widely felt that the sitting councillor had been foisted on the ward. Equally, there was dissatisfaction at the degree of participation of the elected officials in the everyday concerns of their electorate. It was also believed that in one case the deselection was nothing at all to do with revenge but was merely a reward for supporting Roger Godsiff in his campaign to secure the parliamentary selection. The accuracy of these claims is difficult to determine. However, what is significant is the move to construct white politicians as the victims rather than the contributors to this particular brand of local politics.

In this context the discourse of 'white victimhood' deflects attention from accusations of racial inequality in the Labour Party, but its significance goes much deeper. Here white politicians are forced to name their whiteness in a context where it is presumed to be the norm. The paradox is that whiteness is only referred to where it is seen to be a cause of political victimisation. Again, racial politics are inverted so that black activists are blamed for being the perpetrators of these 'injustices'. What is obscured by this kind of discourse is that the politics of patronage is an integral aspect of racialised politics in Birmingham and elsewhere.

### Summary

The contours of Labour politics in Birmingham are complex. Indeed, the processes of racialisation that are occurring within the Party are not simple or crude. Rather they are produced within a situation where the Party has to recognise and show a political commitment to black members and the electoral support that black communities have continually given to Labour. In this sense the Party is being forced to place racial equality on the political agenda, for not to do so could result in disaffection within areas that have long been Labour strongholds. The result is a situation where (i) a challenge has been posed to those white established members who for the past thirty years have been elected with the assistance of the support of black communities, and (ii) pressure is being applied to extend the political agenda of Labour beyond the confines of the shop floor. In this sense the transformations that are going on within Labour politics are echoes of the socio-economic transformations that are occurring within the city. As Birmingham moves towards a post-industrial and post-Fordist economic and social environment, the political identities that owe their origins to the heyday of industrial manufacturing are being challenged. In this sense black forms of political engagement pose a threat to the traditional identity of a Labourism, which was oriented to the plight of an unfragmented – principally white – industrial working class. Crucially, this kind of politics is of limited relevance when it comes to addressing racism and the racial hierarchies that are evolving in the throes of de-industrialisation. The tangle of racial discourses that we have tried to describe here is integral to this situation. These discourses constitute a micro-ideological response to the emerging forms of black politics. What is significant here is their particular effect and form.

## RACE AND CONSERVATIVE POLITICIANS

Moving on to Conservative discourses about race the picture is rather different. As we will see in the next chapter, black Conservatives are emerging as a distinct political phenomenon, but this is on a much smaller scale than has been experienced within the Labour Party. The situation within the Conservative Group is distinct for a number of reasons. First, the Conservatives have not experienced a comparable growth in black participation. Second, the Conservative Group has consistently opposed policy developments that have addressed issues of racial equality in Birmingham. Beyond this the Conservative Party's stance on immigration has tended to limit the extent of its impact within minority politics. Despite recent attempts by the party to attract minority support it still tends to be seen as an 'anti-immigration' Party. Interestingly enough, as we have already noted, the Conservatives have selected black candidates in both local and national elections. They have generally been selected in areas where there are large black communities. These are also areas of traditional Labour support and these black Conservative candidates have generally stood little chance of success, but they have played a symbolic role in the changing face of racialised politics.

Distinctive forms of racial discourse were expressed by Conservative politicians but, as we argue, their responses were far from crude or unitary. In the content of what they do say it is possible to explore the contours of the racialised concepts they use. In all we interviewed sixteen Conservative councillors, four of whom were women. In what follows we want to examine the rhetorical and racialised elements in their accounts. Our general emphasis is that significant shifts are occurring within Conservative political discourses which require sophisticated and careful analysis.

## 'I am not a racist but . . .': the grammar and rhetoric of racialised sentiments

During political debates the Conservatives are frequently accused of being racist by Labour members. In response to this, Conservative politicians go to great lengths to distance themselves from accusations of racism. This is not simply an attempt to deflect criticism nor is it just an attempt to manage impressions (van Dijk, 1984: 117, 1987: 347). As Billig *et al.* (1988: 110) state incisively: 'the recognition of the social inappropriateness of prejudice, are not conversational gambits devoid of ideological content'. A number of the councillors we interviewed said that they took accusations of racism seriously, often claiming that such incidents caused profound emotional upset. These responses need to be explored and not rejected as mere disingenuous repudiations.

A female Conservative recounted a number of incidents where she felt hurt by accusations of racism. In response she maintained that she had a long association with minority communities in Birmingham. Here she describes her relationship to a black domestic helper:

> I have a help who is West Indian. Council Meetings are on Tuesdays and she comes on Wednesdays, she has been helping me on Wednesday mornings for two years. She's a lovely lady – she's got eight children and she's discovered now that they're all grown up that she's got a boring husband. Anyway that's besides the point. I come in [in the aftermath of a Council Meeting] and say 'Evelyn, I'm racist!'. 'Don't take no notice', she says, 'because you get labelled, all you Conservatives' [with being racist]. . . . It is absolute nonsense, one sits there and bites one's tongue.
>
> (Interview, March 1990)

Invoking black friendship is a common rhetorical response to accusations of racism. This example demonstrates the ways in which association with black people, even when employees, is used as evidence of a lack of racist sentiment. However, this rhetorical move is predicated upon a definition of racism as the blind hatred of black people in all circumstances. These conversational moves show clearly that political actors who utilise racialised formulations do not conceive of themselves as racists and sincerely adhere to the rhetorical justifications which they call into play.

Challenges and accusations of racism are also rejected on the basis that they are the result of 'looney left-wing fanaticism'. Such accusations are viewed as senseless and even humorous. A male Conservative councillor reflects on his reaction to being publicly called a racist:

> I find two sides to it: one, I'm going to be hurt by it; two, I find it fun. It's a big joke – everybody in the Council is a big joke. . . . Thirdly, I find it dangerous because if they call me a racist, if they call me a racist and they are calling someone like Adolf Hitler a racist they are saying Adolf Hitler is like [me]. I mean if they are saying that Adolf Hitler is like [me] I find it more dangerous and if they say that [I] am not really that bad, they are saying that Adolf Hitler isn't that bad. What I am saying is that there isn't a sliding scale, which there isn't, it is just you are or you aren't [a racist].
>
> (Interview, April 1991)

The account offered here points to the way in which the politics of race can be dismissed as comic nonsense by those who are accused of racism. The quotation also alludes to the crude and promiscuous way that accusations of racism are made within the political culture. The notion of a 'sliding scale' points – albeit perhaps unintentionally – to the complex ways in which racism is expressed within local politics.

It is important to stress that these responses are sincerely believed without contradiction. Thus, these positions can be sustained in the face of accusations of racism when the person being accused subscribes to the idea that it is inappropriate and undesirable 'to be a racist'. These rhetorical moves are also situated within a particular grammar. The most common feature of this form was the prefixing clause 'I am not a racist but . . .' This was articulated clearly by a Conservative councillor who managed a medium-sized engineering factory in central Birmingham. The following passage records Les Back's first meeting with him:

> I interviewed him at his factory in Birmingham . . . I found the entrance, climbed a set of stairs and waited by the reception of the factory. The Councillor came out, he's a middle-aged man, slender build, dressed in a suit, shook my hand and we proceeded. He then took me through the factory floor and showed me how the washers are made. As we finished our small tour of the factory it became apparent the reason why he wanted me to do this. He said 'I wanted you to see that we don't discriminate either way.' His work-force is probably comprised of about 20-25 per cent of black employees. I saw about 5 or 6 middle aged Afro-Caribbean men, I didn't see any Afro-Caribbean women, I saw a number of Asian men and a number of Asian women. As we walked into his office he said 'I wanted you to see our factory to show that I don't discriminate either way, and that although many people think I'm racist I'm in fact not racist . . . regardless of what you might think, I'm not a racist!'
>
> (Interview, March 1990)

The significance of this anecdote goes far beyond an interesting field-work experience. It captures a significant element in the grammar and lexicon of racist discourse. Indeed, this exercise provided a precursor for the articulation of a whole repertoire of racialised codes and discourses. His insistence that he does 'not discriminate either way' is spoken alongside a multiple construction of black political activity.

An important rhetorical figure in his account is the black Conservative politician, John Taylor. Taylor was trained as a barrister and stood as a Conservative candidate for a parliamentary constituency in Birmingham in 1987 and more controversially in Cheltenham in 1992. He was unsuccessful in 1987 but this councillor was closely involved in his campaign. He said of Taylor: 'He is an educated, refined, pleasant man who you would be happy to invite to eat with you every night of the week . . . his colour is just not important.' Interestingly enough it is around black minority politicians such as Taylor that a series of important codes operationalised. Taylor was constructed as 'a man of impeccable manners', a man who is 'refined'. The pseudo-evolutionary language here exposes an interesting process whereby racist discourses work on themselves. The image of the 'cultured black man', a political insider, acts as rhetorical strategy which makes colour unimportant. This also dovetails into a notion of individualism which is also prevalent elsewhere within this account. Along with other Conservative politicians, this councillor continually maintained that: 'It was not the colour of one's skin that mattered but rather the quality of individuals.' Indeed this construction makes possible the development of more racialised constructs. Images of culture then become central. The result is a characterisation of 'race' which is pseudo-culturally defined (Barker, 1981: 23). Skin colour is replaced by 'culture' as the key signifier in the process of racialisation.

According to this perspective the election of black Labour representatives has led to a 'falling off in standards' within the City Council. Here again the focus on quality leads to the introduction of criminal images of black political organisation and involvement:

> There was one particular councillor who I am not willing to name who was involved in all kinds of corruption and crime. He was drove around in a very big car and had expensive suits – you don't live that kind of lifestyle on a councillor's expenses.
>
> (Interview, March 1990)

He also accused black councillors of embezzling public money and of being interested in financial gain rather than public service. Those black councillors who are active are 'single-issue politicians' who are only concerned with 'racism and calling people racists'. This councillor suggested that:

> The future is a sad image. There will be a growth of ethnic minority politicians who are group oriented, single issue politicians which will lead to falling

> standards . . . the issue of race was one in which people know the truth but were afraid to speak it.
>
> (Interview, March 1990)

These two constructions are closely linked to a discourse on difference. Within this logic black political activists can be defined as either 'cultured' individuals who just 'happen to be black' or 'uncultured', morally degenerate, criminal and corrupt politicians who are defined as having distinct group interests. The interesting and important point here is that these constructions are not placed in a contradictory relationship. Rather, the first facilitates the second in a way that denies skin colour, thus pre-empting accusations of racism. Black Labour councillors were not uniformly constructed by Conservative politicians in this manner, as we shall see. However, numerous councillors used the 'Asian Mafia' discourse we examined with regard to Labour. In particular, it was commonly asserted that 'alien political traditions' had been imported from India and Pakistan.

Interestingly enough these images are also applied to minority Conservative politicians. In the May 1990 local elections the Conservatives fielded three black candidates out of thirty-nine. Their white agent reflected:

> They (Asians) have a tribal approach to politics it is very strange really and I just support them where I can. But the fact of the matter is that they just do not deliver the vote.
>
> (Interview, May 1990)

Claims of 'tribalism' within Asian communities expose a clear connection with notions of 'race', but the important point to emphasise here is the realisation that black candidates ultimately do not produce electoral support.

The important thing about the grammar of this discourse is that it allows for the elaboration of racialised codes alongside a denial that these assertions can be characterised as 'racism'. As we shall see in what follows, these formulations are situated within meritocratic imperatives. The assertion that people should be judged on their abilities alone is a core feature of Conservative political culture. This principle is utilised to argue that 'race' is not significant. A female Conservative expressed this sentiment in the following terms:

> Quite frankly I wouldn't call anybody black . . . I think that it's something that stops us being multi-cultural . . . I don't think the colour of your skin matters tuppence, quite frankly.
>
> (Interview, March 1990)

While this particular councillor rejected the importance of colour, later in her account she expressed deep anxiety about 'fundamentalist Muslims'. The rejection of race thus allows both a means to demonstrate the inappropriateness of racism while enabling a conception of culture as the locus for defining difference. In these circumstances the incorporation of black friends within the rhetoric of particular accounts becomes a crucial way in which this discourse is maintained as a believable set of assertions. Black Conservatives provide a vital emblem which can be offered to substantiate the claim that the main criterion in Conservative politics is quality rather than race.

## 'God, Queen and Commonwealth and Dear Old Enoch': Powellism, race and Conservative politicians

Another key theme in Conservative discourses can be represented by the reassertion of 'old-style Tory values'. This provides the framework for articulating racial discourses which owe their origins to a previous historical moment. As one councillor expressed it: 'I am a Commonwealth man, I'm still the old swear by God, Queen and Commonwealth type' (Interview, March 1990). He was a supporter of Enoch Powell and an avid anti-European. White politicians in his account had a responsibility to be the arbiters of disputes between unruly 'natives'. In the following quotation we see something close to the notion of the 'white man's burden':

> I was chairman of a thing called the Victoria League for Commonwealth Friendship in Birmingham and I was on the central council in London for that . . . with the upheaval (and) with the Commonwealth becoming independent instead of an Empire, at one stage we had to keep the Indians and the Pakis separate. We couldn't put them in the same room or they'd knife each other. Then we had trouble with the South Africans and the Africans and West Indians we had to keep them at opposite ends of the room, you know. So I was used to the coloured and their ways and habits, and how *cunning* the Indians are and how *childlike* the West Indians are in their attitude to life.
>
> (Interview, March 1990, our emphasis)

This inheritance is clearly articulated here, complete with violent ethnic antagonism, 'cunning Indians' and 'childlike West Indians'. This politician operates a whole repertoire of racist constructs which are related to those referred to previously whilst connecting with clearly antecedent colonial forms of discourse. The division within these accounts between 'Indians' and 'West Indians' – or more pervasively between 'Asians' and 'Afro-Caribbeans' – serves as a way of redirecting attention away from white racism to intercommunal conflict. As a senior female Conservative put it:

> You get a lot of racism between the ethnic minorities. It isn't black against white all the time, yes there is some of that there, but you get it between the different ethnic minorities.
>
> (Interview, February 1991)

These formulations were used particularly when faced with political opponents who maintain that black people cannot be racist because of their structural economic and social position. In response to this a Conservative woman comments:

> You go into town (central Birmingham) and you find most of the battles are between Asians and West Indians and then you're told as a white person they [black people] can't be racist. I think that's absolute nonsense.
>
> (Interview, March 1990)

This preoccupation with recounting stories about intercommunal rivalry is closely connected to the discomfort felt when white racism is addressed. Shifting the emphasis to ethnic conflict provides a means to avoid personal scrutiny and the wider prevalence of racist discourses.

The meanings associated with images of Afro-Asian division are mutable and volatile. Whilst a colonial legacy can be invoked to infantilise West Indians and present Asians as inscrutable, it can also result in the realisation of adapted formulations being brought to bear within the political process. An altered version of the racialised contrast between African-Caribbeans and Asians is expressed in the following account of a male Conservative councillor:

> I think there's something intrinsically different in the Afro-Caribbeans. It's not that the Asians are any more intelligent but they are not bolshie if you like. . . . There are super types, but there's quite a few around who are quite bolshie and 'chip on the shoulder' types. But you don't seem to get them with the Pakistani and Indians. . . . Perhaps deep down the Indians are more amenable to the old colonial system. Perhaps there's far more animosity from the Caribbeans to the old colonial system. I'm only suggesting this, I really have no evidence. . . . But we find the Asians learn more easily.
>
> (Interview, July 1990)

There are elements within this account (i.e. black 'super types' and an acknowledgement of 'lack of evidence') which abate racial generalisations. Yet at the same time, a line of argument is developed which seeks to explain the predisposition of racialised groups to the political system in terms of their response to British colonialism. This in the final analysis results in an assertion that 'Asians' have a greater capacity for political assimilation.

In other contexts Enoch Powell's ideas on the consequences of immigration are invoked to give meaning to racial politics in Birmingham. The councillor quoted at the beginning of this section comments:

> Enoch was quite right, rivers of blood, I mean we've had it in Handsworth, and we shall have it again, because the thing that concerns me tremendously is that they're out for power, you see. They're not content to be British and just come along with the rest.
>
> (Interview, March 1990)

According to this perspective, 'to be British' ultimately means to enter into an imagined concept of nationhood which constitutes a way of life. The importance of this is that black inclusion is possible if aspirations for power are contained and if black people remain content with 'just being British'. We will return to this shortly, but the important point here is that even committed Powellites construct accounts that reject race. Consider the following quotation from a male Conservative on the right of the party:

> I am a patriot as I would hope most people are, I am proud of my country because my forefathers made it so; to be anything else would be [being] a traitor I think. . . . Because I am like that I am considered an extremist. The wonderful thing about being British is that we are a mixture and there is no Aryan race, there's no Afrikaner customs, there's no tribe bigotry or Arab clansmanship or whatever they call it – in Britain we are naturally a mixture of all sorts.
>
> (Interview, August 1990)

When asked about British-born black people he is unequivocal:

> They are British. I hope like my own children, who are white, that they keep some sort of pride, some sort of standard that I will be proud of and that my forebears would have been proud of. If I am a racist to say that I am proud to be British and everyone else is inferior, then so be it, but if someone of a different colour was born in Britain, then I consider them to be British. I would hope and pray that they would also consider themselves to be British. I would hope that they would come to be [as proud] as I am of being in this great country. Now surely that's not being racist.
>
> (Interview, August 1990)

This account couples the rejection of the idea of race with a patriotic assimilationism, where electing a British cultural and historical legacy is defined as the means to establish the right to belong to Britain.

Alongside assertions of a racially benign patriotism, however, there are anxieties over the impact and aspirations of black political activists:

> Dear old Enoch was dead right – a lot of the coloured are fitting in well and doing a grand job, no problem, but there are hard cores and especially among the Sikhs and Muslims as I see it, who are determined to have power, you see. And the lefties in the Labour Party tend to be in the colour brigade who are determined not only to come onto the Council and look after the *villages of Birmingham* but to get power.
>
> (Interview, March 1990)

The role of the 'lefties' in giving black people a voice is coupled with a colonialist image of 'villages of Birmingham', internal colonies which threaten to be self-determining and independent. The view that the Labour Party has 'played to' the aspirations of the various segments within minority communities was widely held by Conservative politicians. This was contrasted to the Conservative Party's concentration on the issue of merit and ability.

From a wider perspective cultural symbols provided the key discursive agent in the elaboration of anxieties over patterns of minority political involvement:

> Well, an Indian friend of mine put it rather nicely years and years ago – he's

> an Indian banker, estate agent and all sorts of things like that and he shall be nameless. He said, 'I am very worried.' I said, 'Why what's the matter?' and he said, 'Well, you see all these people coming to Birmingham are from little villages in India and Pakistan', he said, 'where they have no toilets, no knives and forks and if they went to Delhi they would be lost, and instead of coming to Delhi they come to Birmingham . . . the head man comes, finds it's good and you can get hand-outs without working, and he sends the signal back to the rest of the village to come. So in Birmingham now we have got the population of several Indian villages and they were the peasants, you know, way back peasants . . . the bulk of immigrants were from little backwoods villages, and you know, they couldn't read or write or anything like that and *we've had to teach them at extra cost on education because the children didn't know about English, writing or reading English, or anything else. Fair enough, you know, we'll gladly bring them into the system*, but it so happens that they nearly all were if you like pushed or coerced into the Labour camp because we were too unrealistic to realise what was going on if you like.'
>
> (Interview, March 1990, our emphasis)

This extract outlines a number of important points: (i) the idea that the education of migrants and entry into 'the system' is a Commonwealth/post-colonial responsibility, (ii) 'the villages' are placed on a lower point on a scale of cultural evolution, and (iii) the migrants have been falsely led into the Labour Party because of their innocence. Encoded here is a discourse of coloniser/colonised re-articulated in a neo-colonial conjuncture.

This appraisal of the current situation is not merely one which evokes images of a colonial past. There exists an interesting interplay between colonial images and contemporary developments. Whilst the councillor quoted above dismisses the majority of black Labour councillors, a Conservative councillor comments that change will happen gradually:

> I welcomed the first one, Bert Carliss, a West Indian, and I welcomed him with open arms, bless him. You know he's a Commonwealth man. Now, we've got probably twenty of them I suppose on the council, all of them are Labour, but we've got a few coloured candidates now for election, within the Tory Party. But the impetus initially was from these masses of people coming in who were all lefties and out to get what they could from the system without putting anything in. As soon as they landed they went straight to the DHSS and started collecting money. It'll happen [the growth of black representatives], it is happening and it will happen, and it's right that it should when we've got so many coloureds in the city.
>
> (Interview, March 1990)

There is an interesting contradiction here between a construction of black Labour representatives, who were self-seeking and insincere, and support for the principle that black communities should be represented. The same politician argues:

> I think it's good for the city, because we are international. We used to be the industrial heart of the nation, now we're going to be the tourism heart and conference heart and exhibition heart, which means more and more people from all over the world are coming here and a lot of those people will be coloured, and if they meet coloured Brummies in factories, and in exhibition halls, and wherever they go, it's going to be a very nice homogeneous whole, it's going to help rather than hinder. But again, you've got to have these coloureds up to a certain standard. *They come here very rough, the raw material, and we're having to educate them, train them, teach them right from wrong in our view.*
>
> (Interview, March 1990, our emphasis)

In this extract the connection is made between colonial imagery and the shift from manufacturing to service industries. The 'raw materials' are black labourers themselves in this imagined order. Here colonial history and the post-industrial city are symbolised in a metaphorical but highly revealing fashion.

At the same time as being constructed as a 'resource', black people are also identified as responsible for 'social problems':

> One of the biggest problems we have in Birmingham is these chaps from Pakistan families bringing their drugs, the drugs scene never was here, there never was a drugs problem until the West Indians came and then the Indians and Pakis. So there's a bad side to the coin as well as the good; we have to train them in our ways.
>
> (Interview, March 1990)

All these constructs are possible because the dominant referent is culture. The 'good' and the 'bad' are constructed in such a way to allow culturally defined racist discourse to be used. This 'two-handed' style allows racist constructs to be introduced alongside positively connotated attributes. Thus this politician can say without contradiction:

> I've always been brought up on the basis that a man's a man whatever his colour, and you take him as *good until he proves himself otherwise*.
>
> (Interview, March 1990, our emphasis)

The important thing to grasp is that the denial that 'colour' is significant actually facilitates racialised constructions which use cultural references. The 'proving ground' which he identifies in this extract is loaded with racialised discourses and codes.

This material raises a whole series of issues about the impact of political racialisation, intentionality and the agency of social actors. The political culture of Conservative politicians is racialised in mutable and volatile ways. In this sense these racialised discourses provide the means whereby Conservative politicians make sense of everyday political life. Their intention is not to use racism in any crude way, indeed they deny passionately that their ideas are 'racist' in any sense. However, racialised formulations, often revolving around some notion of culture, are integral to their political comprehension of black politics and the issue of racism. The result is that the racial contradictions within the vernacular of everyday politics need not be addressed. As we pointed out in the previous section, the grammar, rhetoric and content of these assertions allow the elaboration of racialised forms while prohibiting accusations of racism.

## 'We have got to do something?': Conservative politicians and race policy

A range of positions are held by Conservative politicians with regard to race policy and the record of Labour in relation to policies about race. Some positions offered by people on the left of the party constitute a distinct departure within Conservative politics. We want to examine this in relation to the position of a particular councillor who has served as the Conservative Spokesperson on Social Services. We will then broaden the discussion to consider a wider range of positions held by Conservative politicians with regard to race policy.

The councillor in question was astutely aware of the way in which his colleagues racialised political issues. In the following quotation he comments:

> I'm spokesman on social services and even now when some question of race comes up, an example being the creation of a specialist Afro-Caribbean or Asian wing within a home for the elderly, I'm aware that it is still expected by those of us on our side that there'll be a media reaction on racial grounds against this. I've found myself having to be very careful on issues like that, not to disguise what I mean, of course not, but to try to make it clear that if I am advancing criticism or opposition it's for a variety of reasons which I try to set out and not just because we have some sort of anti-ethnic minority policy or thinking. I would think that you'd find, you may have found already, colleagues in my group who would put it rather more forcefully than that and who would react against that sort of thing because of the personal belief that they hold about race.
>
> (Interview, April 1990)

As such he places himself on the left of the Conservative Group. In a sense his response is surprising considering the party's open commitment to dismantling the political infrastructure established by Labour to promote racial equality. He stresses:

> You've got to be sensitive to their needs and values and heritage and so forth, and make provision. I've never spoken against specialist provision on grounds of race in any of our social services units. All I would say is that you've got to be careful that you're providing balance and you're providing choice and I would hate to have a situation, for example, in an elderly person's home where somebody from an Afro-Caribbean background is told, 'Right, you go in that wing because . . .', and by contrast a traditional white Anglo-Saxon would be told, 'No, no you can't go over and eat with him', because obviously you're designed to be kept apart.
>
> (Interview, April 1990)

Like previous examples, the dominant theme in his account centres around ideas of cultural difference and anxieties over segregation. His concern is to defend a notion of pluralism as opposed to the evolutionary assimilation proposed by his colleagues:

> I don't believe in imposing cultural values on people. This is something which stems from my early contact with the Hindu group. . . . They operate on this basis. They say we are what we are, we cannot be white men with brown skins, we have our own heritage, beliefs, values and what have you and we're going to cherish that, adhere to it, but from that base and from the strength that gives us we will make an active contribution to the society in which we find ourselves.
>
> (Interview, April 1990)

This kind of cultural, and to some degree political pluralism, is central to his account. He is in qualified agreement with the initiatives promoted by Labour:

> I remember a remark that Bill Gray [Labour Chairman of the Personnel and Equal Opportunity Committee] once made when there was a discussion in I think Finance and Management Committee about whether it is necessary to have an equality policy, and he said something to the effect of 'you people think it would just happen'. That's a remark that's stuck with me because I think there's a great deal of force in it. I think that you can't simply expect, given that a section of society, given that certain elements in the human nature of some, would have racist tendencies, you can't just expect that if you lump everybody together magically it will somehow work itself out. I think you have to have legislation therefore to prevent things like – I've used the word legislation in very general terms – you have to provide for the prevention of over-discrimination.
>
> (Interview, April 1990)

The point at which this councillor diverges from the idea of state intervention is, perhaps predictably, on questions about standards, competition and the individual:

> I'm personally uncomfortable with some aspects of positive discrimination – the idea that you will put somebody in more on the basis of the fact that their particular grouping is under-represented in a particular sector, rather than on the basis of fair competition. I'm uncomfortable with that, I don't condemn it out of hand, because I can see that if you have a history of under-representation you've got to do something at some point to catch up, but I am against the dropping of standards, I think what you've got to do is remove any other and illegitimise obstacles, personal racism of a superior within a department or something of that sort, overt discrimination. Remove that so that people can compete fairly. What I wouldn't do is remove competition.
>
> (Interview, April 1990)

He also disagrees with the idea of specialist units within the City Council to act as advisory services. This is in line with the Conservative Group's Policy Manifesto, but having said this he still argues for the functions a unit of this sort should perform:

> It's group policy to disband the Race Relations Unit in its present form. I would like to see those issues given full weight and taken fully seriously, but within an overall context [of] Personnel rather than put out on a limb. It puts people's backs up. I think for people who are less comfortable with the ideas of integration and proper representation and that sort of thing the creation of those sorts of unit where they are not seen to be doing a particularly effective job or making a particularly significant contribution does tend to fuel intolerance and anger rather than assist it.
>
> (Interview, April 1990)

He views black representatives as performing a positive function, adding that 'you have good and bad councillors of whatever background'. He does warn that there are:

> certain councillors who come from particular wards more because of the support of that community in that particular ward and the strength of that support rather than a general support for that individual as an elected representative . . . but I think there are examples of a departure from the normal party process because of a strong ethnic support.
>
> (Interview, April 1990)

Although there are some similarities between this comment and those discussed earlier, it differs in a number of important ways.

The point here is that ideological work is going on within the Conservative Party. In this sense the discourse of this councillor cannot be simply understood as an exercise in impression management (Wetherall and Potter, 1986). His objections to current political initiatives on equal opportunity are articulated through deracialised (Reeves, 1989) concepts like 'competition' and 'individualism'. The outcome may be the same (i.e. opposition to initiatives on racial equality) but the political style of this discourse is fundamentally different from that discussed in previous examples. These may be little more than 'modern' responses to a politics of necessity. However, the subtle differences need to be comprehended in order to present an overall picture of the accounts of Conservative councillors.

While three out of the seventeen Conservative councillors we interviewed expressed similar sentiments, the majority of our sample were critical and dismissive of the Labour administration's policy on achieving racial equality. Opposition to these initiatives was justified by the claim that the Race Relations Unit constitutes a 'waste of money' and contributed excessively to the large and unwieldy municipal edifice. In this sense, opposition to special initiatives on race was part of the Conservatives' broader commitment to limit the size and machinery of local government. The emphasis in all of the accounts we recorded was that the local state should provide 'value for money' and commensurate access. This was closely connected to meritocratic sentiments combined with market competition. In some cases Conservative councillors claimed that developing policy initiatives on race created racism. This position is clear in the following quotation:

> I don't see a need for a Race Relations Unit. We do have [a need for] an Equal

Opportunities Unit, and I see that as rather different, I see that as being possibly necessary to ensure that on the personnel side that one is keeping to opportunities policies that we [Conservative administration] brought in, that is necessary to stay within the law and not discriminate. But the Race Relations Unit, it does more harm than good. It tends to create racism rather than do away with it.

(Interview, April 1991)

The Conservative councillors we interviewed viewed the initiatives developed by the Labour administration, particularly those on employment, as promoting positive discrimination and 'go over the top to discriminate in favour' of black people (Interview, April 1991). This was presented as an affront to principles of fairness summed up in the words of one female councillor: 'I believe in that it should be the best man [sic] for the job' (Interview, March 1990). Interestingly, 'positive discrimination' was also characterised as counter-productive and patronising to people it claimed to help:

Black people want to be judged on their ability as people. They want to get jobs because of their ability as people, they don't want to get jobs because they happen to be black . . . the black people I speak to, and I know a lot of them, feel patronised. . . . I think we have to first of all ensure that we see black people as people, not as black people, or dark people or coloured people, or whatever – just as people, and I think the more artificial badges you put up by either having an [employment] allocation system for them or providing them with their own old people's homes, or providing them with all-black schools, or even all-black organisations, I think quite frankly, you are delaying the day when they will regarded for what they are, and that is people.

(Interview, February 1991)

Conservative politicians accused the Labour Party of operating *de facto* discriminatory practices in employment by establishing targets for minority employment. As we will point out in the next chapter black Conservatives have advocated a similar critique and this type of argument cannot easily be dismissed. As we shall see, the emphasis on 'ability' and 'competition' has proven attractive to black elites precisely because at the level of rhetoric it offers the transcendence of race.

Another key criticism of racial equality policies is that they artificially alter employment patterns and access to other goods. In one case it was asserted that this 'racial allocation system' was little more that an attempt engender electoral support creating a 'politics of envy' (Interview, August 1990). The position of this section of the Conservative Group is summed up in the following quotation:

We are not in power to tinker around as social engineers, our job is just to get on with providing services. I think if we scrap the Race Relations Unit, the Women's Unit, apart from saving a very considerable sum of money that's spent on them – we would also save on the resentment that they created . . . I think it creates divisions.

(Interview, December 1990)

In addition to references to employment and special service provisions, racial awareness training courses were commonly cited as an example of the misguided nature of the Labour Group's race policy. One councillor commented:

> Going back to racial awareness training, Oh God! that was diabolical. They virtually said that all white people are racists – black people can't be racists. Saddam Hussain and Kurds didn't really come into it at the time I don't suppose. . . . People who weren't racists came out telling me that although they actually weren't [racists] there was actually a lot of pressure put on them to become racists. . . . They still do racial awareness courses but what they call them is something else now. But it defeats the whole object and produces a white backlash.
>
> (Interview, April 1990)

It was claimed that the Labour administration, which some Conservatives characterised as 'well meaning', endorsed counter productive initiatives which merely generated racist responses within the white electorate.

When questioned about a preferred strategy these politicians agreed that the bureaucratic structure for addressing issues of race policy should be dismantled. While often conceding the need for some 'race relations advisers', Conservative councillors stressed that engendering racial harmony was an evolutionary process. A common assertion was that racism was in most cases the product of fear, while others cited the importance of education in bringing about change. The common feature that underpinned these accounts was the argument that the prevalence of racism within British society was vastly exaggerated. Equally, they claimed that it is impossible to legislate for racial equality.

These accounts also incorporated some sense of an acceptable expression of cultural difference. A female Conservative put it in the following terms:

> I think they should be allowed, like the Poles, like the Jews do, to keep and maintain their culture – that's very important within their home. But at the same time I think we've got to ensure that they do speak English even if it is only their second language . . . and until they can speak English then they're not going to be able to play a part in society.
>
> (Interview, February 1991)

Within this logic, cultural difference is consigned to the private sphere while public life should remain unchanged and express British values: 'I don't want the Bishop of Birmingham supporting the Muslim religion, the Sikh religion and all the rest of them' (Interview, August 1991). Interestingly enough, in 1991 the Conservative Group fought the local election on the proposal that they would use money saved from dismantling the municipal structure of race policy to fund the Community Relations Council (CRC). This was contentious at the time because the CRC organisation was facing closure. The significance of this proposal is that it exemplifies the Conservative commitment to organise issues of race policy out of the municipal structure, in favour of favour a community relations strategy confined to a pastoral role.

Conservative approaches to race policy are not uniform but equally there are a number of agreed core features. The most significant areas of agreement centre around the principles of individualism, competition and minimising state intervention. All of these notions are situated within a commitment to meritocracy. The policy initiatives of the Labour administration on employment and service provision are thus constructed as a violation of these foundational principles which are non-racialised. Opposition to policy initiatives aimed at achieving racial equality can thus be voiced through a language that is not racially marked. However, the refusal to accept that racism and racial discrimination are serious social and economic phenomena results in a number of consequences. The predominant Conservative response is that racism should not be challenged and that it will become progressively benign with the passage of time as a result of a 'natural progression'. Racism is conceived as an inflated political issue that is best ignored.

While many of the Conservative politicians we interviewed saw the issue of race as of limited relevance, their political discourse was highly racialised. In this section we have tried to outline the contours of these ideas. Before concluding this chapter, we want to emphasise that Conservative forms of racialised politics need to be seen as highly volatile. Whilst these discourses are constantly shifting and adapting to new circumstances, they also share common grammatical, rhetorical and lexical elements. It is this tension between continuity and change that we have tried to represent.

## SUMMARY AND CONCLUSION

Within the context of the discourses of the Labour politicians we interviewed a variety of racialised issues are of growing importance: this can be seen in discourses over representation and political identity and in discourses characterising black political organisation as criminal (i.e. the 'Asian Mafia' code) or contingent (i.e. the images of 'back-stabbing' Asian Labour Party members who need to be 'policed'). An important theme that runs through our interviews is the argument that the local political system is being transformed by the impact of 'alien' political traditions. These micro-discursive formations are a response to the growing political power of black activists and politicians. In this sense these codes and discourses are resources that can be mobilised against emerging black politicians regardless of their attributes or the circumstances of particular struggles. At the same time the racial identity of white politicians is rarely invoked because whiteness is taken as being the political norm. References to whiteness within the local political system are confined to situations where white politicians are seen as the victims, e.g. in situations where they have been rejected by black party members. This discourse of the 'white victim' provides a powerful way of diverting accusations of racial inequality in the Labour Party.

Black political participation within the Conservative Party is small by comparison with Labour. However, the limited numbers of black Conservatives play a significant symbolic role. Black Conservatives are referred to extensively within the accounts of white politicians, where they are held up as exemplary and contrasted to deviant forms of black participation in the Labour Party. This results in a discourse on culture which pre-empts accusations of racism. The significance of colour is denied while at the same time an 'evolutionary' continuum of cultural forms is imagined. Black politicians are then placed on this continuum. Clear connections exist between colonial imagery and the social construction of black people in Birmingham. These discourses add to a volatile and mutating lexicon of racialised discourses that take on new expressions within the political domain. Complex ideological work is being carried out within the Conservative Party. Amongst the liberal sections of the Party, cultural and political pluralism are significant reference points. Some elements of state intervention are accepted in the area of equal opportunities policy. Objections to special provision are articulated through deracialised concepts like 'competition' and 'individualism'. However, this equally needs to be seen in the context of widespread opposition to state intervention on these issues. For the largest section of our sample of Conservative politicians evolutionary and educational approaches are preferred.

Distinct forms of racialised politics have emerged within the two main political parties in Birmingham. There are, however, also important continuities and shared discursive codes and elements which are common to both parties. For example, black political mobilisations are commonly associated with the import of alien political traditions. These 'traditions' are characterised as being at a lower point on a continuum of political evolution. As a result, white actors speak about having to politically educate black communities. Another shared reference point is the association of black politics with corruption. These racialised discourses cut across party divisions and can be elaborated by politicians regardless of their respective ideological positions.

The developments we have described within Birmingham's racialised political culture exhibit important continuities with previous political discourses on race. Yet at the same time these discourses need to be situated within particular institutional and regional contexts. The growing political activity of black people in Birmingham has prompted a reconfiguration in the way race is socially constructed. Change is bringing about new forms of racialisation as racial discourse feeds off itself while adapting to new situations. The racial discourses which we have described here cannot be reduced to a past ideological inheritance, but neither can they be understood as a strictly contemporary development. Rather, it is important to see that over the past few decades ideas about race have been invented and re-invented in complicated and diverse ways.

The form that this process takes within electoral politics ultimately has to be located within a context where there is a struggle for political influence, i.e. demands for black representation and responses to these demands. This is why we move on in the next chapter to discuss the changing position of black politicians within the political system and their role in the redefinition of racialised political identities.

# 6 The new black politics

In the previous two chapters the emergence of black politicians as a recognisable force in political life has been an underlying theme in the political discourses about race. But we have said little as yet about who these politicians are and how they define their political identities and position themselves in terms of both local and national agendas about race. This is why in this chapter we want to move on and explore the ways in which black politicians are situated within the processes of political change that we have explored throughout this study. There have been few substantive studies of the role of black politicians in the context of British politics. This is in marked contrast to the situation in the United States, where there have been numerous studies of black political elites and their role in shaping urban politics. But developments in the past decade have led to increased interest in the question of how the growing number of black politicians have developed new forms of political identity and helped to reshape the political landscape. It is with this in mind that we want to look in some detail at the new forms of black politics that have emerged over the past decade. Previous discussions of the emergence of black politicians have focused narrowly on either key national figures or on general accounts of the phenomenon. Such accounts have failed to provide an understanding of the broader context in which they must operate politically (Fitzgerald, 1984; Sewell, 1993). In our account we want to focus on the conditions that affect black political activity and participation, the circumstances in which black elected representatives participate in the political process, the constraints that are placed upon them and the forms of political activism that underpin their emergence and impact. We want to emphasise that black politicians are not passive objects of the kinds of racial discourses we outlined in the previous chapter. Here we will examine the kinds of responses and strategies they have developed. We offer a framework that can address the question of the political incorporation of black politicians without reducing their politics to simple co-option (Browning, Marshall and Tabb, 1984, 1986). In line with our general approach, we maintain that it is impossible to understand these new forms of political representation without examining the relationship between institutional structures of political organisation and the configurations of racism within political life. We begin our account by looking at the processes at work within the Labour Party, which has provided the main arena for black political activity. We then look more briefly at the role of minority political activists within the context of Conservative politics.

## BLACK POLITICIANS AND THE LABOUR PARTY

The number of black politicians has grown steadily in the 1980s and early 1990s, at both national and local levels. In the context of Birmingham the number of black councillors rose steadily during this period, and by 1992 there were twenty-one local councillors from minority backgrounds. Since they were all in the Labour Party they made up approximately one-third of the ruling Labour Group on the City Council and exercised a degree of political influence. In this environment the growth of minority representation became a subject of debate within the local political culture. But who were these politicians from minority communities? How did they enter the political arena? How were they perceived by white politicians and activists? How did they see their role within the context of party politics and the changing dynamics of community politics? These are the questions we want to address in this part of the chapter, by drawing on detailed interviews we conducted with minority councillors.

In all we interviewed twenty-three black councillors who were either currently serving as elected officials or who had previously held office. Of these, seventeen were south Asian, four African-Caribbean, one an Yemeni Arab and one an Indo-Caribbean from Guyana. Of the south Asian councillors eleven have links with Pakistan and Kashmir, and seven of these are from the rural district of Mirpur. Five of the councillors had links with India, and one is a Kenyan Asian. These politicians were predominantly male, with only three minority women being elected. In terms of religion, thirteen were Muslim, four Sikh, one Ravi Dassian and two councillors were connected to the black Christian churches. The remaining minority politicians were non-observers or secular.

### Routes into politics

In Chapter 4 we argued that there were chiefly two avenues through which increased black political participation occurred during the late 1970s and early 1980s. These were (i) instrumental negotiations with prominent white politicians, and (ii) ideological challenges inspired by anti-colonial and civil rights movements mediated through left-wing politics. The political biographies of the black politicians we interviewed fit broadly into these two categories, although their cultural and community bases vary greatly. There are, however, some clear patterns regarding the manner in which these councillors became involved in political activity.

From the interviews with black councillors it is clear that they took a number of routes into politics. Three broad routes of entry can be distinguished. While some of the councillors do not fit neatly into these ideal types we want to argue that they allow us to think through the general patterns of involvement. The first mode can be seen as that of the communal advocate. This is associated with the instrumental mode of politics discussed in Chapter 4 and is linked with local forms of advocacy, and is often connected to a local issue based agenda. This can also include a form of political activity that is inspired by involvement in local community issues and campaigns. The second type of entry we characterise as Labour first, often emerging out of involvement in trade unions and constituency Labour Parties. Here the issue of the politics of race is seen as subordinate to the agenda of the Labour Party. The third form of involvement we call black socialist, and is inspired by a hope that black interests can be incorporated within a left Labour politics that includes issues of empowerment and black representation. We want to exemplify these general patterns by looking in detail at the political biographies of black councillors.

The majority of the councillors we interviewed became politically active because they were assuming the role of informal advocates and advisers for neighbours and relatives within their respective local communities. This is particularly true of the south Asian councillors who are first generation migrants. A councillor originally from Pakistan describes his experience:

> There was some people [from Pakistan] . . . and they were having difficulty in getting all the benefits that they were entitled to, in terms of not knowing the whole process or not enough knowledge of English and hence I started in terms of, you could say, a social worker, to help those people, to make sure that they do get these benefits and the like, to which they are entitled to, and this is where I started my career in terms of helping the people.

He continues:

> Later on in 1970 I joined the Labour Party because I also became aware of them, especially in the area of Sparkbrook, the two-party political system, and I was quite aware of them in 1970 and then the third party known as the Liberals, but I decided to join the Labour Party because I was of the opinion that the Labour Party was more in favour of people like my family from the Asian sub-ontinent, in terms of regard for their rights. So I joined the Labour Party and this is when I became much more involved in the organisation of the Labour Party, and then some friends in the Labour Party asked me if I would mind if I should stand as a councillor.
>
> (Interview, July 1990)

Several politicians spoke in similar terms, claiming that becoming a councillor was expected of them as a logical extension of their communal responsibilities. Six of the south Asian councillors described similar kinds of experiences where their knowledge of English and confidence in dealing with bureaucratic state organisations placed them in the role of informal patrons who made representations or assisted with the filling in of forms. Another councillor, who came from Mirpur in 1953, put it this way:

> In those days people from Pakistan were not many, the majority of the people from abroad were illiterate – they couldn't speak any English. I had a little

> English and I was better able to communicate and deal with the local bureaucracy than other people. Things like social security, tax and they used to come to me for help and assistance with these problems. I started to work, initially, in a foundry, I still had problems speaking English, and I basically learned English on the shop floor of the foundry. Working alongside white workers made me stretch my English speaking abilities. . . . From 1955 to 1956 people from the Indian subcontinents started coming to England. I came to realise that one problem for the ethnic minorities was that of religion and keeping our religious life. We also had social problems and day-to-day problems. I didn't join the Labour Party then, I was more concerned with trying to solve these problems at a local level.
>
> (Interview, February 1991)

Five of the south Asian politicians gave similar accounts, commenting that they came into politics through the pastoral role they were performing within their communities. Here involvement in the Labour Party was a consequence of this kind of advocacy work and the ideological character of the parties was of almost secondary importance. Generation and conjuncture are important factors to be taken into consideration. In many ways these politicians represent an elite vanguard within those communities who were gaining access to the Labour Party. This, as we mentioned previously, needs to be contextualised in the increasing desire on the part of the local political leadership, principally on the right of the Party, to bolster their support. Eleven of the south Asian councillors we interviewed came into the Labour Party in this manner. One councillor commented:

> My parents supported the Labour Party although they weren't involved as such because my father always worked, but during the election he was always going to give his vote to the Labour Party. I went with him. We had some immigration problems to start off with some years back and [the MP] actually helped us an awful lot and from then on I was sort of attached to it and have been with the Party ever since. I have been working for the Party from when I was able to vote for them, and I was unemployed in 1982 or 1983 at the change of leadership and that gave me more time to go to meetings and find out what was going on and it really got me involved actually. I was interested, and did show some interest to become a councillor, and my ward actually selected me.
>
> (Interview, March 1991)

The pattern which emerges from these accounts is that the involvement of these politicians in the Labour Party is clearly connected with locally established connections and a political agenda that is associated with practical issues such as access to resources, religious needs and the provision social welfare.

Migrant communities in the initial period of settlement were largely outside of the political system and unscrupulous people could exploit this for their own ends. One councillor reported that it was abuse of this kind during the mid-1970s that precipitated his involvement in mainstream politics:

> There was extortion of money going round and we went to complain and we

> talked to our Labour councillor and MP. They were not interested at all, but it was a very vital disease in our community. People were extorting money out of innocent people who didn't know the law. I can't prove it; we did try but it was just that there were a few Asian people who could speak English and they were informers to the police. They used to go to around saying 'if you don't give me money the police will deport you'. And the police used to come. A guy said to me if you don't give me money I will deport you, and I didn't believe it, the next day they were in my house and they said if we didn't talk to this person I would be deported. But they didn't realise that I was politically active. So after that much of it went underground, and it wasn't so open. . . . There were two or three people involved in this.
>
> (Interview, March 1990)

In these circumstances involvement in politics was closely linked to a desire for civil enfranchisement. The Labour Party provided a means of entry into the political domain, and the means through which activists could argue for civil rights.

In some cases family involvement in independence movements affected political affiliation in Britain. One councillor commented:

> I have some background in politics. My Grandfather was accused by the British of being a subversive and he was arrested by the colonial power. He was a religious leader and he spent most of his life in a British jail. My uncle was poisoned by the British secret police in India and my brother spent ten years in a British jail for political reasons between 1932–1940. So I grew up struggling against colonialism. My family never made any deals on basic principles, we were a very principled family. . . . When I came here I was surprised at the system. I had been denied the right to vote in my own country and as soon as I stepped off the plane on to the runway at Heathrow airport I was given it. One man, one vote! We had been struggling for this for years and suddenly I had it by just stepping off the plane. This had not been given to me in my own country and to people of my own generation. I realised quickly that this is a political weapon and it had been given to me.
>
> (Interview, May 1992)

Other councillors cited the support that the Labour Party gave to the independence movements, particularly the Congress Party in India, as a crucial determinant in their political alignment with the British Labour Party. This, coupled with the overwhelmingly working-class character of migrant communities, meant that – at least initially – there was little choice as to which political party served their interests. All of the councillors interviewed said class was the primary factor in determining their choice of the Labour Party.

Not all of the south Asian councillors entered politics through the locally based negotiations mentioned above. Three of the councillors we interviewed came into the Labour movement through participating in left-wing politics. Some of them had stood as Socialist Unity candidates in the 1970s. Others were involved in Indian Workers' Associations or Kashmiri Workers' Associations and came into the Labour Party via this route. In some cases this was combined with involvement in community politics, but for others this did not necessarily follow.

Three of the councillors mentioned that their path into politics was affected by involvement in education and student politics. Two out of the three minority women councillors mentioned that this political space was important. This is significant given that the forms of advocate politics mentioned earlier are almost exclusively male preserves. For one male councillor from a working-class background, university provided a context where he could be exposed to radical political ideas. He points out that while education offered social mobility within an alienating middle-class environment, it also allowed exposure to anti-colonial writings and a range of radical thinkers. He attended university in 1968 and comments here on its effect on him:

> I was very motivated towards actually succeeding and becoming a professional in the traditional sense. In 1968 what was happening at the university at the time had an impact on me – the business about black power did affect me . . . [I heard lectures on] black power and at the same time one was exposed to all kinds of things, including things like the conference on the Dialectics of Liberation. Almost all students who were on the left read that book at the time. We all read this and it had a tremendous influence on us. At the same time I came across the writings of Frantz Fanon that had a tremendous impact on me. I actually came across the writings of Fanon through listening to a speech of Stokely Carmichael who was talking about Frantz Fanon in May 1968. . . . I think if there was a particular thing which stimulated my interest in politics it was reading Fanon – if there's one single piece of work which one has to look to academically which influenced me greatly it was Fanon's book *Wretched of the Earth.*
>
> (Interview, June 1990)

The type of induction into political ideas is quite different from the locally based orientation mentioned previously. This particular councillor had also been involved in voluntary sector politics but he was also inspired by anti-colonial writers such a Frantz Fanon and the black power movement in the United States.

The politician quoted above is exceptional within the group of black councillors we interviewed. He became involved in the Labour Party during a period when it was hoped that its political agenda could be expanded to address issues of racism. He was consequently closely involved as an activist with developing policy initiatives such as the Ethnic Minority Liaison Committee of the District Labour Party that was set up in 1982. Like many other activists in the early 1980s he entered the Party in the hope that greater democracy within the Party would provide a space for the organisation of black interests (Wainwright, 1987; Shukra, 1990b).

The point here is that a range of political spaces affected the routes through which black politicians entered the local political system. In many ways this can be used to explain the range of responses and positions which black politicians took up within the Labour Group. In particular, the sorts of political agendas that these politicians brought with them need to be contextualised in terms of their political biographies. We found no mechanistic relationship between the economic and social conditions which black communities face and the political agenda being formulated by black politicians. The brief biographies referred to here show the variety that was evident with regard to exposure to ideas relating to colonialism, civil rights and black liberation. Equally these politicians entered the political arena from a range of positions.

Some of the councillors we spoke to were resistant to the idea of being positioned as *black politicians*, maintaining that their background was secondary, if not irrelevant, to their position as Labour Party members. A politician who stood as a candidate for Labour throughout the 1970s and was one of the first minority councillors to be elected comments:

> When I was elected they were trying to get me to say, 'Yes, I am there because I am black.' I said, 'No.' I so happen to be black, that is what I would like to think. I wanted to take a more positive role. I believe in a multicultural, multiracial society. In the place I came from in Jamaica there were people of all races and colour. I want to live in a society where there is a more equitable distribution of resources . . . I just wanted to see if it was possible for a black person to get into the mainstream of British life and be successful. I wasn't one of those individuals who were just seeking attention.
>
> (Interview, August 1990)

The important point to stress here is that there are a range of positions held by councillors with regard to the significance they invest in the notion of race or difference.

In broad terms, thirteen of the councillors we interviewed can be seen as falling into the communal advocate category. Four councillors fit into the Labour first category. Six councillors can be positioned in the black socialist route into the Labour Party. Whilst these categories are merely heuristic and do not fully capture the complex processes which shaped the personal biographies of individual politicians, they help to highlight the broad contours of how black political activists made their entry into the Labour Party. As we shall argue later these differential routes into party politics had important consequences for the formation of political identities among black politicians.

## Representation and black sections

The councillors we interviewed held disparate positions in relation to the issue of what black representation meant to them. This can be seen in the range of views they expressed in relation to the issue of black sections. As we have already noted, a majority of the black councillors we interviewed were opposed to the formation of black sections. Such opposition cannot be taken at face value, since it is important to explore what this opposition meant and how it affected the dynamics of black political mobilisation. It is to this issue that we now turn.

For some black councillors, particularly those we have characterised as communal advocates, their opposition to black sections was connected to an antipathy towards the politics of the Labour left. One female African-Caribbean politician commented that she was initially interested in the black sections movement but became disillusioned because she felt it was little more than an organ of the 'white left'. A long-serving councillor put it the following terms:

> So far I have praised the Labour Party. But the problem is that Labour doesn't educate its own people. There are misfits within the party. Generally there are two kinds of misfits – 'the yuppies' and the 'left intellectuals'. These people started out working class and they became educated and tried to be middle class but the middle class wouldn't accept them. Then they came back to the working class and they don't accept them so they are caught in-between you see?
>
> (Interview, January 1991)

For these councillors black sections were the product of this intellectual left politics. The same councillor, who heads a Muslim welfare organisation, continues:

> You can see from this morning that the people come to me – do they come to the black section? No! They are totally separate from the working-class people and so the people don't want black sections. It is just a few intellectuals trying to tell the people what they should be. This is what was wrong with the Labour Party in the past and the division between left and right, they never thought of what the man in the street, the little man in the street, wants. He doesn't want a black section.
>
> (Interview, January 1991)

Black sections were also opposed by some politicians because they were seen to invoke an illegitimate and privileging notion of race. This division is in evidence in the following quotation from a south Asian councillor:

> I voted against black sections. They use that badge as a privilege, we don't want a party within a party. I don't want a special place for me because I am black. I want a fair chance and not a priority. Black sections still exist in Birmingham but not in my ward. People should be looked at because of their ability and not the colour of their skin.
>
> (Interview, June 1992)

This objection is connected with a notion of universalism that is underpinned by the idea that it is impossible to combine self-consciously black interests with a generic socialism. The same south Asian councillor comments:

> I classify myself as an ethnic minority politician who supports everyone's interests. I wouldn't use the term 'black'; I don't think that is right. I am not for creating black sections in the party. I don't believe in black and white skin. I believe in only people who have sympathy with everybody.
>
> (Interview, February 1991)

Here generic socialism is concerned with providing for the everyday aspirations that working people have regardless of race. A female councillor connected this position with a desire not to be patronised on racial grounds:

> The point is I think that black people face the same kind of problems in their daily lives as white people, housing, social services, education, the Poll Tax, all that. They're the same problems. . . . As a black person what I feel is I don't want to be patronised, I don't want people to bend over backwards for me, I want my basic rights. One of those rights is to be respected and accepted as a black person; now if that means that the Labour Party has got to change its ways to recognise black people then it's got to do that. How it does that is another debate; whether it does that through having black sections that's fair enough I don't mind that, because we've got women's sections. But I also feel there is a danger, I don't want to be boxed, I don't want to be classified, I just want to be recognised as a person. Yes, I happen to be black but I'm also a lot of other things, so I think the only thing that I feel about some of the Labour Party having black sections is that becomes 'Oh right well we'll discuss that because it's from the black section' and it's a black people's issue, it should be everybody's issue.
>
> (Interview, April 1990)

In this account black sections are constructed as a legitimate strategy but one to which this particular politician would not subscribe. Other councillors suggested that black sections within the Labour Party would lead to political segregation:

> I don't believe in black sections. I've never ever believed in separatism. I've seen that in America. Martin Luther King, as good as he was, he was fighting for the black people . . . but there were poor people, white people, as much as poor black people in the ghettos of America who never had attention of Martin Luther King. He never ever mentioned the poor whites. He never ever mentioned the poor and sick whites or lack of medical care. I'd never ever support black sections. In any case I don't believe that you should belong to something in something. Either you belong to the Labour Party or you don't belong to the Labour Party. I don't think that because you belong to the Labour Party and you're black you have priority. I don't believe in that, because I should explain that to you . . . I'm a black man. If I want a school in my ward and a white man, a white councillor wants a school in his ward, what do I say? Do I say 'I'm a black man I should have priority before he got his bloody school.' Do I say that? No! I say I belong to the Party as much as him, let us assess the situation, which school should be built first. If I've got priority – give it to me. If he's got priority give it to him. Would black sections bring about that? The hell they would!
>
> (Interview, March 1990)

Other councillors, speaking from a similar political position, characterised the black sections' controversy as merely 'banner waving' and only concerned with the 'ghetto politics of black issues'. Their politics was formulated around the principle that politically constructed notions of race should be abandoned in favour of a transcendent colour-blind socialism: 'We want to go out there and fight for our rights and we say forget about the colour, let's have equal rights as human beings' (Interview, March 1991).

There are a number of core features of this stance: namely, a universalism that is defined in relation to equal access to resources, a rejection of race as a privileged form of political consciousness or need, and a meritocratic approach to political priorities whether they be about selections for political office or the allocation of resources.

From a different position black sections were also criticised for not being culturally specific. A south Asian councillor commented:

> I am a strong believer that there should be representation of the black community within the Labour Party, but that representation has got to be more of a grassroots thing. [Black sections was] a policy made by the individual few who really see themselves as the sort of, basically the intellectuals of the party. One of the problems of the black sections has been that they have not taken into account the cultural identity of the black movement. People were just saying 'you're black', and what it doesn't do is the fact it doesn't give you a geographical belonging to an area. . . . It is a set-up in the form of protection against the oppression of racism we feel and face. But really, I think the black movement ought to be a bit more than that and have a bit more of an identity.
>
> (Interview, November 1990)

There is an interesting dual process evident here: on the one hand, a political definition of race is being rejected, whilst on the other, culturally defined interests can be defended and expressed. As a result it is very difficult to define exactly what minority representation means in the context of the Labour Party. The political significance of race is played down while references to minorities and cultural difference can be discussed when placed outside of the internal structures of Labour politics.

Amongst the politicians who supported black sections there was a range of attitudes with regard to their usefulness as a political strategy in the 1990s. In particular some questioned the relationship between the black sections movement and left-wing models of political activity. A south Asian councillor commented:

> I still support the concept the black sections, but I do not support that they should be the mouthpiece of black people. I think the black sections should be just talking about equality, nothing else. It took me four years to come to that experience or idea. But I think it's too much the mouthpiece of left-wing politics and it shouldn't be. I think there's a debate going on in the black section, there's a big fight going on in the black section, that it shouldn't be a mouthpiece for white left-wing issues, it should be mainstream, it should be part of mainstream.
>
> (Interview, March 1990)

The major advantage of the black sections approach to politics was that a politically defined notion of inclusive blackness had the potential to override divisive structures of caste and interethnic conflict. He continues:

> [Black sections should have] united everybody and got rid of the first obstacle, which is the caste system; then among Asians the divisions by religion are very strong and apparent. The Sikhs won't sit with us and we won't sit with the Hindus. The second is that there is some sort of misunderstanding between African-Caribbean and Asian. [Black sections means] you sit down together and you talk about your experience. So it unites us, the very first section thing was about unity. But there are people in the Asian community saying 'we're not black, we're Asian'. We have had those people for centuries, those are people who are saying we're part of the Aryan race, we have a far superior race, we've got nothing to do with these blacks because they are just inferior.
>
> (Interview, March 1990)

Such arguments notwithstanding, support for black sections amongst the black councillors we interviewed was limited. The strategy of using black sections as a way of extending black representation proved to be a limited strategy in the context of Birmingham. In the following quotation a south Asian councillor reflects:

> The party leadership and the local leadership got a bit scared, even here, people like Hattersley and Howell and others used the media, saying that black sections and things like that are dividing the party and the Labour Party should be one party. I don't see it that way. They use the media to scare a lot of black people away from black sections. We're not able to build a campaign, you need twice as many people to do the work, if the work is only left to a few people it collapses.
>
> (Interview, March 1990)

Whatever the reasons for the limited impact of the black sections movement in Birmingham the debate about this issue serves to highlight the very real differences that existed among black politicians and activists about the best way to increase their influence in the context of the Labour Party.

## Labourism as a sovereign political identity

As we will go on to show, black politicians within the Council do not uniformly submit to the idea of the primacy of political affiliation to the Labour Party. But this is an issue that remains important in political debate. The then Leader of the City Council, Dick Knowles, recounted a story of when one of the black councillors stood up during a debate and proclaimed 'I am not here because I have a black face, I'm here because I am a socialist and a trade unionist'. He continued:

> I said to him afterwards, 'you are the most awkward bugger sometimes but I never felt as proud of you as I did today.' Because he meant what he said, that

> he was here because he was a trade unionist and a socialist not because he had a black face.
>
> (Interview, March 1990)

The preoccupation with defining a 'sovereign Labour Party identity' is related to a desire to constrain the political agenda to the conventional bastions of Labourite politics. This is also linked to a concentration on the primacy of class as opposed to other forms of political identity.

It needs to be emphasised that many of the black politicians we interviewed also adhered to this kind of politics. This type of politics is most clearly expressed in the following account from an African-Caribbean councillor:

> I think there is something wrong if every time we don't get our way we say 'Yes, it is because we are black'. I think we alienate people sometimes; all right when the argument and the evidence is there by all means, you go to town on it [racism] and make sure it doesn't happen. The militants they will do that, they will try and stir up: 'Yes you will never get justice in this country because you are black!' They are not saying it is because you are poor and . . . you rarely get justice in this country if you are poor.
>
> (Interview, August 1990)

The agenda of the Labour Party is viewed as being adequate with regard to issues of race and not in need of modification. He continues:

> I think the reason that you get people in the Labour Party is to tell them about socialism and what the Labour Party stands for, it doesn't matter about their culture or what language they speak – it is about the philosophy of the Labour Party. . . . I think you have to leave people to the state that they are, yes it might take a bit longer but. . . . What I am saying is that we have got something to build on, we don't start behaving as if we are in South Africa in Britain. I think it is a very great shame we don't look at ourselves. We are here fighting as if we were fighting in South Africa and by doing that we are entrenching ourselves.
>
> (Interview, August 1990)

The maintenance of a sovereign Labour political identity is not only relevant to the issue of constructing black sections. It impacts on the position of black councillors within the Council. We are not suggesting that black councillors are somehow duped by their white counterparts. Rather, we are arguing that the politics of these councillors need to be understood within the context of the culture of the Birmingham Labour Group. The premise of this political culture is that black politicians must be 'first and foremost members of the Labour Party'. This actively militates against the development of a self-consciously black caucus. The result is that black interests and Labourism are reproduced as mutually exclusive forms of political consciousness.

There is immense pressure within public meetings for black politicians to place themselves squarely within the ideological boundaries of the Labour Group. In line with the sentiments outlined above, some black councillors comply with this and do not question the terms of the political agenda. This manifested itself dramatically during the Gulf War. During a Council meeting that was held during this period two incidents occurred that implicitly questioned the commitments and loyalties of left-wing black African-Caribbean and black Muslim Labour coun- cillors. The first focused on the issue of 'showing the flag'.

With the declaration of war the leadership of the Council decided to fly the United Nations flag above the Council House as a gesture of solidarity with the troops fighting in the Gulf. During the course of the meeting the Conservative members produced seventeen Union flags. An amendment was put to one of the Committee Reports asking for the United Nations flag to be replaced with the Union flag. A Conservative councillor captured the sentiment of the amendment in his speech:

> It should be the right of the city to fly our flag, it is our flag, we are all British . . . I believe it is time to take it back from the National Front. It belongs to all of us whether we belong to Labour, Liberal Democrat or Conservative parties . . . I don't understand why people are asking us not to fly our flag. [He then mentioned a sense of embarrassment that he has felt travelling around the country over the incident.] This I understand from the press has not just happened in this City Council. If people are offended by us flying our flag then I ask why?
>
> *Shouting from the Labour benches: 'Who?'*
>
> I don't see what the problem is with flying the flag. I have been told that it may cause problems within the immigrant population as they used to be called . . .
>
> *Shouts from the Labour benches*
>
> I'll withdraw that . . . there are forces from twenty-eight nations in the Gulf . . .
>
> *Shouts from Labour benches*
>
> I therefore ask the Labour members opposite as to why our flag isn't being flown.
>
> (Fieldnotes from Council Meeting, 5 February 1991)

Perhaps the most important symbol in this speech is that of 'the flag', which becomes closely associated with a commitment to the nation. This is rhetorically directed towards those who are assumed to have divided loyalties, i.e. black communities in general, but within the context of the Council Chamber it is specifically aimed at black councillors, particularly those members who are Muslim. The atmosphere within the chamber was intense and it seemed to trigger defensive statements from Muslim councillors about their commitment to Britain.

Later on in the meeting the Conservative Group put forward a motion that would convey the good will of the people of Birmingham to troops fighting in the Gulf. The motion was amended by the Labour Group in a long and detailed way. In the debate that followed a Muslim councillor spoke and within the content of his speech we can see a resistance to the war alongside a passionate commitment to Britishness. He started his speech by stating that he is against the war, which he stated 'is a war for oil'. He said that he was born in Pakistan but stated unequivocally:

> I am British and a Brummie and I am very proud to be British and a Brummie. I am also a Muslim. I believe that giving my life for England is the greatest thing that anyone can do. If I had a thousand lives I should die a thousand times for Britain.
>
> A prominent white Labour councillor: 'Good man'
>
> But this is an unjust war it is a war for a new world order. But it is not just me who is saying this . . .
>
> (Fieldnotes from Council Meeting, 5 February 1991)

He went on to say that America had invaded and illegally occupied small countries and he asked where the United Nations were when the Kashmiri people were asking for their freedom:

> I started to pray for peace and harmony the moment I saw mothers and wives waving to their children as the forces were leaving from the Gulf. I started to pray. I hope and pray that common sense will prevail. Why can't politicians use their brains rather than their guns and sorties? It was Gandhi who said when someone asked him 'what did he think of western civilisation?'. He said 'it will be a good idea' [Labour members laugh]. I believe in the power of prayer. I pray for peace justice and harmony.
>
> (Fieldnotes from Council Meeting, 5 February 1991)

The Labour Group decided to send an amended motion of good will to the troops and to fly the Union Flag above an adjacent building to the Council House until a second flag post could be erected. This indicates (i) the preoccupation of the Labour Group to present itself as moderate and (ii) points to the pressure placed on black councillors to publicly show their loyalty and commitment to Britain. Indeed it was rumoured during this time that a prominent Labour figure suggested that the ten Muslim Labour councillors walk into the Council meeting in procession behind a Union Jack.

The location of black politicians within what we have referred to as a sovereign Labour identity means that it is difficult within the terms of this culture to establish sectional interests defined in terms of difference, whether defined in terms of political notions of race or religion.

## Patronage and clientelism

The position of black politicians also needs to be understood within the patterns of patronage that operate in political institutions. Since the Labour Group came to power in 1984 they have made a sustained attempt to secure the support of the black Council members. This support has been maintained, even in times when the leadership has de-emphasised support for policy initiatives on racial equality. This cannot be simply explained in terms of the dominance of the political identities discussed above. The support of the black councillors has been maintained through complex micro-political negotiations. Within the vernacular of local politics this is referred to as 'patronage'.

The specific meaning of the notion of patronage in this context relates to negotiations whereby political support is offered in return for political positions and resources. The result is elaborate – often highly secretive – political negotiations, particularly in the aftermath of an election and before the annual general meeting of the Labour Group where political positions are decided. A prominent and influential white councillor put it this way:

> How do political groups survive? They do so on the basis of patronage. We are not a homogeneous body, made homogeneous because we all swear to a particular set of policies. I am afraid it doesn't work that way, it never has done, it is unlikely to work that way. It doesn't matter if we are talking about the right or left or the centre or whatever, in the end it is all about personalities, it is all about patronage, it's about checks and balances that you can put into place by having people in particular positions. That is how it's run, it has been run for years and years in that fashion, and not just Birmingham all over the country, and it is not just the Labour Party it is the Tory Party as well. The political machine has, and will always, operate in that fashion.
>
> (Interview, April 1991)

What we want to do here is discuss the manner in which black politicians are positioned within these patterns of patronage.

The sheer size of Birmingham's local authority structure has meant that decision-making and budgeting is devolved to the major service committees. The chairperson of each committee is thus in a highly influential position, often controlling large budgets, part of which enable the funding of voluntary sector organisations. This is particularly significant in relation to the black community organisations which often receive funding through these means. Although the committee structure is constantly changing there are between eighteen and twenty main committees. These committees are not of equal significance. There are ten main service committees and these include Finance and Management, Economic Development, Education, General Purposes, Housing, Social Services, Personnel, Leisure and Urban Renewal.

A key question in relation to the position of black councillors, therefore, is the issue of what role they play in these committees. As one councillor commented:

> What you've got is the emergence of candidates in the inner city wards, candidates who in many instances have come out of the membership manipulation of the ward, and therefore, in my view, aren't always the most capable of candidates that the minority ethnic community could put forward, which then has its effect here in the City Council. There are few, and this is a very damning remark, there are few black councillors, at this moment in time,

> [whom one could] consider for a major chairmanship. . . . It needs a chair of committee that has political vision, has the ability to drive it [policy] through the bureaucracy of the City Council. There are very few, very, very few of the minority ethnic members of the City Council who have those capabilities. Mind you the same could be said for a very large number of the white members of the Labour Group. The question was particularly posed in respect to the minority ethnic members.
>
> (Interview, April 1991)

The lack of prominent minority councillors is viewed as being the result of the character of the local mobilisations that have occurred within inner city wards. Here it is being asserted that the instrumental form of politics being operated within these communities is leading to a situation where 'poor quality' politicians emerge. This claim needs to be evaluated in the context of the racial discourses discussed in Chapter 5. The notion of ability is contestable and possibly invested with dubious racialised assumptions. However, a tension exists in the way the local leadership related to black councillors on the Labour Group: on the one hand, the right-wing leadership was dependent on their support in order to retain political control, whilst on the other hand there was deep ambivalence over sharing positions of power and influence.

The allocation patterns for key political positions since 1984 reflect this ambivalence. In 1984 the Labour Group appointed one black chairman, Sardul Marwa, who headed the Race Relations and Equal Opportunities Committee. In addition to this there were two black vice-chairs (Women's Committee and the Appeals Committee) and three black councillors chaired the Department Consultative Committee. The pattern that was established in 1984 endured throughout the 1980s. Black councillors were given minor committees such as Appeals, Department Consultative and Joint Consultative and a limited number of councillors were promoted into major service committees.

Another clear pattern that emerges from an analysis of committee chair allocation is that the number of black councillors in prominent positions remains constant while the particular politicians concerned may change. This results in cycles of promotion and removal. This produces and amplifies rivalry between black politicians. For example, the allocation of Sardul Marwa to Chair of the Race Relations and Equal Opportunities Committee in 1984, was in part the result of pressure applied by a group of black councillors who wanted to exclude another candidate who had been supported by the leadership. However, in 1986 Sardul Marwa was removed as chair of this committee in favour of a white Councillor, Bill Gray. This occurred simultaneously with the promotion of Councillor Muhammad Afzal as Chair of the Urban Renewal Committee. The patterns of patronage here involve compensating moves that enable the endorsement of particular black councillors to occur concurrently with rejection of others. As we noted in Chapter 4, Phillip Murphy, an explicitly radical black representative, was disciplined and removed as Vice-Chair of the Race Relations and Equal Opportunities Committee in the summer of 1986. This resulted in a heated debate locally, and as a compensating move he was replaced with another black councillor.

Between 1987 and 1989 the level of black incorporation stabilised with two minor committees and one major committee being chaired by black councillors. Two other councillors held the office of vice-chairs during this period. It was essential for the leadership to retain the support of black councillors in order to retain control of the Labour Group. This was established through allocating black councillors to prominent service committees. In this sense an unwritten reward system operated whereby councillors who are in favour are suggested by the leadership to sit on particular committees. This system of rewarding support is not simply applied to black councillors. In the period 1986–1987 councillors who were seen to be on the left were allocated few committees and key left-wingers who were chairs of important committees were deposed.

With regard to black councillors the pattern that has emerged during the last ten years is that particular councillors who are in favour are given up to six committees, while others are given one or two committees. In the aftermath of the conflicts over his involvement in black sections in 1988, Phillip Murphy was excluded from attending all committees. In this sense the pattern of committee allocations reflects a process whereby particular black representatives are incorporated within the Labour Group whilst others are marginalised. The incorporation of black councillors is always contingent on their support of the leadership.

Councillors also receive an allowance for attending council meetings. In this context, the allocation of a number of committees to a particular councillor has a financial dimension. In 1988 the left-wing councillor Lynne Jones wrote a paper which was sent to the National Executive of the Labour Party entitled 'Manipulation, patronage and corruption in the Labour Group'. In this document she claimed that by deposing twenty-one left-wing members, the forty-six right-wing members of the Labour Group were taking a larger proportion of the committee places:

> After the AGM, the average number of committees carrying attendance allowance (including joint boards) allocated to 'the 46' was 3.23 compared with 2.29 for the '21'. Subsequent removal of the '21' from committees means the current figures are 3.49 compared with 1.90.

During this time the Conservative Government was preparing legislation that would result in councillors being paid a flat rate allowance. She concludes:

> It is appalling that we as Labour members should be placed in the position of having to welcome Tory legislation as the only means of curtailing the excessive use of patronage so evident above.

These patterns of political clientship were used to establish the support of black politicians. A black councillor comments:

> There is a financial element – I knew one Asian councillor who was on a

> number of committees, although he was very ineffective actually. I think it was a financial incentive, so he can attend every day of the week. At the moment it is £19.50 per day . . . you attend your meeting, sometimes they only last five minutes and you have your £19.50.
>
> (Interview, May 1990)

The allocation of positions and committees provides crucial resources that can be used in bargaining for political support. These resources have to be passed through the General Meeting of the Labour Group in the aftermath of an election, but once a dominant coalition has been established through informal negotiations they are effectively in the gift of the leadership.

In 1990 an important shift took place and for the first time two black councillors were allocated policy committee chairs – Muhammad Afzal (Urban Renewal) and Najma Hafeez (Social Services) – and in addition to this two further councillors were retained as chairs of non-policy making committees. This development seemed to suggest that a possible breakthrough in political incorporation was imminent. Both councillors were also contesting the selection for the parliamentary seat of Small Heath vacated by the retirement of Denis Howell. This protracted battle resulted in Muhammad Afzal falling from favour within the Labour Group. At the Group Annual General Meeting in 1991 Afzal was not returned as chair of the Urban Renewal Committee and he was removed from the Group Officers Executive of the Labour Group. As a compensating gesture a south Asian supporter of Roger Godsiff replaced Afzal on the Group Officers Executive.

These shifts in support and the urgency of retaining control within the Labour Group have implications beyond the sphere of electoral politics. In addition to the allocation of political positions, voluntary sector funding plays a crucial role in the political dynamics to which were are referring. A former black member of the City Council described the political relevance of voluntary sector funding:

> There will always be patronage, they will always want something back. You have the whole question of getting people grants and immigration cases and if you are there and you have got power you can do those kinds of things. In some ways it has happened to me; I have been expected to get people grants, I've got something like thirty people grants in the time that I was on the City Council and you are expected to deliver for people and in some ways it is your duty to solve their problems, and the old-style politics is very much like that; they do things for you and expect things back and there is also the village-style politics in the ethnic minority communities. You know it is the situation where I'd become a leader and then I get twenty people to follow or to act as my supporters. I get them in the Labour Party and then I become the blue-eyed boy.
>
> (Interview, July 1991)

This means that political struggles can be fought out over the relationship between voluntary sector organisations that are associated to particular politicians.

One councillor whom we interviewed claimed that the chief mechanisms whereby control of minority councillors is exercised were through voluntary sector funding and the allocation of committee chairs. He claimed that this was a means whereby powerful positions could be retained by white politicians through dividing black politicians. We found a number of cases where voluntary sector funding provided a strategy for establishing alliances with councillors who were connected to particular community organisations. Equally, we found examples where funding was withdrawn from organisations in a punitive fashion because the politician linked to the organisation fell from favour or challenged for political positions. In the aftermath of Muhammad Afzal's challenge for the parliamentary candidacy in Small Heath, two organisations linked with him had their funding withdrawn and their practices scrutinised. These grants are discretionary and their allocation and withdrawal are legitimate, in this sense there is nothing corrupt or illegal about such tactics. But what is clear is that the patterns of voluntary sector funding are complexly interwoven with the establishment of political allegiances and patronage.

## Black councillors and political life

Once in the Council House, black councillors encounter a municipal culture that can be alienating and on occasions hostile. It is striking when one enters Birmingham's municipal centre, the Council House, that until very recently it has been an exclusively white preserve. As one walks through the corridors of the building pictures of political notables are displayed and they are overwhelmingly white and male. The municipal culture itself is invested with a whole set of cultural assumptions about the heritage of its politicians. For example, it was not until 1986 that halal food was provided at civil functions. By this time there were seven Muslim Labour Councillors on the Council, and the provision of food for them was met with considerable hostility in the local media. The *Birmingham Evening Mail* reported the dispute under a headline 'Row Over Curry On The Rates'. It claimed: 'Free snacks and meals for Birmingham's seven Asian councillors are to cost city ratepayers £11,000 a year, it was revealed today' (*Evening Mail*, 13 September 1986). More recently wide coverage was given to the impropriety over a planning application for a restaurant owned by then councillor Ghazandar Khan. The *Birmingham Evening Mail*'s headline read '"Nod and a Wink" Tandoori' (*Evening Mail*, 11 July 1991). The controversy led to the resignation of the Labour Chairman of the Planning Committee and further fuelled stereotypes of the corrupt nature of black politicians (*Birmingham Post*, 6 August 1991).

Events such as these serve to highlight the ways in which the everyday experiences of minority politicians are shaped by intrinsically racialised processes. This is why in this section we want to examine the experiences of black politicians and their accounts of the role of racial and other forms of identification in shaping their experiences within the political system. The first point to note is that the experiences of black politicians are both diverse and complex. For example, while many of the politicians we interviewed identified subtle forms of hostility and ambivalence within the political arena, others claimed that they experienced little racism. One south Asian councillor put it this way:

> The black thing? Well, you know I never experienced prejudice or anything, discrimination or anything, you know. I have always got on with people and that, and always got whatever I wanted to do, I have got things done and that. You probably had the skinhead in the younger days and that, and all the games and that coming up, but I never felt the need to form a black section, or to get the blacks together, I never had that feeling. Never had the need. I always thought that society was doing all right and we were getting and doing the things and if you are in the right enough eventually you will come through, it is just a matter of perseverance.
>
> (Interview, February 1991)

The notion of a black political identity galvanised in opposition to racism was seen to be simply irrelevant for this politician. Others claimed that very subtle forms of racism are present within the political process at all levels from candidate selection, electoral campaigns and daily political life.

One example cited to us in the course of our interviews with black politicians is the issue of the pressures faced by minority politicians in the context of meetings. It also became evident to us through observation of Council meetings that black councillors as a group do not participate actively in either open debate at committee level or within the monthly full Council meetings. As an experienced black representative comments:

> Obviously, to start with I was nervous, and that over the years I have become quite confident. I know when to speak, who to speak with, what are my rights. There are I would say six or seven black councillors who'll never speak, even at committee meetings. There are still many councillors I would say, in the black community whom I have never seen speak at a committee meeting.
>
> (Interview, March 1990)

In the context of political debate in committees and in full Council we found crude references to racist formulations and hostility to black members based on racialised grounds. In the observational research we conducted in these meetings we found on one occasion that a Conservative politician referred to a white politician as the 'Nigger in the wood pile', meaning that the white politician in question was really responsible for sentiments being expressed by a Labour colleague. On this occasion the assertion was challenged and the comment was withdrawn. However, in response the Conservative member replied:

> It was not meant to be offensive. It is a phrase that my grandmother used and I am sure that some of the wives of members opposite will use.
>
> *White Labour Politician*: 'Shame, Shame.'
>
> In no way will I be classed as a racialist. I have some good friends from ethnic minorities. The more reasonable ones will take no offence.

*Labour benches*: 'Ooooh'

*White Labour Councillor*: 'Shame, shame.'

Incidents like this are infrequent and challenges are construed by some politicians on the right as left-wing fanaticism. Often in debate references are rehearsed to the way radical black councillors will respond, e.g. 'No doubt Councillor X will say this is racist'. This allows politicians to incorporate a dismissal of accusations of racism into their accounts. These function as ideological disclaimers in the same way that accusations of racism can be dismissed as impossible because the speaker has black friends. The fact that racist formulations are still publicly used is important within the everyday culture of politics. More interestingly, however, the suppression of these assertions in public debate results in another level of racist practices which are coded within politics. This often revolves around reference to racialised language skills. For example, in Council meetings multilingual south Asian councillors are heckled and asked to give a translation in English of their speech. This kind of very crude abuse obviously has an effect on how freely black members can participate in debate. In the theatre of politics this constitutes a racism that is whispered in committee meetings and heckled from the sidelines of debate

This kind of exclusive activity is not just confined to personal expression. During the controversy over the publication of Salman Rushdie's book *The Satanic Verses*, the Muslim councillors delivered a petition on behalf of the Muslim community. On 4 April 1989 a rally was held in Small Heath Park and between 1,500 to 2,000 Muslims gathered to express discontent at the publication of the book. There was a call from key figures in the rally not to vote for councillors who did not support opposition to the book. Mohammad Niwas, of the Sandwell Muslim Organisation, was reported as saying at the rally:

> The councillors are representing us. We voted for them but they are not taking our views into account. . . . We organised this demonstration on a weekday to show the strength of feeling that Muslims have against this book. Many people have left work and closed their businesses to come here.
>
> (Quoted in *Birmingham Post*, 5 April 1989)

The march ended with 400 Muslims gathering outside the Council House to present a petition before the monthly general meeting of the City Council. However, the response within municipal politics to the petition revealed much about the racial dimensions of the political culture. As a female Muslim councillor comments:

> It is sheer intimidation and it happens all the time. Councillor Muhammad Afzal, who has an accent . . . Afzal got up started to read the petition out, there were many interruptions from the opposition. There was all kinds of abuse like 'speak English', 'you are in England now'. This offended me greatly, he hadn't finished because there were too many interruptions. I was very angry because it was just pure racism . . . no doubt about it. They weren't interested

in the issue it was all about language and pronunciation they weren't interested in what was being said. That is just one indication of how difficult it is sometimes even to do your duty.

(Interview, August 1990)

In these circumstances black councillors are faced with the dilemma of having to address the concerns of their political constituency while having to confront politicians who are often dismissive and hostile.

It is not simply that Asian members who are classified as having 'foreign' ways and 'language problems'. Similar kinds of arguments are made against outspoken black members who raise issues related to racial equality on a consistent basis. For example, an outspoken black member of Caribbean origin, is consistently labelled as being 'a single issue politician' or less sophisticatedly as having a 'chip on his shoulder'. He pointed out:

You see they try to label you. It's very subtle. Your are expected to rise to this, to beat your chest as it were. It happens with some of my colleagues in the Labour Group. It is quite interesting, actually, because there are some times when I purposely stop myself from getting up and speaking on a particular issue. You see, if they can understand you then they can control you. People don't come right out and say we object to you because you are black. It is much more complicated than that. No, you get turned into a troublemaker and the whole thing gets turned into an 'individual problem'. So there are some times when I quite consciously say nothing.

(Interview, May 1991)

As we noted previously the overwhelming proportion of black councillors represent inner city wards. These are areas where mass recruitment occurred within minority communities. A pattern that emerged throughout the late 1980s and early 1990s was that politicians coming to the Labour Party through a black socialist route were not being selected in these wards. Experienced candidates who had stood in left-wing marginal wards were not being selected for winnable marginal seats. This meant politicians entering politics on the left were being squeezed by having to compete for electoral priority. This often resulted in issues of gender and race being placed in direct conflict. A black councillor commented on his own constituency:

We had run women candidates and black candidates at a time when it was thought to be a dangerous thing to do in the context of Labour Party politics, it was only when we started to win the ward that we stopped running black candidates. We had a very able candidate who did well in the selection but the local party chose a woman over him because the issue of gender had priority over the issue of race in this particular selection and I find this a very cynical position.

(Interview, February 1991)

These complicated struggles over political priority are crucial to understanding the schisms that are emerging between black male left-wing politicians and their white counterparts. Often this is underpinned by a feeling that there are few constituencies where black socialists can be successful candidates, whereas it is felt that white women have a wider set of opportunities. This is summed up by the following quotation from a male south Asian politician:

> There's another argument recently developed; women are saying 'Look we're not going to shortlist anybody, we're going to shortlist women', and that excludes black people from those marginal seats . . . and the women said 'Well if you give us a black woman we don't mind'. Why can't we turn round and say 'We're interested in equality, if you don't support us then we look at right-wing politics.' Why should we say that we have to support women, we have to support lesbians, we have to support homosexuals. . . . If you're a black woman fair enough. But they know we haven't got many black women who are politically active, they're trying to exclude us.
>
> (Interview, March 1990)

This quotation demonstrates some of the tensions that exist between the political aspirations of some black male activists and issues of sexuality and gender party. In Birmingham, as elsewhere, there is a real dilemma with regard to the degree to which previously excluded groups can achieve peak political representation without being drawn into a competitive politics of relative priorities, which may also involve asserting a hierarchy of priorities in order to promote specific interests.

Allegations of harassment and intimidation are not merely confined to thc Conservative opposition. Councillors we interviewed also reported that similar processes operated, albeit with less frequency, within the ranks of the Labour Party. Two occasions were recounted in these interviews where black councillors stated that they were jeered in public debate from their own benches. Others also complained about being passed over in the context of public debate where the Lord Mayor, a Labour Councillor, has discretion concerning when members are invited to speak. These claims were supported in our observations of public meetings where on two occasions we witnessed black councillors being side-stepped in debate. This reflects a dangerous convergence within the political culture between white politicians on the left and right of the political spectrum. In these circumstances, challenges relating to racial discrimination within the Chamber can be dismissed with some degree of cross-party consensus as gibberish, paranoia or ultra left-wing dogma. A south Asian councillor put it this way:

> Some of the councillors come from [suburban] wards, like Longbridge, they don't understand the problems that black people face, in fact they are racist themselves. They are even more narrow minded than the Tories.
>
> (Interview, March 1990)

Here issues like racism within the political culture can easily be dismissed. Equally, this is not just confined to those on the right of the Labour Party. Left-wing black councillors also commented that when black candidates were proposed for posts assertions about the language skills of black candidates have been used made in public. A black left-winger recalls:

> There was one particular meeting where we were preparing the left-slate for the AGM. One of my colleagues [a south Asian councillor] was being put forward for a committee chair and one of my left colleagues stood up and said 'speaking quite frankly' that [the councillor's] command of English was not good enough. I was extremely angry then; there it was suggested that a black right-winger was incompetent. This was all nonsense. In the past I have been extremely concerned to keep the left caucus unified, but these comments were downright racist, [the south Asian councillor] speaks five languages. I wonder how many [the white councillor] speaks?
>
> (Interview, May 1992)

We are not suggesting that Labour politicians uniformly subscribe to these formulations. However, it is relevant to note that such views seem to be held across the political spectrum and that they have an effect on the everyday political interactions that involve black politicians.

The subtle forms of racism at work within political institutions have two consequences for black politicians. First, they do not seem participate equally in public political life. Second, outspoken minority politicians are caricatured as deviant radicals whose comments can be easily dismissed as being beyond the realm of 'reasonable politics'. Here again silence is a strategic means through which these caricatures may be avoided. In both cases black politicians have to work within a political culture that militates against them. In January 1990, for example, Phillip Murphy called for City Council speeches to be translated into the two major south Asian languages, Urdu and Punjabi. This he claimed would enable south Asian councillors to participate more fully in the political process. At the time this was constructed both amongst politicians and in the media as another leftist prank from someone who is viewed as a political extremist. In view of what we have discussed here this gesture has more than just a symbolic resonance. It alludes to the way in which racism is subtly registered within Birmingham's civic culture. He commented:

> We are talking about making Birmingham an international city, and here we have a City Council with a large ethnic population and it seems to me it would show them tremendous respect.
>
> (*Wolverhampton Express and Star*, 12 January 1990)

From the interviews and observations we have conducted there is evidence to suggest that black politicians do not experience access to the political process in an equal way to that of their white counterparts.

## Alliances and factionalism

While the existence of political patronage and racialisation is undoubtedly significant, black representatives themselves are bringing their own responses to this process. The black members do not speak with one voice; but having said this, the question of organisation around a notion of 'blackness' is still a powerful political idea. A councillor of south Asian origin commented:

> Some people would say that black is a political colour and will cover anybody who is not white. Others, like the Asian community, are more reserved and say we are not black, we don't have a black skin. But my opinion is that, call it whatever you want to, the problems we face whether Asians or West Indians are similar: that is, racism. We should all stick together under one name.
>
> (Interview, March 1990)

The development of a strong inclusive black caucus within the Labour Group has not been realised, and the prospect of such a political development does not seem imminent. With one exception, all of the councillors we spoke to expressed dissatisfaction with the degree of influence they had in the political process, often claiming that if they could act as a united caucus they would be able to apply much greater pressure for change. Over half of the black politicians we interviewed said that they would want an effective and united black caucus. We have already tried to point to how the nature of local Labour politics militates against this with regard to the way political identities are constructed and through patterns of political patronage. In this section we want to explore how the internal diversity of the group of black councillors contributes to this situation. Finally, we point to the emerging patterns of political incorporation, drawing some conclusions from the relationships we have analysed and identifying some of the key factors producing political change.

In the context of our research there were no clear patterns with regard to the relationship between ethnicity and lines of political support amongst black councillors. Rather, what emerged was that issues of ethnicity and religion always need to be understood in relation to other factors such as ideology, personal interest, factional affiliation. There was no mechanistic relationship between, say, Kashmiri Muslim councillors and a particular political aim and agenda. The political machinations of the Labour Group were infinitely more complex than can be captured by any simple model of ethnic mobilisation. Having said this, there were some clear features of local black politics which created a situation where the development of a unified black caucus proved difficult to establish.

Black politicians are thus constantly having to position themselves in relation to the wider power bases within the Labour Group. A black councillor who joined the Council in the mid-1980s reflects on his own illusions about how to organise politically in this context. With an academic background and an interest in policy creation he initially thought the logical step was to write a strategy document and circulate it amongst his black colleagues:

> I wrote a paper – I put all the ideas of what blacks should be doing [in it] and all the policies we should be pushing. Can you imagine it now? I mean I did all that. And circulated it to the black councillors. It's important – that kind of naivety – again you can see having a kind of academic background is dangerous, because I thought that writing a paper was a sensible thing to do, if you write a paper as a basis for the meeting. . . . We had the meeting on a Friday night and on the Monday morning I call for a meeting with the group officers. I realised that they were calling me before them because obviously someone

> had given them a copy of the paper. I was very bitter about it, very very bitter that they were calling me to account because I was trying to organise . . . I realised then that there were nine black councillors there [in the Council House]. Labour's majority was such that if nine black councillors voted against Labour they'd lose. I think I was stupid enough to actually put this in the statement. Admittedly I didn't circulate the paper to anyone other than the black councillors, but what I didn't know was the treachery of [some of the black councillors].
>
> (Interview, June 1990)

In this kind of context, where black politicians are vying for positions of political favour, incidents like this provoke intense personal conflict. The patterns of personal antagonism amongst the councillors themselves are thus central to the question of why a united caucus has not developed. Intense feelings of betrayal leave a powerful legacy in the everyday political encounters that take place. This is often coupled with a questioning of the authenticity of particular councillors and the sincerity of their commitment to representing the interests of black communities.

Councillors we interviewed did express some sense of division on crude African-Caribbean and south Asian lines. This division is invoked by some councillors as a way of explaining why these two racialised groups do not share political interests. One commented for example:

> If I suggested that we have a black group in the Labour Group, you know a caucus group, I would have been thoroughly stoned for that idea by the people. But you see we're a very significant group on the Labour Group, if you take the African-Caribbeans, Indian Asians and Pakistani Asians, but there is so much fear within and I hate to say this because there's so much racism between the black groups. The Asian group are not very comfortable with the African-Caribbean group. I know there is friction amongst some members of the Asian group and I think that's really sad because we're not able to organise.
>
> (Interview, August 1990).

The divisions should not be over-generalised, because we also found politicians who were very much opposed to exploiting the notion of African–Asian differences. However, it would be irresponsible not to discuss the importance of these distinctions in prohibiting meaningful alliances. For example, one African-Caribbean political activist argued:

> The only thing about the Asians is that they are only black when they need West Indian support – I know we are all prejudiced . . . I hate West Indians too, but I hate them because they are so stupid and they don't see that it is the Asians that are getting rich, while we stay in the same place . . . they are the people who are making the money – not us. The Asians take our business and we let them, and the same thing is happening in politics, the same thing is happening here. We have mass recruitment and it is the Asians who are taking

> it for themselves. There used to be an understanding in my [ward], because it is a mixed ward, that the Chair would be white one year, black the next year and Asian the next. Now they are trying to take all the posts and the management committee. It is the same thing again, the same thing all over again. The people who are in charge of race relations, they are all Asians, and when things are going out from the city, they are leaked, so it is the Asians who make the best of it.
>
> (Interview, March 1992)

These crass narratives of intercommunal hostility provide a backdrop to political life and the lack of dialogue amongst the black councillors. The important point to stress here is that the racial discourses outlined in Chapter 5 can be utilised by black politicians themselves against rivals. The 'Asian Mafia' discourse is clearly present in the following quotation from this politician:

> I was talking to an Indian friend of mine the other day and he said that the problem with Indian councillors in Birmingham is that they still think they are back in India. He told me in India when someone gets elected they all get a little something, it is like a tribute system, whereby people pay to get things done, you know, councillor [a south Asian politician] gets a little bit of money here and a little bit of money there, and this was an Indian man who was telling me that – an Indian man was saying that about the Indian councillors in Birmingham.
>
> (Interview, March 1991)

This quotation bears all the hallmarks of the racialised codes present in white political discourse. In particular, the conflation of the notion 'Indian' with south Asian as racially marked collectivities. Interestingly enough the politician being referred to in this account has no connections with India at all.

These discourses are not only utilised across racial divides. They are equally utilised in disputes between south Asian politicians where accusations of corruption and membership irregularities may be utilised strategically for personal ends. Equally, there are important divisions within south Asian groups. The issue of caste can be crucial, for example, in providing the basis for mobilising supporters and ensuring a strong basis of support.

In the May 1992 elections Labour did very poorly, losing eleven seats and narrowing their majority in the Council House to five votes. Many Labour strongholds had their majorities dramatically cut, including the seat of the Leader of the Council, Dick Knowles, whose majority in Sparkbrook fell from 3,000 to 442. The result of these losses meant that the hegemony of Labour's right-wing leadership on the City Council was severely disrupted. Beyond this 64 per cent of the seats lost by Labour belonged to politicians aligned to the right-wing faction of the Labour Group. The seven black candidates who contested the election were all re-elected and four of them had majorities of over 1,000. This turn in electoral fortunes created an environment where the local leadership had to respond to the shifts in political make-up of the Labour Group. The number of black councillors rose temporarily to twenty-one. With the position of the leadership in question, the black councillors were in a highly influential position with the potential to exercise influence in determining the local political agenda.

It was in this context that it was suggested that a gathering of the black councillors should take place to discuss strategy. This suggestion had been made in previous years, but given the new circumstances a number of councillors who had supported the right were interested in the possibility of an inclusive black alliance. However, this proposal was discredited by a senior black politician in an informal meeting, and it did not take place. In the votes that took place at the AGM of the Labour Group it was clear that a small number of black councillors had struck an alliance with the leadership in return for some key political posts. This is important because it demonstrates the complexity of these negotiations. Given that the Labour majority was only five, it meant that if small numbers of black councillors acted in concert they could wield substantial influence. Rather than open this caucus up to a wider inclusive group, five south Asian Muslim councillors were able to station themselves in a strong position without sharing their influence. As a result, this group of councillors, who had recently been poorly treated by the leadership voted steadfastly with the controlling group, even backing long-time rivals. In opposition to this a rival Muslim caucus supported the left on a number of key votes. The important point we want to emphasise here is that, in the context of a situation where a formerly strong controlling caucus is weakening black councillors are in a stronger position to bargain for influential positions. Whilst these realignments yielded important gains for some black councillors, they did not herald the emergence of a caucus that could have potentially argued for much larger scale change.

## Black politicians and the left

Browning, Marshall and Tabb (1986) have suggested on the basis of their research in the United States that responsiveness to minority political mobilisation is dependent on the nature of the coalitions that are formed with whites. But what is clear is that such alliances are inherently difficult to establish. A clear example of the difficulty in establishing stable alliances can be seen in the complex relations between black politicians and left-wing Labour politicians. In the mid-1980s a number of left-wing black activists developed an alliance with white colleagues in order to push for initiatives on racial equality. This move was, in part, the result of the failure to unite black Labour councillors behind a coherent political agenda. The caucus was known as the Summerfield Group, after the community centre in which its members met. The Group was relatively successful in helping to prioritise questions about racial equality and equal opportunity. But it soon became clear that the left itself did not have a well defined and coherent agenda on racial equality.

One common source of conflict is the perception that the left have used black representation in order to fulfil their own objectives. This has caused considerable resentment. In the following extract a black councillor talks about what he views as the 'pretensions' of the left on racial equality:

> I think a lot of the white politicians patronise us. My own experience in Birmingham is that at least I think the right is honest. There are people who are in the right wing of the Labour Party who are very good anti-racists, there are some left-wingers who – it is hard to believe – but they're racists. My own experience in Birmingham is that the soft left has used blacks. The left have pretended that they represent black people, that they are part of us. But as soon as you don't support their views you are a traitor. You have to prove to them that you are a much better left-winger than they are before they can stamp you as a good left-winger.
>
> (Interview, March 1990)

Other black activists have questioned whether the situation for minority communities would be significantly different if a shift towards the left occurred, and expressed the worry that one form of political patronage would be traded for another.

A key area of tension between the left and minority politicians is the question of mass recruitment and machine politics that we referred to earlier. For many on the left the machine politics operated within minority communities is intrinsically corrupt and politically incomprehensible. In an interview a white left-wing councillor said:

> I don't know why some of the Muslim comrades are in the Party. I certainly don't know, it seems as if the Labour Party is just a vehicle that is open to them. I'd like you to ask them why they are in the Labour Party.
>
> (Interview, May 1991)

Such views were expressed by a number of left-wing activists we interviewed. One of the consequences of this tension became apparent in a parliamentary selection process that took place during the early 1990s. Anxiety was focused on the manipulation of postal votes and as a result a Party officer included with the application forms for postal votes a slip of paper asking the applicant to swear on the Koran that the vote they were casting was their own. This was issued within a constituency that had a reputation for being left of centre. The ideological underpinnings of this gesture are closely connected to the racial discourses outlined previously and point to the inability of the left to understand the complex forms of political mobilisation that occur within British Muslim communities.

It is also clear that in some inner city areas attempts to prioritise the interests of black minorities did not receive unanimous support from the left. A key area of tension was the question of what priority should be given to issues of gender as compared to race.

The result is a very complex politics of priorities whereby leftist gender politics can converge with racial exclusion and black empowerment collides with sexism and homophobia. Here we are trying to point to the complex debates that can lead to a situation where the political aspirations of black men become incompatible with those of white women and men on the left. The end result is that black male and leftist candidates are consigned to unwinnable seats or selected for the candidate panel without being adopted.

Processes such as these point to the inherent problems that face attempts to construct alliances in a political environment where there are competing claims to priority. Any assumption that minority politicians are somehow aligned to one specific definition of Labour politics misses the complex forms of everyday political mobilisation which have shaped both how black politicians perceive themselves and how they are perceived by other political activists.

## ONE NATION CONSERVATISM AND MINORITY POLITICAL ACTIVISM

The 1980s saw a marked growth in the involvement of minority communities in the Conservative Party. During this period there were signs that Conservatives were keen to embrace black Tories as a way of demonstrating the Party's meritocratic commitments. The loudest ovation at the Party's 1985 Conference was received by a previously unknown forty-nine-year-old black woman from the Harrow West constituency Party. Lurline Champagnie brought the conference to its feet earning rapturous applause after proclaiming that she was: 'A Conservative, and black and British. And I am proud of all three.' This signalled a new development. In the early 1980s the Conservatives had attempted to develop a racially inclusive stance. The controversy over the Conservatives' election poster in 1983 that showed a young black man alongside the caption 'Labour says he's black, Tories say he's British' was illustrative of one element of Conservative politics about race. The advertisement was widely criticised and a number of minority publications refused to publish it. In an attempt to convey a message of non-differentiation – 'with the Conservatives, there are no "blacks", no "whites", just people' – it merely ended up constructing blackness and Britishness as mutually exclusive categories.

Throughout this period black Tories were treated as a novelty in the press. The *Sun*, for example, run a story about Birmingham-born, black Conservative John Taylor. He argued that the Conservative Party was the natural home of Britain's black communities, given the party's emphasis on enterprise and self-help (*Sun*, 27 May 1987). Taylor himself contested the 1987 General Election as a candidate for the Labour stronghold of Perry Barr and in 1992 stood unsuccessfully in Cheltenham. He thus became an important symbol both for the Conservative Party as a whole and for minority activists within it.

As early as 1976 the Conservative Party took steps to encourage black participation, when an Ethnic Minorities Unit was set up as part of the Conservative Central Office's Department of Community Affairs. The aim of the Unit was to establish relationships with minority communities through the construction of Anglo-Asian and Anglo-West Indian organisations. These were multiracial forums dedicated to fostering connections with minority business people and professionals. The Anglo-West Indian Society was only a partial success and was confined mainly to London. The Anglo-Asian Society was, however, active throughout the country. By 1983 it had 1,000 members in fourteen branches, including a number in the West Midlands. At its height the Anglo-Asian Society had approximately thirty branches, and its activities centred mostly on social functions rather than political debate (Sewell, 1993: 63). In London the driving force behind the Society in the early years was Narinder Saroop, who had been a Conservative candidate for Greenwich in the 1979 General Election. By the mid-1980s, however, the genteel atmosphere in Anglo-Asian Society meetings was transformed into bitter struggles over the control of the organisation. A dispute occurred between Saroop and Jay Gothel who eventually succeeded Saroop as Chairman. Then in 1985 Saroop deposed Gothel – both of whom were Hindus – by recruiting primarily Sikh supporters. So many of Saroop's supporters turned up to the meeting held in Conservative Central Office that the room allocated for the Annual General Meeting proved too small and as a result it was conducted in the carpark underneath. Subsequently the establishment of Saroop's control over the Anglo-Asian Society became known as the 'carpark coup' (*The Times*, 4 December 1986). After regaining control Saroop brought in a prominent Sikh, Professor Mohinder Paul Bedi, a child psychologist, as Deputy Chairman. In 1986 Bedi challenged Saroop and the Anglo-Asian Society was again beset by internal conflict and acrimony. Conservative Central Office became anxious over possible adverse publicity and this was compounded by the allegations that Bedi was sympathetic to 'Sikh terrorists' and demands for Khalistani independence from India. In December 1986 a working party, chaired by Sir Peter Lane, of the Executive Committee of the National Union of Conservative Associations, took the decision to dissolve the Anglo-Asian Society. Bedi and his supporters claimed that they had been the victims of a smear campaign (*The Times*, 19 December 1986).

The One Nation Forum emerged in the wake of these controversies. A multi-racial organisation whose members are selected by the Party Chairman, it was envisaged as an advisory body to the National Union. Constructed in this way, the organisation is much more tightly controlled by Central Office, but also this means that its members had direct access to Members of Parliament and Government Ministers. The objectives of the One Nation Forum are more clearly defined than its predecessors. It has four main objectives: to discuss issues which relate to ethnic minority communities and to write reports for appropriate Ministers; to respond to requests for information from Ministers and the Party Chairman; to encourage participation from ethnic minority communities and to increase membership; and finally to spread Conservative philosophies within minority communities. In this sense the Forum calls upon a legacy of 'one nation' Toryism, and focuses on consultation and advice whilst also performing a crusading role bringing the Conservative message to minority communities.

The West Midlands branch of the One Nation Forum was formed by members who had been involved in the initial meetings based in London. The Birmingham-based branch flourished and grew to around a dozen members who meet every six weeks to consider issues of strategy and send reports to Central Office. The group is predominantly drawn from the south Asian community, some of whom were formerly members of the Anglo-Asian Society. But it also includes people of Afro-Caribbean, Greek Cypriot, Chinese and Polish origin. The chairman of the

West Midlands branch, Demetrios Marcus, commented in a local newspaper: 'We want to find ways of breaking down the barriers that exist between ethnic communities and the Conservative Party' (*Birmingham Post*, 29 April 1991). An increase in the number of black Conservative candidates standing for election has also accompanied the formation of the One Nation Forum.

As early as 1980 black Conservatives contested local elections – this was the year when Saheed Zafar stood in Aston, only to be beaten into third place when he polled only 289 votes. Zafar stood again in 1982 (Handsworth) and 1983 (Sparkhill), polling greater support but not coming close to being elected in these inner city Labour strongholds. While failing at the ballot box Zafar became a non-Council member of the Education Committee in the 1982–1983 Conservative administration. As we noted in Chapter 5, white Conservatives claim that black Tories are unable to deliver the vote. However, by the early 1990s the Conservatives were putting up three or more minority candidates in local elections. In 1992, a year when Labour did poorly, there were six minority Conservative candidates in local elections. In three cases black Conservatives cut Labour majorities to 500 votes. In the Sparkbrook ward, the Leader of the Council, Dick Knowles had his majority cut to 442 by the south Asian Conservative A. U. Hassan. The possibility of black Conservatives being elected in these Labour strongholds is debatable. What is clear is that considerable inroads have been made into previously staunch support for Labour amongst black communities. In addition, a small number of minority politicians have deserted the Labour Party in favour of the Conservatives. The controversial ex-Labour county councillor for Spakhill, Mohammed Rafique, joined the ranks of the Conservative Party in 1991 claiming that he was disillusioned with the Labour Party's 'double standards' (*Birmingham Evening Mail*, 29 April 1991).

In the General Election of 1992 the Conservatives fielded two black candidates in Birmingham and these campaigns took on additional significance in view of the resistance within the Labour Party to pressures to field a minority candidate. Mohammed Khamisa stood in Roy Hattersley's Sparkbrook constituency and Abdul Qayyum Chaudhury stood against Roger Godsiff. Khamisa failed to lessen Labour's majority but still commanded 24.8 per cent of the vote. When this London-based barrister met Margaret Thatcher at a Party function he is reported to have said: 'We are the true Conservatives – scratch an Asian and you find blue blood' (*Birmingham Post*, 2 April 1991). Chaudhury in Small Heath fared better than his colleague. He managed to increase the Conservative proportion of the vote by 3.8 per cent. All these developments show that black politicians have made minor advances into Conservative politics.

Jewish Conservatives are not represented within the One Nation Forum despite the fact that there are a small number of prominent Jewish Conservative councillors. It is claimed by black and white Labour councillors that particular Jewish Conservatives harbour and express anti-black and arguably racist sentiments. There are also a number of Jewish Labour members and it is equally claimed that anti-Semitism is at times manifest within Birmingham's black communities. This adds to the complexity of Birmingham's political culture. Some Jewish councillors themselves play down the significance of their faith and ethnicity. A prominent Conservative politician comments:

> I see myself as Jewish but I don't see myself as essentially representing Jews, there is no Jewish vote in Birmingham. I mean the problem of course is people confuse immigrants with being black. I look back at different generations of my people that have been persecuted, and in England you have got to go back to the days of Oliver Cromwell but I'm not going back that far. I am talking about in Eastern Europe and in Germany and the Arab countries where if you had the bad luck to be born there, your life was a misery . . . . Now I'm very very lucky to be here and whilst I want to retain the great things about my own cultural background, I don't want to shove it down anybody else's throat.
>
> (Interview, July 1990)

This councillor is a strong supporter of the Conservative principles of individualism and merit and emphasised the 'double responsibility' of migrants to 'foster their own culture' while contributing to the wider civil society. He argues that 'racial guilt' plays a part in the local political culture:

> I think that parts of Britain have a conscience towards the black immigrants the same way that Germany has a conscience about Jews. They will take certain decisions in Germany to help the Jewish community, perhaps unfairly, because they have a conscience that they've done the Jews badly in past generations. And I think we have the same problem here . . . there is a bending over backwards to deal with the immigrant issue.
>
> (Interview, July 1990)

The resolution offered in this particular account is an adherence to the principles of equal competition on the basis of merit while keeping issues of religious and cultural heritage confined to the home. For this politician the fact of Jewishness has no relevance within the political sphere, making participation in organisations like the One Nation Forum redundant and irrelevant.

We interviewed six members of the West Midlands One Nation Forum, three of whom had stood as councillors, and tried to establish the ways in which these politicians became politically active, how they saw key political issues and their opinions of counterparts in the Labour Party. In what follows we want to examine the content of their accounts.

Perhaps the key theme that comes through from these interviews is that ethnic minority Conservatives came into politics via a number of routes. Four of the politicians had been actively involved in voluntary forms of community politics. In these cases their involvement was due to the fact that they belonged to a professional elite within minority communities. These activists were self-employed lawyers, accountants and business people. Their participation in the Conservative Party was a result of being approached by professional peers who were involved in local Conservative Associations. Two of the people we interviewed had been active in the Midlands Anglo-Asian Society. Other members of the One Nation Forum became involved in politics via local contacts with

Conservative Associations, particularly in the context of election campaigns. What became clear in our interviews was that involvement in the One Nation Forum and the Conservative Party more broadly was closely linked to minority business networks. Black Conservatives became established in particular associations and from there further invitations could be made to peers. This was particularly true for the Conservative Associations in the inner city areas of Birmingham.

In the context of the interviews we explored a range of political issues with these politicians, attempting to develop an understanding of their political orientation. When asked what had attracted them to the Conservative Party a number referred to an association with individualism and freedom. A Greek Cypriot commented: 'I find more sort of freedom of choice in conservatism . . . the individual freedom . . . you can develop your own ideas' (Interview, July 1991). Equally, the Conservative emphasis on family values also resonated with the importance of the notion of the family within migrant communities. One politician born in Poland commented:

> Well, as I grew older it was more or less Maggie [Thatcher] that crunched it, the importance of the family, etc., you know, and getting on and going out there and grabbing it, not laying on your back and waiting for somebody to give it to you, and I thought that's what it's all about, there is nobody who really owes you anything, you know you get what you go for and if you don't go for it that's it, that's your problem.
>
> (Interview, August 1991)

In this sense it is quite clear that Conservative arguments around the family, self-help and individualism can connect with the aspirations of sections of migrant communities.

All of the people we interviewed claimed that they had experienced no hostility or discrimination in the Conservative Party and one summed up the situation in the following terms:

> We are happy, we are active members of the Conservative Party and are very happy to see change arrive. There are no two ways about it, we are treated as equals and in certain instances they really do look to us for guidance because we have strong families, we have strong religious beliefs, all to do with the good, nothing to do with the bad. The moment you start being a revolutionary if you like then obviously you are going to get a bad name, but no, I am very pleased.
>
> (Interview, June 1991)

It is interesting to note that the one black activist who came from a Labour supporting, working-class background, was attracted to the Conservative Party because of its emphasis on class mobility and professional status.

The One Nation Forum is conceived by these political activists as a place in which reasoned debate can take place and where black Conservatives can present themselves as exemplars of their respective communities. In this sense there is a real tension between the way these politicians subscribe to an idea of colour-blind meritocratic philosophy while presenting themselves as experts on their communities. The stress on individualism and merit winning through is clear in the following quotation from an African-Caribbean activist:

> I think really if you have a long-term perspective, [you are] ambitious and you are determined, prepared to put the, as I say, the trivial comments that are made about you and sort of show willingness to achieve and be strong, then obviously, yes, you should and can earn the respect and that perhaps goes back to the phrase: we have got to work twice as hard as an English person. I think that means success is going to be there at the end of the road, then I think that it is worthwhile fighting for it.
>
> (Interview, October 1990)

What is interesting about this account, and others offered by black Conservatives, is that there is a recognition that racial discrimination exists, yet it is viewed as an obstacle to be overcome through personal industry and seemingly colourless notions such as 'thrift' and 'hard work'. These are all easily incorporated with Conservative values and the shifts of emphasis in political culture that were taking place in the 1980s and 1990s.

These political discourses are underscored by a kind of Conservative universalism:

> I believe that . . . nobody is white, nobody is black, the point is basically people are people, you know, they are either accepted for their social behaviour or they are not, and this goes back to what I say, if a lot more kids were educated to that way of thought, then we wouldn't have this problem.
>
> (Interview, October 1990)

All the politicians we interviewed emphasised that they did not want to have special treatment and that they merely wanted to achieve success on their own merit. They derided tokenism and the special treatment associated with the 'race relations industry' and emphasised integration and 'opportunities for all'. Even where these politicians argued for special provisions it was always couched within the language of universal access. A Muslim Conservative commented:

> I have said [in] discussions that I have about Islamic schools with my own community . . . that when you have Islamic schools make sure that there is an integration within the school of not just Pakistani or Muslim children but also non-Muslim children, so that children who are studying there realise that we are living in a multiracial, multicultural society, and if they're segregated there is that danger that when they leave school at the age of 16 or 18 that they would have to break down a great barrier with regard to communicating or getting on with people. So it is very, very important that the doors are open to everyone.
>
> (Interview, June 1990)

This principle of universalism is applied here to the question of blasphemy and the controversy over Salman Rushdie's book:

> If blasphemy is not allowed against Christianity then why should it be allowed against any other religion, and obviously Islam is one of the major religions of the world and denying that to the Muslims is very, very wrong. Blasphemy laws should not only apply to the Christians but should also apply to the religions of all the ethnic minority people living in this country. That is the only way to have a happy and well integrated and well-understood society.
>
> (Interview, June 1990)

This kind of philosophy is not shared by other members of the Forum who are Christians. A Polish member put it this way:

> When in Rome do as the Romans do. I have had it out with most of the Asians round there [his ward], they want to build an Asian school, and I say well go and build one – go and build one, get it funded, call it what you like, but you don't take a Church of England School and say this is now an Asian or a Muslim school or whatever it is, because religion in the UK is Church of England and that's what should be taught and if you don't like it, you lump it.
>
> (Interview, August 1991)

He continues here to reproduce an account of cultural difference being confined to the home that is very close to that of new right ideologues like Ray Honeyford:

> He [ethnic minority householders] can have that culture in his home but the parents should teach him that is not how it works when you go out there, there is a different culture out there and you have got to abide by those rules that exist out there. When it comes back into the house he can do what he likes because it is your house, you can practise all your cults if you want, but as soon as you walk out of your house you have to fit in to the British way of life. Colour doesn't come into it, it is what the person makes of himself. Some Conservative Asians are Conservative first and Asian second, they still keep their identity . . . but when they get out of their house you couldn't tell the difference apart from the skin that they were other than conservatives.
>
> (Interview, August 1991)

This kind of debate was also repeated around issues relating to commitment to England that surrounded the remarks made by the prominent Conservative politician Norman Tebbit, who claimed that minority communities displayed their ambivalence to Britishness by supporting Pakistani or the West Indian cricket teams over England. Three of the people we interviewed reported the distress that the 'cricket test' had stimulated within their communities. The politician quoted above concludes:

> You see Tebbit had the right thing, when there is a cricket match which flag do you wave? Now that is the right attitude you see – who do you support – you are either a Brit or you are not.
>
> (Interview, August 1991)

These sentiments display a tension between the various political positions held within the group. This is best characterised as a division between a universalistic as opposed to a sectarian perspective, respect and tolerance of cultural and religious difference in public life, which is counterpoised by a distinction between public assimilationism and private difference.

The activists we interviewed gave a variety of responses to the question of immigration control and the association of their party with anti-immigrant politics. A south Asian Conservative claimed that the most oppressive forms of control were implemented by the Labour Party and that the Conservatives had demonstrated their opposition to racism by opposing Enoch Powell in 1968. Another south Asian activist said that while immigration control caused family distress, it was widely felt in the community that it was correct. In particular, reference was made to the fact that marriages in the community were failing because young people were being brought from the Indian subcontinent and that there was an incompatibility between young people who had grown up in Britain and their suitors from India and Pakistan. These responses were presented as elaborate ways of disavowing the Conservative Party's responsibility for legislation that had militated against minority communities in Britain.

These activists claimed that the Labour Party had exploited the vulnerability of migrant communities who were primarily undereducated and working-class in origin. Black Conservatives spoke of the difficulty they faced finding widespread support in their own communities because of the Labour Party's monopoly on black political support in working-class districts. A south Asian Conservative recounted her experience of contesting a staunchly Labour inner city ward:

> There was one Pakistani woman who was very happy to see the leaflet that I gave her, not realising that I was standing for the Conservatives. She wasn't able to speak or read English so she said, 'What party are you standing for?' and I said the Conservatives, and she tore the leaflet in front of my eyes.
>
> (Interview, June 1990)

While it is clear that black Conservative candidates have increased support for the Conservative Party, the possibility of actually being elected in the inner city wards still remains remote. In fact the only member of the One Nation Forum to be elected was from a white minority. In 1991 Jan Trojnacki, who was born in Poland, was elected as a Conservative Councillor in the middle-ring, predominantly white ward, of Brandwood. However, one activist in particular commented that Birmingham Conservatives were not willing to put up black candidates in predominantly white areas and as a result they were consigned to standing in unwinnable inner city wards. A former minority Conservative candidate put it in these terms:

> They [white Conservatives] couldn't care less. It is something I want to condemn them for, I feel that if they are really serious about it . . . why not give one of the safer seats. Usually it is the hopeless ones like Handsworth, Small Heath, Sparkbrook, Sparkhill. What happened to Quinton, Edgbaston?
>
> (Interview, April 1991)

There are real tensions here, and worries about whether the commitment of the Conservative Party to minority interests is merely gestural. Although these sentiments are rarely expressed, the unwillingness to adopt black candidates in outer city Conservative strongholds is clearly demonstrated in the pattern of wards where minority Conservatives have contested elections.

There are equally signs that the types of racialised responses to increased black involvement in the Labour Party are being repeated within Conservative associations. Many of the black Conservatives we interviewed shared with their white party colleagues the racialised constructions of black Labour councillors discussed in Chapter 5. Some talked about the poor quality of these representatives, others made references to black Labour politicians' lack of language skills. A minority Conservative here comments on south Asian Conservatives who were formerly members of the Labour Party:

> Now I know that they are not Conservatives as such, their ideas are not conservative, never have been and never will be, and they are slowly infiltrating the political groups . . . money changes hands left right and centre. . . . I wanted to through a meeting here of local Conservatives and get a guest speaker. I would have been grateful for any member of parliament. . . . Now we get the ethnic groups they want a Minister, and it must be a Minister because a Minister will draw 300 and for that Minister to come there the person who has invited him is now the personal friend of the Minister, so that part of the community knows to respect that man because he is a personal friend of the Minister.
>
> (Interview, August 1991)

This account is very close to what we identified as the 'Asian Mafia' discourse in Chapter 5. This was accompanied by assertions about white children being the subject of intimidation and violence in predominantly Asian schools as 'evidence' that racism works both ways. The same activist made the following comments about John Taylor:

> I mean, I know John Taylor personally. If you could say that every black was like John Taylor you'd have no problems. It's like saying if every white was like so and so you would have no problems, you have good and bad but he is apart from his colour, as good a Conservative as the next, you see the only difference is that he is black, but there is nothing in John Taylor apart from his colour. On the other hand . . . I know blacks who would say that they haven't got anywhere because they are black, and that's the opposite to what Taylor is, that's the difference see. The ethnics here don't help themselves because for the good ones that nobody hears about there is always one or two bad ones that hit the headlines and spoil it for the rest.
>
> (Interview, August 1991)

There are clear similarities here with the accounts of white Conservatives discussed in Chapter 5. But it is also clear that within the political discourses of minority Conservatives there are the added tensions of how to handle the pressures of identifying with a political party that has a specific history in relation to race and immigration issues.

The above arguments, however, need to be viewed in the context of the public outcry at the expression of openly racist sentiments about John Taylor's selection in November 1990 in Cheltenham and his ultimate defeat in the 1992 General Election. The politics of refusing the importance of colour, adhering to the maxim 'the best person for the job', simply could not be sustained in the aftermath of these events. This not only threw black Conservatism into crisis, it also undermined the liberal agenda on race that was set by John Major. The Prime Minister proclaimed in support of Taylor that he had no 'truck with racism' (*Glasgow Herald*, 11 December 1990), yet the potency of racism at the ballot box, even when encoded, seemed beyond question. Taylor himself, while receiving much support, was subjected to racially abusive hate mail. Bill Galbraith, a Conservative member in Cheltenham who was eventually expelled, openly opposed Taylor's candidacy and called him a 'bloody nigger' (*The Sunday Times*, 9 December 1990). Interestingly enough, in a television interview he suggested that Taylor could be an appropriate choice as a Conservative candidate in other contexts:

> Perhaps . . . in Birmingham or somewhere where he comes from, but not to enter the zone of this town [Cheltenham] as a black man and stand for Parliament. Believe you me I think he is treading on rather curious zones.
>
> (*BBC News*, 4 December 1990)

This revealing quotation suggests much about the future of black Conservative politics. While many Conservatives did rally to support Taylor, maintaining that ability and not colour was the crucial issue, his eventual defeat signalled the extent of the problems faced by black Conservatives in gaining acceptance. The 'curious zones' which Galbraith refers to are not merely confined to Cheltenham. There is a real tension between the pervasive belief amongst minority activists that the Conservative Party will offer opportunities based on merit irrespective of colour and the racially circumscribed realities that black Conservatives are positioned within. The cartography of racism means that in Cheltenham, outer city Birmingham and elsewhere it is electorally implausible to be 'black, British and Conservative'.

We do not want to inflate the importance of black Conservative political activism. The level of involvement is still comparatively small and overshadowed by the Labour Party. However, the significance of the developments outlined above is not only a matter of pure numbers. Black Conservatives have an influence that is more than symbolic. In the United States, for example, the election of Clarence Thomas to the United States Supreme Court, highlighted the ways in which Conservative black political figures act as powerful symbols, incorporated into complex expressions of racism. Equally, the emergence of such figures poses a challenge to the orthodoxies of black political life (Morrison, 1993).

The spectre of black Conservatives arguing against race policies constitutes an equally powerful political symbol. In 1990 Glory Osaji-Umeaku, the Nigerian-born editor of *Ethnic Enterprise News*, led a campaign to repeal the 1965 Race

Relations Act on the grounds that it is patronising to treat black people as a 'special case'. Journalist Donu Kogbara, in a scathing piece entitled 'Why I feel betrayed by the race industry', expressed revulsion at 'the trendy white liberal view' and argued:

> Many of us do not want legislation. What we want is simple. We want schools to give our children discipline and good education – not the liberals' beloved multicultural learning. What we want is a meritocracy that will ensure true equality of blacks and whites.
>
> (*Daily Mail*, 13 June 1990)

These are important developments, but the events in Cheltenham are clearly at odds with the notion that adherence to Conservative principles of individualism and meritocracy can simply override the enduring potency of racialised politics.

As we noted in Chapter 5, the Liberal Democrats in Birmingham have had little significance with regard to political participation of minority communities. However, at a national level the Asian Liberal Democrats was launched in April 1991 by Paddy Ashdown to encourage Asians to 'take their rightful place in the heart of British political life' (Our Different Vision – Asian Liberal Democrats, 1991). The aims of this organisation – which largely centres on London – are to increase Asian representation on public bodies at all levels and to develop policy initiatives on racial attacks, equal opportunities, parity of Asian languages with European languages and to create racially equitable forms of European integration and immigration laws. There are some signs that this nationally inspired campaign will have some effects in Birmingham. In October 1991 Faiz-Ur Rahman Choudhury stood as a Liberal Democrat candidate in a by-election in the Sparkbrook ward. There is little sign, however, that their strategy of concentrating on white outer city areas is about to change. As a result there is little prospect in the foreseeable future that minority participation within the Liberal Democratic Party will rival either the Labour or Conservative Parties.

## SUMMARY AND CONCLUSION

The scale of black political participation has transformed the character of local politics in quite fundamental ways in recent years. As one council officer commented:

> I haven't the slightest doubt that in Birmingham there will be, within a decade, a huge and significant change in the political control of the city .... We will have, in my opinion, more black councillors and more Muslim black councillors, both in the business community and the political community in Birmingham, in my opinion, exercising powers which they have so far exercised with extreme restraint, whether it be over religion, diet, when people have holidays, curriculum, supple- mentary schools, whatever; and we haven't even begun to see that.
>
> (Interview, April 1991)

If this projection is accurate, the kinds of patronage and control we have discussed within this chapter might not continue to be the dominant form of black political incorporation in the city. This in itself is not surprising, given the fact that the impact of black minorities on the local political system is a relatively recent phenomenon and subject to rapid change. We may not have seen the secure establishment of 'black political regimes' on the model of major cities in the US (Reed, 1988), but it is also clear that the racialisation of local politics is proceeding apace.

In view of this it would be an oversimplification to view the politics of black Labour councillors and black Conservative activists as ultimately an accommodation of necessity brought about by predominantly white political institutions. Equally, it would be incorrect to proclaim the dawning of an era of progressive incorporation in the political process (Keith, 1990; Fitzgerald, 1990; Miles 1988). What is emerging is a complex struggle for political influence and representation within multiracial cities such as Birmingham. Whether this will mean a transformation in the local and national politics of race is unclear. What is certain is that black political representation, at a local level at least, is secure and will constitute a significant force in the future. What we have tried to do in this chapter is to explore the emerging political identities of minority representatives. In the context of the Labour Party, the allegiances of black politicians are defined in the context of an institutional political structure which insists on the primacy of what we have called a sovereign Labour identity. The complexity of the politics that is produced is far beyond the capacities of a framework that conceives of social divisions as divided along ethnically or racially plural lines.

What we have shown is that the divisions that exist and the forms of patronage that have been constructed mediate the degree to which political mobilisations along ethnic, or any other lines, are feasible. The situation is not static, and there are no guarantees that these patterns of support are fixed. As a black councillor commented:

> The thing is that black people came in the Party supporting a white figurehead, or whoever, but what happens in politics all the time is that people sow the seeds of their own undoing. My colleagues may support the leadership now, but there is nothing written in stone that they always will. I have often told them [the Leadership] they don't know how lucky they are, they don't know how lucky they are!
>
> (Interview, February 1992)

It is also clear, however, that the local political culture remains deeply racialised, with the result that subtle forms of political racism are present that militate against black political participation on equal terms. The majority of the black politicians we interviewed subscribed to a universal generic socialism that did not privilege race, often emphasising the importance of individual merit, ability and need. This concern was also shared by the black Conservatives we interviewed. However, it is also evident that the pervasiveness of racialised politics means that these principles are at odds with the political cultures themselves, where racism is sometimes subtly and at other times crudely inhibiting the development of a truly multiracial democracy.

# 7 Political change and policy agendas

Bearing in mind the account of political and social change outlined in previous chapters a key question remains: What is the relationship between policy change and political mobilisation and participation? Or to put it another way, how far can we assume that political mobilisations by minorities produce changes in policy agendas and priorities? It is to this issue that we now want to turn, in order to analyse the intersection between new forms of political mobilisation and policy agendas about racial equality and equal opportunity.

This has been a recurrent theme in the analysis of racial inequality and public policy in a variety of national contexts. For example, in the United States a key theme in historical accounts of civil rights legislation and affirmative action programmes is the question of what impact, if any, did the Civil Rights Movement and the urban protests of the 1960s have on the policy agenda. While there is by no means agreement between researchers working on this issue, it does seem clear that black political mobilisation and participation was a key factor in the important changes in urban service provision that took place during the 1960s and 1970s (Button, 1989). In the rather different environment of contemporary Europe there is also growing evidence that minorities are actively attempting to use political mobilisation as a means to transform the policy agenda to take account of their needs and interests.

In previous chapters we have touched upon some key features of the impact of new forms of racialised politics on policy agendas. We highlighted, in particular, the impact of pressures for greater representation of minority interests on political party structures and on public policy agendas. In this chapter we want to look at this dimension in more detail and to examine the dynamics of policy change during the past decade or so. Our main concern is to examine the processes which led to the development of programmes and policies concerned with aspects of racial inequality and urban deprivation, but we shall also touch on the likely avenues of future policies and the relationship between pressures for greater minority representation and new strategies for tackling racialised inequalities. Additionally, we shall examine the ways in which competing ideologies about equal opportunity and anti-discrimination practices are articulated both in theory and practice.

This is an opportune time to look at this issue, since all the indications are that after a period of rapid policy change in this field we are now faced with a period of retrenchment and retreat. After the wide-ranging public debate that went on throughout the 1980s and the initiatives of many local authorities it seems relatively clear that in recent years there has been something of a move away from making equal opportunities a priority issue. There is also a growing backlash against equal opportunity initiatives from sections of the new right, which has sought to undermine both the intellectual as well as the political justification of these initiatives (Green, 1990; Levin *et al.*, 1992). At the same time, even supporters of equal opportunity policies seem unclear about what kind of policies should be pursued in the present political and policy climate. The changing role of both central and local forms of governance has raised questions about the role of public policy in this field.

It is not surprising, therefore, that there are demands for a rethinking of the role of equal opportunity initiatives as we look to the future. Initiatives by both the Thatcher and Major administrations to promote the reform of the public sector and increase accountability have pushed the debate about the role of equal opportunities in new directions. Debates about the Citizens' Charter and active citizenship have also highlighted the need for a rethinking of the role of the state in protecting civic and social rights and remedying social and political inequalities. Although this has not been widely recognised as yet, it is also clear that these debates take on a particular form in the context of an increasingly multi-ethnic society.

In this environment a number of key questions have come to the fore. What are the political processes that have shaped the development of equal opportunity and anti-discrimination policies? What objectives do these policies have and how far have they succeeded in meeting them? All of these issues are complex and there is a real difficulty in providing a rounded answer to them, since there is at present little research-based discussion about them. In this chapter we shall tackle them by drawing on the research discussed in previous chapters. We analyse some of the key policy changes that we have seen in this field over the past decade and their implications for the wider political agenda about anti-discrimination policies. Additionally we shall look at attempts to rethink the role of equal opportunity initiatives in an environment where public policy is coming under critical scrutiny.

## EQUAL OPPORTUNITY, ANTI-RACISM AND PUBLIC POLICY

Over the past three decades the public policy agenda about race has been premised on the achievement of equal opportunity through race relations legislation and related policies. Initiatives and policies developed by governmental and quasi-governmental bodies, such as the Commission for Racial Equality, have attempted to define a legislative and administrative framework for tackling racial inequalities in such areas as housing and social services. In this context it is not surprising that one of the key components of the politics of race in Britain has been the enactment and implementation of legal measures to tackle racial inequality.

Successive Race Relations Acts, central and local government initiatives and policies developed by quasi-governmental bodies such as the Commission for Racial Equality have attempted to define a legislative and administrative framework for tackling racial inequalities in such areas as employment, housing and education (Jenkins and Solomos, 1989). But what is clear is that the effectiveness of such measures is by no means universally accepted. Measuring the extent to which legislation can deal effectively with the complex processes through which racial inequalities have been produced and reproduced is notoriously difficult. We still know relatively little about the workings of the race relations legislation and related social policies. What seems clear, however, is that the effect of the race relations legislation in diminishing racial inequality has been limited (McCrudden *et al.*, 1991). Indeed, the CRE has itself spent much of the past decade lobbying unsuccessfully for a stronger legislative framework.

Some of the reasons for the limited impact of the legislation can be traced back to the ways in which public policy to deal with racial inequality has been framed. The initial attempts to tackle racial discrimination can be traced back to the 1960s, and took two basic forms. The first involved the enactment of legislation to control immigration from the New Commonwealth and the setting up of welfare agencies whose task was to deal with the problems faced by black migrants and to help the white communities understand the migrants. The second stage of the policy response began with the passage of the 1965 and 1968 Race Relations Acts, and was premised on the notion that governments should attempt to ban discrimination on the basis of race, colour or ethnic origin through legal sanctions and public regulatory agencies charged with the task of promoting greater equality of opportunity. The linking of immigration controls with integrative measures was a significant step, since it signalled a move towards the management of domestic race relations as well as legitimising the institutionalisation of firm controls at the point of entry. In 1965 the Labour Government passed a Race Relations Act, which enunciated the principle of ending discrimination against black immigrants, and their descendants, on the grounds of race. Although fairly limited in its scope the Act was important in establishing the concern of the state with racial discrimination and as an affirmation of the broad objective of using legislative action to achieve good race relations. This led in turn to further Race Relations Acts in 1968 and 1976, which have established the legal and political framework for initiatives to tackle racial discrimination and inequality to this day.

On the basis of this legislative framework a variety of policy responses have been used since the 1960s to deal with racial discrimination and to promote equal opportunity for black migrants and their descendants. Successive governments have stated their commitment to this broad objective, and have developed policies which have promised to tackle various aspects of direct and indirect racial discrimination, to promote greater equality of opportunity and to remedy other social disadvantages suffered by black minority communities in British society (Braham *et al.*, 1992; Solomos, 1993). These policies have been held together by the notion that the main objective of equal opportunities policies in this field is to secure free competition between individuals and eliminate barriers created by racial discrimination.

Yet, research findings have shown that in practice the impact of public policy in this field has been limited even within the parameters of this narrow definition of equal opportunity. Recent research on such diverse areas as housing, employment and welfare indicates that equal opportunity policies have had only a limited effect on levels of discrimination, though they have reduced its more direct forms. Similar arguments have been made about the impact of equal opportunity policies aimed at tackling gender discrimination (Cockburn, 1991; Kahn and Meehan, 1992).

## LOCAL AND NATIONAL AGENDAS

During the 1980s, despite the unwillingness of successive Conservative Governments to introduce new initiatives in this field, a combination of urban unrest and massive social and economic change helped to keep racial inequality and the role of public policy in tackling it firmly on the political agenda, particularly in local politics. A variety of policy initiatives and programmes developed by a number of radical local authorities since the 1980s have been based on the manifest premise of providing equal access to employment, education, housing and public services generally (Ball and Solomos, 1990; Braham *et al.*, 1992). What is interesting, however, is that such initiatives run counter to the attempts by the Thatcher and Major administrations to reorganise local government. Public policy since the 1980s has been based on the principles that there will in future be a considerable reduction in (i) the role of local authorities as direct service providers in education, housing and related fields, and (ii) the ability of local authorities to develop alternative policies and practices to those that are part of the national political agenda.

A number of radical Labour-controlled local authorities during the 1980s attempted to go beyond the limits of national policy. Under pressure from both the left and from the growing number of black political activists in the Labour Party they sought to develop two sets of racial equality initiatives: (i) measures to remove discriminatory barriers to full equality of opportunity, such as rethinking job qualification requirements, placing job advertisements in the ethnic minority press, and (ii) attempts to facilitate and encourage minority group participation in education and the labour force by means of additional education and training, and the use of Section 11 of the 1966 Local Government Act to create new posts and related actions. The general principle behind such measures is that action should be taken to overcome the effects of past discrimination in order to allow certain sections of the community to catch up with the experience of other employees or applicants, and to remove those barriers which have the effect of excluding some people from employment opportunities. These initiatives took different forms according to local political circumstances, but there is evidence that they did have a measurable impact on both the employment profile of local authorities and on key aspects of service delivery.

What has become clear in recent years, however, is that within the constraints imposed by the 1976 Race Relations Act and the present political climate, those local authorities that want to develop positive measures to tackle racial inequality are forced to work within very narrow limits. These limits do allow for some radical initiatives to be taken, but those authorities that have attempted to go down this path have found themselves criticised for going too far in the direction of positive discrimination. It is also clear that local initiatives to tackle racial inequality have become heavily politicised and the subject of intense political debate. Such controversies have in turn helped to create a political climate which is much less friendly to the development of equal opportunity initiatives both locally and nationally than was the case in the 1980s.

It is worth noting, however, that we still know relatively little about the political mobilisations and struggles that have gone into shaping both national and local policy agendas about racial inequality and disadvantage. It is with this in mind that in the rest of this chapter we want to explore the interface between the political changes that we have explored in previous chapters with the new dynamics of policies and initiatives concerned with racial inequality.

## POLITICS, POLICY AND MOBILISATION

In comparison with many other Labour-controlled local authorities Birmingham maintained a reputation of being controlled by the centre right of the Party throughout the 1980s and early 1990s. Nevertheless, it has witnessed important policy transformations in relation to racial equality and equal opportunity issues. It thus represents an interesting example of the tensions and conflicts that have shaped local and national policy agendas in this field over the past decade. By exploring these tensions we shall thus be able to shed some light on processes that go beyond the parameters of our own concerns.

Policy changes in relation to race are the product of a complex range of historical and contemporary processes. Indeed, in the context of Birmingham it is evident that policy changes have taken place in a political environment where increasing minority representation and an awareness of the potential electoral impact of minority communities acted as a spur for change. As one senior Labour politician, who was involved in the Council's race and equal opportunity initiatives from the beginning, put it:

> A lot of the councillors who are in this Council House at the moment wouldn't be elected if it wasn't for the power and the voting power of ethnic minority communities in Birmingham.
>
> (Interview, July 1990)

Within this political environment it is clear that policy changes in this field are not simply the product of some rational process of managing change. Rather they are the outcome of political mobilisations, actions in relation to specific issues and of participation in political institutions. Indeed, it would be no exaggeration to say that much of the interest within the local political system in the question of racial inequality and policies to overcome it has rested on the development of the new politics of race outlined in previous chapters. The priority given to issues of race policy needs to be contextualised within the shifting patterns of alliance and leadership within the labour movement and the electoral fortunes of the Labour Party.

As we have argued earlier, in Chapter 4, the outbreak of urban unrest in 1980–1981 and 1985 was an important push towards changes in both the political representation of black minority communities and the policy agenda. Part of the symbolic impact of the unrest can be gauged from the following statement by a senior Labour politician:

> I think the more black councillors we've got the more likely that issues that the black community are feeling strongly about are likely to be raised in the Labour Group and the Labour Party and should be addressed before they get to a riot situation.
>
> (Interview, March 1990)

The intersection between increased black representation in urban politics and the outbreak of urban unrest is in some sense the key to the development of racial equality initiatives. We will argue that the intensification of Labour's employment policy was closely linked to a desire to gain credibility with Birmingham's black communities. Certainly, if we look at a range of local political environments it is precisely around the concern with political representation and urban unrest that many of the early initiatives in this field were formulated and implemented.

Furthermore, the articulation of new policies about racial equality contributed to a transformation in the social and political relations which have shaped policy. It would be misleading to see policies about race as simply being shaped by the political environment, since the actions and conflicts around the formulation of policies to tackle racial inequality have themselves been an important site of struggle over the definition of what we understand by the politics of race at the present time. In particular, we want to examine the relationship between the political sphere and the bureaucratic structure of local government. In this sense we argue that the interface between council officers and elected representatives is crucial if we are to understand the forces which either inhibit or facilitate change.

The mid-1980s can be seen, therefore, as a key turning point in relation to policies about race and equal opportunity. Certainly, it was during this period that the question of racial discrimination in areas such as employment, housing and service provision came to the fore in local political and policy agendas. In the case of Birmingham the formal commitment of the City Council to positive measures in this field can be dated to July 1983 when it adopted a formal statement about equal opportunities in employment. Indeed, a Conservative administration was responsible for these early attempts which concentrated on monitoring the ethnic composition of the city's workforce under the remit of the Personnel Department. Within the municipal structure employment has been by far the most dynamic area of policy change. This in many respects reflected a degree of shared commitment by Labour and Conservative Groups to the idea of equality of opportunity. As we saw in Chapter 5, however, attitudes to how this ideal should be achieved varied enormously within the respective political parties. It was with the election of a Labour administration in 1984 that policy initiatives on racial equality gained pace and public attention.

The first substantive institutional change was the establishment in 1984 of a Race Relations and Equal Opportunities Committee and a Women's Committee. This kind of strategy grew out of the wider political debate, both locally and nationally, about the role of local authorities as agents of change in the fields of race and equal opportunities (Ball and Solomos, 1990). But it also reflected the growing pressure on the local authority to respond to the demands of black communities. Additionally demands were being made by black Labour activists and their associates in Birmingham for a voice in the formulation of the policy agenda. A key document produced during this period was a discussion document entitled *Birmingham Labour Party and Ethnic Minorities in Birmingham: Labour Party Politics and a Multi-ethnic Society in Modern Birmingham*. This pamphlet was produced by the Ethnic Minorities Liaison Committee of the District Labour Party in May 1983 and was highly critical of the resistance on the part of the Birmingham Labour Party to put agreed policy commitments to the electorate. The point here is that the construction of race policy within the Labour Party provided an important site for political struggle. The unwillingness to include radical initiatives like the establishment of a Race Relations Unit, employment targets, multicultural education programmes and forms of positive action were due to assumptions about the unpopularity of such initiatives with members of the Labour Group, the trade unions and the electorate. The controversy around this incident had a clear effect on the construction of the election manifesto of 1984. The newly elected Labour administration came to power with clear manifesto commitments on race policy. The following passages from the 1984 manifesto reflect the tone and content of a policy agenda that was in large part established by district party activists:

> A Labour Council will undertake the following action as an equal opportunity employer: seek to achieve proportionate employment of ethnic minorities, women and disabled at all levels; keep records on the ethnic origin of all job applicants; carry out a survey on the ethnic origin of all present employees; give appropriate race relations training to those involved in recruitment; advertise job vacancies in the ethnic minority press and women's papers, making use of minority languages; state in all job advertisements that the Council operates an Equal Opportunities Policy . . .
>
> The Labour Council believes that the curriculum must reflect the diversity of cultures in our society and must positively counter racism; that this multicultural curriculum must apply to all subjects, all age groups and all schools and colleges; there should be in-service training for teachers with particular emphasis on training in racism awareness and greater recruitment of ethnic minority teachers . . .
>
> The Labour Council will take positive action to ensure that there is equality of opportunity for ethnic minorities in all its initiatives such as the West Midlands

> Enterprise Board, NEC and business developed through Co-operative Development Agencies.
>
> (*It's Your City – Fight For It: The Labour Party Manifesto*, 1984)

As we shall see, these promises were unevenly translated into practice. However, the establishment of specialist units within the centre of the municipal structure provided a key policy strategy.

The institutionalisation of the Council's commitment to a higher profile on race equal opportunity issues was also reflected in the formation of the Race Relations Unit in 1984. Initially the Unit had a budget of £120,000, a senior manager and five staff. Over the years that followed it expanded both its remit and the numbers of people employed, and by the early 1990s it had a budget of in excess of one million pounds. The role of the Unit was initially seen as that of serving the Race Relations and Equal Opportunities Committee. In the decade since its formation the committees it has reported to have changed but the Unit has remained at the heart of debates about policy change in this field. Its objectives have evolved over time, and they are currently grouped around three broad headings:

- to address issues relating to racism and discrimination in the delivery of the local authority's services to the community;
- to develop corporate strategies, policies, procedures and practices to tackle all forms of institutional racism within the local authority which inhibit racial equality for the local black and ethnic minority communities;
- to ensure the involvement and participation of black and ethnic minority communities in local authority decision making through consultation and liaison.

(BCC, Race Relations Unit: 1991)

Such broad objectives make little sense, of course, outside of the political culture and everyday political machinations, negotiations and silences which characterise the formulation and implementation of policies on race and related issues. But they do serve to signal the very wide range of problems with which the Unit is concerned at an everyday level. In this sense its remit has been confined to a monitoring, community and advisory role; the Unit has had little direct power to effect change. This needs to be understood within the broad municipal structure of the authority where decision-making power is devolved to large service committees such as Education and Housing. It is within this structure that officers with a remit for race policy work are located within service committees as Departmental Policy Advisers. It is important to stress that these officers and the Unit as a whole are confined to an advisory role.

Initially the Race Relations Unit reported through the structure of the Race Relations Committee to the Chief Executive. The Unit was situated within the Central Executives Directorate of the Council which co-ordinated policy development and concentrated central decision-making powers. It is important to note, however, that the development of the structure for race policy in Birmingham was shaped by the political transformations we have examined in previous chapters. It is perhaps not surprising that the institutional changes outlined above were the subject of heated debate and controversy from the very beginning. For example, the Race Relations and Equal Opportunities and Women's Committees established in 1984 as flagship new committees to implement policies on race and gender equality were merged in 1987 with the Personnel Committee to become the Personnel and Equal Opportunities Committee. Because this decision was taken in the aftermath of a poor electoral performance by the Labour Party it was seen as an attempt by the Labour leadership to project an image of Birmingham that contrasted to the 'loony left' characterisation of Councils such as Lambeth and Brent, and to ensure that it did not lose support among its traditional white working-class base. Moving race policy structures into the Personnel Department meant that the Unit no longer had a direct line to the Chief Officer. Some officers we interviewed felt that this created an intermediary management structure which made the development of initiatives such as writing policy documents more difficult. This situation lasted until 1991 when responsibility for race relations was transferred to a newly created Community Affairs Committee and its Sub-committee on Race Relations. But it remained a source of conflict and debate within the Labour Group throughout this period.

In practical terms Birmingham's race policies have been organised for much of the past decade in such a way as to emphasise the Council's self-image as a local authority committed to change but at the same time different from the more radical authorities in London. Birmingham's Labour administration was preoccupied throughout the 1980s with presenting an image of a balanced and well-run local authority, what its leadership referred to as 'sensible socialism'. For many on the left of the party and for black political activists the main implication of this stance for the development of racial equality initiatives in the city is that they have been less than strident. For the leadership, however, its strategy represented an attempt to (i) produce a practical policy agenda on race and equal opportunities, and (ii) avoid what it saw as the rhetorical and divisive politics of the more left-wing local authorities in London.

At one level it is important to acknowledge that the policies pursued over the past decade have resulted in some noticeable changes in both policies and practice. For example, the Council's strategy in relation to employment has produced a noticeable transformation in the employment profile of key departments. Birmingham, like other local authorities, has been relatively successful in opening up jobs to previously underrepresented groups.

A key concern of the Council from the very beginning was with the question of how to transform its own employment practices. Its strategy was encapsulated in its commitment that 20 per cent of staff recruited by the Council should be from an ethnic minority background. This target has been pursued in one way or another since 1986, and it has become a key component of the Council's commitment to what it sees as a practical strategy to change its own employment profile to reflect the ethnic composition of Birmingham as a whole. Bill Gray, at the time Chairman of the Race Relations and Equal Opportunities Committee, announced the policy in the following terms:

What we are saying is that from now on, regardless of other considerations, 20 per cent of recruiting must come from ethnic minorities. We are going to monitor recruitment, and managers will have to explain if they have not recruited 20 per cent. It is no good just talking of being committed to an equal opportunities process – we have to demonstrate that we mean what we say

(*Birmingham Evening Mail*, 12 July 1986)

In large part the establishment of this target was pushed through by Bill Gray in a situation where Birmingham's black communities had lost confidence in the Labour Council in the aftermath of the disturbances of 1985. In the period since this target was announced, ethnic monitoring has been carried out in order to ensure that all departments were moving towards meeting it. In March 1987 the Council published its strategy on *Equal Opportunities in Employment Policy* which identified a programme of action in relation to recruitment, selection, positive action and training and redundancy. This was accompanied by a move to write equal opportunity criteria into the performance contracts of senior managers. The Chief Officers of service departments also make regular reports to the Personnel and Equal Opportunities Committee, sometimes resulting in embarrassed and heated exchanges with members. An officer we spoke to suggested that part of the cause of the impasse that is sometimes experienced at committee level is the tendency for elected members to blame officers for lack of commitment with regard to engendering racial parity. Officers, on the other hand, blame elected members for a lack of coherent political direction.

There is substantive evidence that this strategy has been successful in challenging discriminatory practices, leading to the increased employment of minorities in key departments of the Council. According to the 1983 ethnic monitoring survey, 6.1 per cent of Birmingham City Council's total workforce was drawn from black communities. Participation in this survey was relatively low, with 61 per cent of the workforce participating in the monitoring exercise, and some departments like Museums and Art Galleries and Planning recorded less than 2 per cent minority employment (BCC Ethnic Origin Survey, August 1984). Other departments demonstrated larger levels of minority employment. For example, the Engineers Department recorded 15.9 per cent of its workforce as being drawn from black communities. A black officer commented:

The City engineers came out top in 1983 because it was in this area that the Council's cleaners were found. In white-collar jobs there were very few black people and those who were employed there were in low-grade posts. There was massive underrepresentation of black people in the areas of the City's workforce.

(Interview, April 1994)

Ten years later the situation had been transformed radically, the figures from the 1993 monitoring exercise showed that the proportion of the city's workforce drawn from black communities had increased to 15.4 per cent (Report of the Assistant Director (Equal Opportunities) to the Personnel Committee, 21 April

1994). A significant percentage of employees did not complete the monitoring forms (33 per cent) but this makes the two sets of figures comparable and a good indicator of employment change over the last ten years. A number of departments are approaching the target of 20 per cent minority employment and some have completely transformed their ethnic composition. For example, in 1983 black employees made up 8.2 per cent of the Social Services workforce. By 1993 this had increased to 28.2 per cent. Other departments have been less successful, including the Environmental Services Department where black workers made up 9.3 per cent of its employees. Having said this, in every department of the City Council significant increases have occurred in the overall employment of black people. These figures are made more significant when one realises that Birmingham City Council is the largest employer in the region with a workforce of close to 40,000.

While these changes are of undoubted significance, others we interviewed claimed that the general figures masked underlying patterns of inequity. A white officer commented:

> If you look at the numbers of people who work in the city, there are large numbers of people of black people who work in the City Council. As you go up the hierarchy of employment to the top you find that the people there are predominantly white and predominantly male. This is starkly contrasted by the people who are working in the Council House after 5.00 p.m. where practically all the cleaners have black faces.
>
> (Interview, January 1990)

An examination of the grades of black employees seems to support the assertions being made here. The largest concentration (15.4 per cent) of black employees is in the lower manual employment bands and these are almost exclusively women. The secretarial and administrative bands (Sc 1–2, 3–4, 5–6) account for 40.5 per cent of black employment and again the largest proportion of these employees are women. Of the higher grades only 2.9 per cent are at the PO 1–2 level who earn between £17,000 and £20,500, and 9.2 per cent are at SO 1–2 with salaries between £16,000 and £18,500 (June 1994). Beyond this the most senior-ranking officers are concentrated in race-related jobs or within the Race Relations Unit as policy advisers. These distributions raise some questions about the qualified success of these initiatives. Beyond this the abolition of Section 11 funding under recent changes in local government finance looks likely to affect adversely the whole black workforce.

Equally significant is the degree to which the culture of the workplace engenders racial equity. One black officer commented:

> It is all very well making policy pronouncements, but you have to take it much further than this. It is just not enough to have fine pieces of paper. . . . In employment, for example, you need to take a whole view. Employment issues are not just about recruitment and selection. If you recruit ten black people and ten years later they are in the same position, that's not equality.
>
> (Interview, March 1992)

Along with initiatives on selection, policy guidelines have been generated for managers to counter racist and sexist harassment at work. In addition, codes of practice have been established to enable the observance of religious festivals for non-Christian employees. However, people we interviewed claimed that these measures have done little to protect black workers who at times experience the workplace as a hostile environment. A black NALGO union representative comments:

> The problem with Birmingham City Council is that they produce things that are very good on paper, but the employment structure for those people falls into two basic categories: There are white middle-class managers and black working-class lower-grade employees. The problem is not that the city's equal opportunities policies are problematic or poor, but rather it's the structure of the City Council that is at fault. When there is an alleged case of racist harassment it is white middle-class males who are sitting in judgement of other white middle-class males.
>
> (Interview, March 1991)

This person goes on to suggest that this has several consequences for the victims of racial harassment:

> Cases of racism at work are numerous and the common syndrome that I've found is that cases of racism become translated into interpersonal problems. In situations where there have been cases taken up against the city, victims have got very little. Black people who have enough courage to go through the procedures have been incredibly courageous, and have been subjected to enormous amounts of stress. Black workers are made out to be 'trouble makers' and all kinds of stereotypic notions of black people are used. In most cases I have dealt with the manager gets away with it and I have to make some kind of settlement.
>
> (Interview, March 1991)

The same interviewee went on to argue that the complaints procedure in incidents of alleged harassment puts all the responsibility on the victim, who is then expected to take his or her claim through line managers. Other officers we interviewed reiterated the point made here: 'The City Council goes to extraordinary lengths to avoid any accusations of racism being levelled against them. This comes down to the whole question of a cultural change within the organisation' (Interview, January 1991).

At a more general level, senior officers within the authority expressed some confusion as to the overall strategy of the authority with regard to race policy. One of the key problems with the implementation of policies through the authority was the issue of sheer size. During one interview an officer quipped 'When you find out what we are doing as an authority I'd appreciate it if you would let me know' (Interview, January 1991). This general confusion at a corporate level led by the early 1990s to the articulation of a broad Race Equality Strategy in Service Delivery which signalled the commitment of the Council to a strategy against discrimination in all aspects of its work. The strategy formulated by Chief Officers was aimed at providing a corporate set of values:

> The central purpose of the Race Equality Strategy is to eliminate the problem of racial discrimination. Racial discrimination can be either direct or indirect . . . . All service departments must develop policies and procedures within the corporate framework to eliminate direct and indirect forms of discrimination where these exist or manifest themselves. In tandem, all policies, procedures and practices employed within service departments, their administrative structures and professional activities should be reviewed and changed if they can be identified as being discriminatory.
>
> (BCC, Race Equality Strategy, October 1992)

The history of this initiative is in many ways indicative of some of the apprehension experienced within the authority over the development of race equality policy. This strategy was the result of a review by chief officers of the equal opportunity policy. Initially members of the Race Relations Unit and Women's Unit were not included in this review. Although black officers were subsequently included in these discussions it was suggested to us that this was symptomatic of the lack of comfort felt by senior officers within the organisation regarding these issues. A number of officers we interviewed commented on how the organisational structure of the local authority was constantly being reviewed but little was done to monitor the effectiveness of existing policies. Specific equal opportunity initiatives have been set up in relation to housing, education, social services and urban renewal but it was widely felt that the authority had done little to monitor their implementation or co-ordinate an overall effective strategy. One officer suggested this overview of the situation:

> The problem is where does the direction come from? Officers blame the politicians because they say they can't get their 'act together'. But the truth is there are Chief Officers who are not completely comfortable with these issues. As a result the City lacks direction. It is not because we haven't got good policies on paper but what we need is a corporate strategy which is not just about saying 'how great Birmingham is' but how we should monitor the level of change and the effectiveness of policies at the level of practice. Otherwise all we are going to have is more of the same: reports come to committee and nobody does anything about them after the meeting is over.
>
> (Interview, August 1994)

The point being made here is that Birmingham has been very successful with regard to writing policies and presenting an image of itself as an authority that is in the forefront of developing race equality policies. However, what is hidden in these often spectacular public relations exercises is the thorny question of how far have race equality initiatives been embraced at all levels within the municipal structure?

It is clear that anxieties over the direction and nature of race policy prevail. In many ways this can be summed up as attempts from the centre of the organisation to set policy agendas in the context of an organisational culture that was generally resistant to change exhibiting an unevenly developed commit- ment to realising racial parity. In interviews conducted with politicians and community activists alike it was widely acknowledged that since 1984 the Labour administration had enshrined excellent 'paper policies'. However, it was widely felt that these had little impact in bringing about change at the level of practice. Throughout this period a series of local scandals emerged which exposed the distance between the authority's expressed commitments and the achievement of these goals. Little over a year after the Labour authority launched its target of 20 per cent minority employment, a black secretary, Margaret McKane, won a case of racial discrimination against the City Council's Chief Executive's Office (*The Voice*, 18 August 1987). In the following sections we want to attempt to point to some of the features of the debate over policy within the political sphere and the dilemmas faced by council officers and administrators. Beyond this we will point to some of the factors that inhibit change.

## COMPETING VIEWS OF RACIAL EQUALITY

Whatever the extent and impact of the policies that have developed over the past decade it is evident that there is no unanimity within the local political culture – amongst politicians and local government officers – about the kinds of social policies that should be pursued in order to deal with racial inequalities. An important factor that needs to be considered, therefore, is the changing nature of political discourses about racial inequality. Within the context of the changing politics of race during the past decade the pursuit of strong initiatives to promote racial equality and equal opportunities has led to competing ideas about this issue. This is perhaps not surprising since, as we have argued in previous chapters, notions such as 'racial equality' and 'equal opportunities' are essentially contested and take on particular meanings within wider social and political contexts. But it is worth exploring aspects of these competing positions in order to see how they have helped to shape the overall policy agenda.

In the particular context of Birmingham there have been divergent perspectives within both the Labour and Conservative parties about (i) what the Council should be doing to tackle racial inequality and discrimination, and (ii) the strategies that should be developed to put policy commitments into practice. Though in general the Labour Party was committed to the initiatives on equal opportunity it produced in 1984, there are noticeable differences in emphasis on this issue from within both the right-wing and left-wing sections of the Party. While all members we interviewed subscribed to the strategy of equality of opportunity in employment, others, particularly on the right of the Party, voiced disagreement with broadening anti-racist strategies:

> The difficulty is the distinction between gesture politics and real politics .... [Sometimes I feel] my colleagues are playing to the gallery. I remember we had one budget meeting for the City Council televised and the leader was

> attacking the Government for pinching many millions from the City's expenditure. This was wiped off the television screen by the Chairman of Race Relations Committee who had banned [white] Sindy dolls in nurseries. . . . The overwhelming view on the [Labour] Group was that we didn't want to get into that [kind of politics] and the real world was more important. We owned and managed thousands and thousands of properties in the urban areas where there were horrendous problems. Those were the things that mattered to people whatever their ethnic background.
>
> (Interview, January 1990)

Regardless of the accuracy of this trope, it shows quite clearly a commitment to a colour-blind generic socialism which essentially reduces the politics of race to class issues. It should also be remembered that some black councillors subscribe to this position, as we saw in Chapter 6. These views were not uniformly adhered to amongst Labour councillors and a large minority of politicians, including many black councillors and those on the left of the Group, suggested that the city's 'paper policies' were not going far enough.

More noticeable differences in relation to the question of race and equal opportunities can be seen within the Conservative Party. It would certainly be misleading, as we have noted in Chapter 5, to see all Conservative politicians as holding to one view of the politics of race. Rather, it is evident that there are a variety of political discourses about race within the Conservative Party. Among the Conservative politicians and activists whom we interviewed in the early 1990s we found that the question of what kind of policies should be pursued in relation to equal opportunity and racial equality led to quite diverse responses.

One of the key arguments articulated by Conservative politicians was either direct or indirect opposition to legislation as a tool of social change. As one senior Conservative politician argued:

> I personally do not think that you pass laws and it makes people view equal opportunities in any other way. You can't change people's attitudes and minds by laws, you have to change it by other means. Now we do have a number of women Chief Officers; as far as I am aware they're excellent. At times there has been a question of 'oh, we must appoint a woman here, we must appoint a woman there, must make sure we appoint a black person for this job'. Now that's not a very good reason for appointing them because they're either a woman or a black person. We need to appoint people because their abilities are right.
>
> (Interview, July 1990)

Such arguments represent a key strand in Conservative discourses about racial equality and equal opportunity policies.

What has been evident throughout the past decade, however, is that Conservative politicians were often articulating a complex mixture of arguments, ranging from opposition to immigration to support for modest forms of equal opportunity policies. As recently as April 1987, for example, amid scenes reminiscent of the debates about immigration which took place during the 1960s, the Conservative opposition accused the Labour Party of being soft on immigration and of ignoring the impact on the city of the arrival of too many immigrants. Councillor Alan Blumenthal argued: 'We have come to the point where the city is suffering the problems of unemployment, bad housing and race relations' (*Birmingham Post*, 8 April 1987). While these remarks were prefaced by the statement that 'in the majority of cases, we are very lucky to have these people here', they led to a bitter debate in which Labour councillors accused the Conservatives of pandering to racism and undermining the efforts of the city to promote better race relations and greater equality of opportunity. While the Conservatives rejected the argument that they were giving credence to racist arguments, this exchange symbolised the nature of the differences between the Parties about the kinds of policies that were necessary in this field.

Throughout the late 1980s and early 1990s there have been numerous clashes between Conservative and Labour politicians about key aspects of policy. There was, for example, strong opposition from the Conservatives to the implementation of a 20 per cent recruitment target for ethnic minorities by the Council. The leader of the Conservative Group, Neville Bosworth, opposed such a move on a number of grounds:

- First, he saw it as a move towards positive discrimination, and as therefore potentially divisive;
- Second, he argued that it was immoral to introduce colour and creed into decisions about the allocation of jobs;
- Third, he argued that jobs should go to the person with the best qualifications, ability and experience.

(*Birmingham Evening Mail*, 17 September 1986)

Arguments such as these are at the core of Conservative discourses about race. But in the context of political debates about what kinds of policies and initiatives are necessary in order to tackle racial inequality they take on a particular form and have important practical consequences. Perhaps the most important of these was the constant pressure on the Labour leadership to pull back from some of the more radical initiatives it sought to develop.

As we saw in Chapter 5, one clear example of this was the controversy linked to the 'racism awareness' courses that were organised by the Council in the mid- to late 1980s. In August 1987 a furious debate took place about the Council's attempt to ensure that its employees attended 'racism awareness' courses. A local Conservative MP, Dame Jill Knight, criticised the courses, arguing that they amounted to indoctrination and referring to allegations that Council staff needed psychiatric help after taking part in the courses. She was supported in her criticisms by Councillor Blumenthal, among others, who spoke of the courses in terms of 'Orwellian' techniques of brainwashing (*Birmingham Evening Mail*, 25 August 1987). Although the courses were initially supported by the Labour Party, the Leader of the Council responded to these criticisms by distancing himself and the Party from what he saw as the radical 'anti-racist' ethos of such courses. The content of such initiatives often become blurred and inflated in the theatre of political debate. Indeed, the local press is often willing to oblige with sensationalist coverage further exacerbating confusion and the distortion. In this sense, race policies provide easy prey for less than supportive right-wing newspapers.

While there are clear divisions within and between political parties on the matter of race policy, we also found that the council officers we interviewed had a range of attitudes with regard to how to address issues of racial inequality. Some officers claimed that the bureaucratic culture of the authority produced severe inertia with regard to the issue of race. One commented: 'What is necessary is a complete transformation in the whole culture of the Council House or of the Council as a functioning bureaucracy' (Interview, October 1990). This respondent claimed that resistance within the municipal culture was the product of the attitudes of middle managers and a lack of commitment to changes in work practices and suggested that some departments of the Council showed more resistance to change than others. Service committees within the city demonstrated a range of emphases with regard to race policy. For example, in Housing, a Race and Housing Section was established to look at issues of racial harassment and other tenant related issues, and in Social Services, a Positive Action Unit was established. Yet other departments, such as Treasurers and Engineers, demonstrated minimal activity and some of the people we interviewed claimed that such departments had little commitment to achieving racial equality. We also encountered the view that within service departments themselves there was variation with regard to issues of race and racism. A white council officer reflects:

> Take for example Social Services. It is an odd department because on the one hand there are some very good officers, but on the other I have stumbled across extremely racist managers.
>
> (Interview, October 1990)

The point that we want to make here is that while there are broad patterns of policy development within the authority these should not be generalised within the culture of service departments. While the bureaucratic structure of the authority is shifting with regard to issues of race, the pace of these changes is slow and is maturing at an uneven rate within specific policy contexts.

Shifts in policy stance have to be seen, as we have tried to show in previous chapters, against the background of changing political ideologies and new forms of mobilisation and participation in politics. Hence, it is vital to be sensitive to the diversity of political attitudes to racial equality within the local political culture. It is perhaps this diversity that helps to explain the 'stop and go' approach to developing a racial equality strategy that has characterised the situation in Birmingham over the past decade. Periods of intense activity have been followed by periods of inaction, even stagnation, leaving officers and local community activists unsure of the Council's commitment and direction.

One interpretation of this situation, commonly articulated by radical black political activists, is that senior members of the Labour Group see initiatives on racial equality as politically dangerous electoral liabilities which can be sacrificed in politically uncertain times. Whatever the merits of this argument it is precisely this feature of policy change which has affected the intensity with which racial equality initiatives have been practised. One feature of this process is the relationship between key political actors, their constituencies and the officer structure.

## DILEMMAS OF ADMINISTERING EQUALITY

As we have noted, since 1984 there has been a noticeable growth in the number of officers working in all departments of the Council on questions of racial equality and equal opportunity, and there has been a noticeable growth in the number of officers from black and ethnic minority backgrounds within the Council. Both of these developments were closely tied in to the pressure that became evident in the 1980s to create specialist race units and professionalise race-related work. However, we argue that it is important to see these developments in the context of a broader institutional structure which is predominantly white.

In practical terms the most noticeable change was the growing number of black officers working on race and related work within the local authority. As one senior officer pointed out to us:

> It's very rare now to have a corporate group of senior officers meeting without having at least one or two black people in the group and that's quite a new experience for many senior local government officers; same with women in the group, it is now very rare to have a meeting with senior members without one or two black members, and a growing number of women there, and that does affect the way those groups operate without a doubt.
>
> (Interview, October 1991)

However, the Chief Officers group has remained exclusively white and in interviews we have conducted with black officers it was suggested that senior officers demonstrate anxieties over their presence. A black officer commented:

> I think some people do want to move, they do want to change but they are frightened of being called racist. White people haven't been sacked through being openly racist yet. What are they afraid of? I think they have to ask themselves the question, why are they frightened of this? Is it something about themselves, or about their racism? They don't come right out and say it, that's for sure.
>
> (Interview, May 1991)

We do not want to suggest that there exists a simple reluctance to address race policies on the part of white senior officers. It was suggested, for example, that for senior officer participation race initiatives could be strategically important for career development. As issues of race policy become a key component of the work of all metropolitan councils, experience in this area can become an important element for an ambitious officer to have on his or her curriculum vitae. In this kind of situation complex combinations of resistance and change occur simultaneously, producing a tangle of outcomes and it is increasingly difficult to identify those who are resisting and and these embracing change. In the context of the interviews we conducted with senior officers it was clear that they had learned the 'language of equal opportunities' and this was demonstrated in the ease with which they discussed issues of race and gender inequality. In this sense their discourse was much more sophisticated than that of their political counterparts. With this in mind, it is important to try and situate race policy initiatives within the officer structure and see how this relates to political leadership.

Policy initiatives are set within the sphere of electoral politics and we have already pointed to some of the complex struggles that can take place. However, the implementation of the agenda set by elected members is the responsibility of council officers. Therefore, one must see policy outcomes as produced through a complex interplay between these bureaucratic and political machineries. Officers in this setting can be differently disposed to embracing the agenda of politicians. A white officer commented:

> Broadly, there are two kinds of council officer. There are 'officer officers', who are simply interested in maintaining their own power and autonomy. There are decisions made in certain departments that the Leader of the Council doesn't even know about. On the other hand there are 'political officers' who have some idea or some commitment to the notion that officers should be facilitating politicians and the political agenda of politicians.
>
> (Interview, October 1990)

While this classification needs to be viewed as a gross simplification, it does correspond with patterns we recorded during our research. The situation was further complicated by the fact that officers who were committed to facilitating a political agenda were often closely linked with particular political personalities. In this sense there was not one political agenda within the Labour Group with regard to race, rather competing politicians and factions vied for influence over the implementation of policy.

Initially, race policy was overseen by a black councillor, Sardul Marwa, who was Chairman of the newly created Race Relations and Equal Opportunities Committee. It was widely felt amongst officers and politicians that Marwa had provided insufficiently coherent leadership and as a result he was replaced with Bill Gray, an experienced white councillor who some referred to as a 'political heavyweight' with a strong and charismatic presence. Initially there was strong support for Gray even amongst radical black councillors. Gray's enthusiasm and leadership were responsible for the establishment of the city's employment targets. During this period Gray established strong connections with officers in the Personnel Department with whom he worked closely. As a result of the merging of committee structures in 1987 the Race Relations Unit reported to the Personnel and Equal Opportunities Committee and the Personnel Department moved into the Central Executives Directorate. The merging of these machineries into one structure brought together competing visions of the strategy for race policy.

This can be summarised as, on the one hand, a commitment to 'mainstreaming' race initiatives within the context of service committees and, on the other, the construction of a race relations structure which ultimately would have representation at the chief officer level with an organisational structure of its own.

This 'mainstreaming' position is summarised in the following quotation from a white personnel officer:

> I mean the dilemma is I think if you want to change the direction of the organisation there is something to be said for creating a specialist unit to go and irritate the organisation, to tell them 'Look we've got to change', to be a nuisance in a positive and constructive way and give a real message that we mean business here. But there comes a point where having a specialist unit becomes counter-productive in my view; it actually starts working against a mainstream policy it encourages managers to say race relations isn't my business, that's the job of the Race Relations Unit.
>
> (Interview, October 1991)

However, in interviews we conducted we encountered suspicion of such a move which claimed that this would mean that the influence of black officers in particular would be reduced and questions were raised about the motivations of white officers in suggesting such a strategy. In particular it was claimed by those critical of the position being outlined here that if race initiatives were not explicitly stated they would be ignored by the City Council. The officer quoted above continues:

> You have got all the staff in the units, you've got all the elected members who have committed themselves to that cause, all of them passionately believe that if you abolish the Race Relations Unit you are really saying well we will stop caring about equal opportunities. Now I think the opposite, I think you are saying we care so much about [race policy] and we have invested so much in it, we are now going to make sure it permeates the mainstream of the organisation.
>
> (Interview, October 1991)

It would be incorrect to confine this type of position only to white officers. In the following quotation a black officer argues:

> Some black policy advisers are arrogant .... There is a strong platform, there is some commitment. The problem I have is how do I make this a reality. Anybody can declare anything.... You see you have two schools of thought. Birmingham is a progressive authority and therefore we have to work within consensus. Then you have the extreme view 'We'll clobber the Chief Officers if they don't do what we want them to do.' The truth is not at the extremes.
>
> (Interview, March 1992)

This officer favoured the placing of responsibility for race initiatives in the hands of service officers and questioned the ability of race advisers to create workable initiatives in areas where they had little knowledge of the practicalities of specialist service areas. Within accounts like these, references to a notion of the 'ownership' of race policies were invoked, where it was suggested that white officers need to 'own' these issues 'with both their heads and hearts' (Interview, March 1991). However, some black officers claimed that 'white ownership' had become synonymous with 'white leadership'. There is a real tension here around the influence that white officers, and for that matter politicians, exercised over the issue of race policy. In our research we encountered suggestions that white politicians like Bill Gray, for example, used issues of race to further their political careers. Equally, we recorded accounts from black officers who suggested that the political coalition which was established with officers in the Personnel Department had inhibited the work of the Race Relations Unit.

This situation shifted as the political leadership of Bill Gray was challenged. The details of these machinations are far from clear, but with the emergence of a new Community Affairs Committee structure in 1991 the relationship with officers in Personnel altered and the Race Relations Unit came under the auspices of a Race Relations Subcommittee chaired by Khalid Mahmood, a young black councillor. It is also important to note that in the aftermath of the May election Councillor Abdul Rashid, a prominent and moderate black councillor, lobbied Labour Group members to sign a petition supporting the construction of a full race relations committee. Not all black councillors signed the petition, and in some cases, when it was clear that the initiative would fail, signatures were withdrawn in order to preserve the chance of being allocated political positions.

After an initial burst of activity which resulted in the Race Relations Unit being moved away from the remit of the Personnel Department, the pace of activity slowed. Khalid Mahmood encountered severe rivalries and he was absent from Birmingham's politics for long periods, and eventually he was replaced and he left politics altogether. Councillor Kazi took over the Subcommittee and it was widely believed that his association with Bill Gray meant that he lacked independent vision. It is true to say that during this period there was limited activity within the Subcommittee. Ultimately, Bill Gray was to contest the leadership of the Labour Group and in the aftermath of his failure lost the position of Chair of the Community Affairs Committee. He was replaced by Councillor Najma Hafeez. As we noted previously the Chair of the Joint Race Relations Subcommittee was Councillor Abdul Rashid whilst Councillor Afzal maintained his position as Chair of the Personnel Committee. These shifts are important because they illustrate the complex relationships which are formed between officers and political factions. The pursuit of particular policy strategies needs to be situated within a shifting political terrain.

In this situation black officers particularly those in the Race Relations Unit must respond to these vicissitudes. One officer commented:

> We have created a facade that race relations have strengthened. We go all around Europe, host conferences blowing Birmingham's trumpet but the reality of the situation is very different and it is the black people in the City Council who then become the targets while it is others who are making the real decisions.
>
> (Interview, April 1991)

Another commented:

> We [black officers] have been used as a buffer, but we have not been just content to be used as a buffer. I quite realise that my position is to stand between the City Council and the community out there, but on the other hand we have been stifled within the City Council.
>
> (Interview, March 1992)

The accuracy of this observation was confirmed by this comment from a member of a black voluntary sector organisation:

> The City operates like a huge chain and all the links in the chain are white except when it comes to voluntary sector funding or race relations and then the last link in the chain is black! So black people get turned against black people.
>
> (Interview, May 1991)

The expectations of black people both within and outside the organisation are being raised, whilst white senior managers appear incapable of facilitating change in line with these aspirations. The line managers of senior black officers expect them to dissipate the frustration that is widely felt, while black people in the workforce and in the community expect black officers to deliver results. On occasions black officers are also expected to be 'representatives' of their 'communities'. In the context of a committee meeting we recorded an exchange where a white officer suggested that a black colleague should be part of a consultative group because 'of the people they are and not just for of the offices they hold' (Field Notes, January 1991). In this sense black officers are objects of a 'skin game' which positions them as racial exemplars. This carries within it a 'burden of representation' but also the racial anxieties of some white officers. These apprehensions produce a situation where key white officers on the one hand want to acknowledge a black presence whilst on the other they are deeply resistant to radical change. The consequence is that the structural position of black officers places them in a situation where as one person commented: 'It is impossible for me to be black and an officer.' Too often the focus of blame and accountability is levelled at people in this position.

Within the wider political context black officers working for the City Council are often the target of criticism by minority organisations for the failure to develop more radical policies to deal with racial inequality and discrimination. It is perhaps not surprising, therefore, that it was evident in interviews we conducted during 1991 and 1992 that the morale of officers working in the Race Relations Unit and race advisers working within service departments was very low. One question that arises from all this is: Why does the Race Unit in Birmingham survive? This is a particularly pertinent question in view of the fact that throughout the country similar units have been closed down or have had their names changed. Within groups of black officers there is a great deal of debate about the utility of specialist units. Here a black officer comments:

> The time has long passed where we need separate units, they have served their

> purpose and it has got the issues on the agenda. We don't want marginalised units, they can't be effective because they can never really implement initiatives. These issues have to be at the core of things. I want to see more than commitment . . . . How do you measure commitment? You can only measure commitment by what is achieved.
>
> (Interview, May 1991)

Despite such pressures the Unit has survived and it seems likely to play a role in the shaping of policy in the near future. There seem to be two crucial factors at work in this situation. The first is the delicate balance that exists within the ruling Labour Group, with black councillors increasingly playing an important role in shaping the struggle between the centre right and the left of the party. The second is the emergence of an umbrella organisation of black voluntary groups called the Standing Consultative Forum. In this context it would be politically problematic to abolish the Unit, or to downplay completely the commitment to racial justice and equality. There is, however, a feeling by those working in the Unit and in other positions within the Council that there is a lack of commitment with regard to making the Unit effective within the organisation as a whole. The end result is a general feeling that the issues of equal opportunity and racial equality are being marginalised. Perhaps the survival of the Race Relations Unit is connected with a wider suspicion that the City Council as an organisation is not ready for the 'mainstreaming' of racial equality and in this situation there is a reluctance to sacrifice an organisational strategy that appears to belong to a past era. A black officer concludes:

> There have been some changes, which is good. But we have not been operating in these structure for very long and no one tells you the rules and the result is that we are in but we are not very effective. . . . It is a new experience for us but we don't know the tricks, the subtle ways organisations like this work, but we are learning fast.
>
> (Interview, May 1991)

In summary, we have tried to show how the development of race policy initiatives needs to be contextualised within complex shifting relationships between council officers and members. It is only when this complexity is unravelled that the combination of change and entrenchment experienced in Birmingham can be comprehended. Alongside these institutional machinations new forms of community consultation have emerged. It is to this issue that we now turn.

## CONSULTATION AND THE POLITICS OF COMMUNITY

A key aspect of Birmingham's race policies in the late 1980s and early 1990s has been the attempt to use consultation with local community groups as a key aspect of policy implementation. The Council has been trying to set up an effective forum for ethnic minority organisations since 1987. As we commented in a previous chapter, early attempts to establish such an organisation degenerated into ethnicism and intercommunal conflict. The idea behind this strategy was to provide a democratic framework for black and ethnic minority organisations to lobby for their interests and to give voice to their concerns. This eventually took the form of the Standing Consultative Forum (SCF), which emerged as an umbrella organisation in which all of the diverse interests of Birmingham's black and ethnic minority communities were represented in one form or another. Initially the forums were facilitated by the Race Relations Unit and the political impetus behind this was in some ways related to anxieties over the absence of any structured communication with minority groups. More widely the outbreak of urban unrest in Huddersfield during this period focused the minds of the local political community on the importance of having some kind of mechanism to consult with minority organisations.

The emergence of this organisation needs to be seen in the context of a contraction in funding to the black voluntary sector and the widely held view that the City Council was intransigent and lacked commitment with regard to putting its pledge on racial equality into practice. The SCF provided a means through which pressure could be applied on the City Council for change. A black voluntary sector activist comments:

> The city structures are closed to us so what we did was to go out to communities and organise within communities. Some saw the umbrella groups as a kind of divide and rule strategy, but you can't expect thirty-two ethnic groups to come together as one group. It was tried in 1985 and it failed. What we are trying to do now is provide the context where community groups can speak for themselves.
>
> (Interview, March 1992)

An immediate question raised here is the degree to which such organisations have the authority to represent Birmingham's diverse black populations. Views on such a strategy varied, with some voluntary activists claiming the initiative was little more than an outmoded form of 'community relationism'. Others maintained that political mobilisations inside the Labour Party and the local state were needed in concert with pressure from outside in order to bring about long-awaited change.

Initially the City Council was slow to fund the SCF, and gave it largely administrative support through the Race Relations Unit. However, by the early 1990s the SCF grew in strength and became a site of public discussion about the Council's racial equality policies. A key concern of the SCF, from the perspective of the Council, was both to provide channels of consultation and to give legitimacy to the policies pursued under the broad heading of racial equality or equal opportunity. These two developments are not connected but it is important to note that the CRC had not been functioning effectively for a considerable period before its demise, making the emergence of the SCF all the more significant. This was made more urgent by the demise of the local Community Relations Council which had its funding withdrawn amid controversy and allegations of mismanagement. Each ethnic minority community was encouraged by the Race Relations Unit to form an umbrella group to represent specific community interests through the SCF. By the early 1990s bodies such as the African and Caribbean People's Movement, Bangladesh Islamic Projects Consultative Committee, Black Led Churches Liaison Committee, Chinese/Vietnamese Consultative Council in Birmingham, Hindu Council of Birmingham, Pakistani Forum and the Sikh Council of Gurdwaras in Birmingham claimed to represent over 500 ethnic minority organisations in Birmingham. In this context it is difficult to assess what this notion of representation meant in practice. But it is the case that the SCF became by the early 1990s an important channel of political debate and negotiation within the new politics of race in Birmingham.

A feel for the debates going on within the SCF at this time can be gauged from its 1992 Annual General Meeting. Three hundred and fifty people attended this meeting in the summer of 1992, and many members could hardly hide their anger at what they saw as the Council's lack of commitment to racial equality. One commented poignantly: 'We pay our poll tax! We pay nearly a quarter of the city's wages, we have a right to services which are sensitive to our needs' (SCF Annual General Meeting, 27 July 1992). Such anger was not surprising, since tension had been building up between the SCF and the City Council for some time. This came to a head in June 1992 when the various umbrella groups threatened to break away from the SCF unless they were given more support and recognition. In a letter to the leader of the Council, Dick Knowles, they argued:

> It would appear to be the same old story with the City and its relationship with Black Minority Ethnic Communities, in that City Councillors are only interested in making promises at the election time and not carrying them out when in office. This is what is now felt at the heart of the community and I am afraid will eventually result in a lack of support for the City from our communities.
>
> (Letter to Dick Knowles, 18 June 1992)

The Council eventually warded off the threat that the organisations represented in the SCF would withdraw their support by promising them extra support and a greater voice in the formulation of priorities. But this event symbolised the increasing tension in relation to what community groups saw as the manipulation of consultation as an aspect of symbolic politics used to give legitimacy to local authority policies.

Such tensions are also suggestive of the distance that many community groups feel from local power structures, despite the growth of black representation over the past decade. In particular, the Council's relationship to community organisations has been shaped by suspicion that some groups are more likely to gain access to financial and other resources than others. This is largely because community politics in Birmingham, as elsewhere, involves competition between voluntary groups and organisations for funding from both local and central government. The use of grants is inevitably part of complex manipulations involving councillors, officers and representatives of community groups. A black officer in the Council described this process in the following terms:

> There are some cases where officers are forced to make grants for political

> reasons. You see people in positions to influence things like that are very careful what they do, and even if they are granting for political reasons there will always be a legitimise case for the grant. The crucial thing is where the emphasis is placed when there are a number of legitimise cases.
>
> (Interview, April 1992)

In a political context such as this the implementation of policy change inevitably involves close links between politicians and community organisations. It is perhaps not surprising, therefore, that in the local political folklore there are constant accusations about the misuse of grants to favour some groups as opposed to others in equal need. This is compounded by the feeling that particular sections of the black voluntary sector are being hit very hard because of their lack of good connections to political leaders. As a black activist explains:

> The African-Caribbean voluntary sector is being starved of funds. Some organisations are being closed that have been in existence for nearly twenty years. We had the so-called riots and that brought us a lot of bricks and mortar but that's all. The Handsworth Employment Scheme, Harambee Advice Centre, the Handsworth Law Centre, all these organisations have had their funding cut.
>
> *Question*: Does funding act as a political tool?
>
> It is not a tool it is a whip. It is a whip to make people fearful, it is a whip to keep people in line. . . . Many organisations are actually scared to say what they think . . . organisations that are critical of the city are treated in a vicious way – a vindictive way. We want to get away from the city as much as possible because we don't know where we stand, you never know where you stand from one year to the next – one year they give you money the next year they take it. While they are starving the black voluntary sector of funds they opened a new Citizens Advice Bureau on the edge of Handsworth [laughs]. That about sums things up right now.
>
> (Interview, May 1991)

In addition, voluntary sector activists also commented that the city had introduced more draconian forms for monitoring and reviewing grants. It is beyond the concerns of our research to examine in detail the politics of voluntary sector funding. However, we found clear evidence which supported the sentiments expressed in the above quotation.

For many on the left of the Labour Party the realities of community politics and the messy machinations involved proved to be a disappointment. As one Labour politician with an interest in racial politics explained:

> The problem was that white liberals put black people on a pedestal and we were disappointed that black leaders weren't progressive, brilliant trend-setters. One of the problems is that there is a wide range of black organisations. Those organisations have their own local interests. . . . You have to remember that people were involved for very different reasons and some of them were very self-serving.
>
> (Interview, July 1991)

What is interesting about this quotation is that it exposes the strange combination of romanticism and condescension that is part of the images that the left has of black politics. The assumption that black community groups should somehow have progressive altruistic interests as opposed to self-serving ones is itself the product of these discourses and it has had an impact on the kinds of policies pursued over the past decade.

The development of the SCF constituted an important shift in political strategy. However, this needs to be evaluated in the context of a severe contraction in the funding of the black voluntary sector. This exposed some of the clear connections between the local political system and community politics. In this respect the division between the municipal 'inside' and 'outside' hides points of connection and contingent political articulations. In this case funding operates as a crucial feature of these connections. The result is that consultation with the voluntary sector needs to be evaluated within the twin processes of financial constraint, which some suggest inhibits the frankness of criticism, and the establishment of a forum which offers municipal accountability.

## MARKETS, CITIZENSHIP AND EQUAL OPPORTUNITIES

It is in this overall context discussed in previous sections that we must see the development of new strategies about racial inequality which prioritise the role of the market. The Conservative Government's political agenda for local government in the 1990s has emphasised the application of private sector values within public sector services. This has resulted in pressures on local government to become more cost-effective and accountable. Local government is being forced to move from the role of 'service provider' to that of 'service facilitator'. This is compounded by the changes in the financing of local government. The overall result is that local government is having to justify its existence and the relevance of the services it provides. Beyond this, local authorities are under increasing pressure to contract out work to competitive tendering, thus relinquishing their powers as a direct employers. This has serious implications in view of the relative successes that Birmingham City Council has enjoyed in the area of equal opportunities and employment. For example, under current legislation it is increasingly difficult to insist that subcontractors operate equal opportunity principles. This, potentially, will have massive consequences for the policy agenda established during the 1980s, making it more difficult to sustain the considerable changes that have been achieved with regard to the ethnic make up of the authority's workforce.

Following from the pressures on local authorities to become more customer-sensitive and embrace the ethos of 'charter culture', many local authorities, like Birmingham, have been forced to reappraise their role and the nature of their services. The maxims of the charter culture are that local authority services should be effective, customer care regarded as paramount and performance constantly reviewed. What effect is this shift having on equal opportunity policies and initiatives? In particular, will this emphasis on 'the customer' have any impact on the quarter of a million black residents living in Birmingham?

It is quite clear that Birmingham is taking these central-government-led initiatives very seriously. In the early 1990s it employed Jonathan Nicholas Consultancy at a cost of £100,000 to provide a series of workshops on quality assurance which were attended by 200 of the city's top managers. During the presentations a number of corporate initiatives were stressed including: sensitivity to customers, equal opportunities, efficiency, effectiveness and value for money. The managers were expected to take responsibility for these changes and actively incorporate them into their specific services. The rationale behind the consultation was that the participants would become better managers, take ownership, listen to consumers and staff, achieve greater productivity, deeper involvement and an improved quality of working life. Some managers who attended those sessions suggested that this was yet another cosmetic 'policy spectacle' which allowed them little opportunity to participate in discussion.

The changing terms of policy change were made clear in the early 1990s, when there was a clear move towards performance indicators which will be negotiated with officers and departments. Interestingly enough, it seems that the Race Relations Unit and the Standing Consultative Forum have an important role to play in this process. The SCF in particular is applying pressure to make the city more accountable.

The financial constraints that have occurred simultaneously with the changes in local government finance are another crucial element in the current situation. The financial pressures to deliver a competitive service may be at odds with some of the expressed aims of Birmingham's Labour Council. In an era of fluctuating priorities it is hardly surprising that the morale of people working in the area of racial equality in Birmingham is low and that frustration within the authority is endemic. It seems unlikely that the recent emphasis on customer accountability, quality and efficiency will change this situation for the better. On the contrary, many officers working in this field within the Council see the marginalisation of racial equality in the city as inextricably connected to these changes.

In addition to activity inside the management structure of the authority, Birmingham has developed a list of guiding values for the organisation. These are summarised in five key points:

- We place a high value on ensuring that you receive high quality services and that you have a *say* in which services are provided and how;
- We want to improve *access* to all our services;
- We want to make sure that people are treated *fairly*;
- We want to develop Birmingham as a City of *opportunity*;
- We intend that Birmingham will be a City of *safety*.

(BCC, Value Statement, 1992)

What is striking about this development is the degree to which these notions reproduce elements which have been fostered in the context of equal opportunity initiatives throughout the last decade (Jouhl, 1992). The debate on 'quality' has appropriated elements from equal opportunity discourse without embracing fully the implications of trying to achieve equality of outcome. For example, one of the key concerns of the 'charter culture' is the effective monitoring of performance. Ethnic monitoring of employment, and even service provision, has been one of the cornerstones of equal opportunity policies. At one level, therefore, these initiatives could be seen as replicating aspects of what has been advocated by people working in the area of equal opportunities for the past ten years.

But there is also a fear that the new developments are creating a situation where equal opportunity initiatives, especially within service provision, can be simultaneously acknowledged and marginalised. The consequence of this subtle process is that the 'charter culture' uses the language of fairness, consultation and equity while ignoring substantive evidence of inequality and the need for new initiatives.

In this setting it is perhaps not surprising that it is widely felt that there can be no quality for Birmingham's black citizens without equality (Jouhl, 1992). The aspirations of black communities may well be raised by the rhetoric of the 'charter culture' and there certainly appears to be a growing self-awareness within the sphere of voluntary sector politics. The current emphasis on consultation, in particular, may open up spaces where the aspirations of black people in the city can be heard.

In this situation the rhetoric of greater customer care seems of little relevance to a quarter of the city's population. The result may be seen as a token bow in the direction of racial justice alongside an inability to appreciate its implications. In 1992, for example, the City Council articulated its broad commitment to racial equality in a policy statement which began with the following broad principles:

> The City of Birmingham is a multi-racial, multi-ethnic, multi-faith and multi-cultural city. The City Council is committed to a policy of racial, ethnic and cultural pluralism which reflects the permanence of, and positive contribution made by all communities to the City's heritage. In keeping with this commitment the City Council believes that every section of the community should have the right and freedom to practise their own customs and beliefs and to maintain their own culture, values and traditions without interference or imposition if social justice and equality are to be achieved.
>
> (BCC, Racial Equality Strategy, October 1992)

What is interesting about these general principles is that they combine an acknowledgement of the fact that Birmingham is a 'multi-racial, multi-ethnic, multi-faith and multi-cultural city' with a commitment to social justice. What remains unclear as yet, however, is how racial justice is to be achieved in practice.

As these complex and fractured political mobilisations are threatening to achieve greater effectiveness, the efficacy of the local state to deliver change is being severely curtailed. The result is that black politicians and officers may gain greater influence in the local political system but the local state no longer enjoys the autonomy and power it possessed in the heyday of local authority anti-racism in the 1980s. To put it crudely, the increase of minority participation at the municipal level has occurred simultaneously with a lowering of the political stakes as the local state has been progressively dismantled by central government.

## SUMMARY AND CONCLUSION

In this chapter we have concentrated on an exploration of the interplay between political change and policy initiatives dealing with key aspects of racial inequality in employment and access to services. We have tried to show (i) that policy changes cannot be analysed in isolation from the political transformations that we have looked at in previous chapters, and (ii) that the everyday dynamics of policy formation and implementation involve competing views about both the nature of racial discrimination and of what needs to be done to counter it. In the course of developing these arguments we have provided an analytical framework which prioritises the role of political representation and mobilisation in the formation of policy initiatives concerned with racial inequality and related issues. Additionally, we have argued that the dynamics of policy change in recent years have highlighted the limited forms of political empowerment of minorities.

The above points indicate the central dilemma we face in the present environment in thinking about the role of local and national policies concerned with tackling racial inequalities: namely, how to come to terms with the contradictions and limitations which seem to be an integral part of the pursuit of equal opportunities and anti-racist policies. There are important conceptual and political debates about the meanings of equal opportunity and anti-racism and their relation to wider social and political objectives. But it is also clear that these issues cannot be settled in isolation from an analysis of the political mobilisations and struggles which take place around them. It is also important to bear in mind the nature of institutional and organisational processes and their role in influencing the shape of policy agendas and outcomes. Rather than seeing policy change as essentially a bureaucratic process, it is important to see it as the product of a complex variety of pressures and mobilisations both within and outside of the political system.

Returning to the issue we flagged at the beginning of this chapter, namely the relationship between increased minority representation and policy change, the main conclusion we would draw from this account is that there are clear limits to the role of minority politicians in effecting change. A constant refrain that runs through the interviews we conducted with both black and white politicians and activists is that it is (i) not possible to see black politicians as sharing political values and objectives, and (ii) rarely the case that they are able to act in a concerted way to influence political decisions. As we noted in the previous chapter, minority councillors have co-ordinated their actions through establishing small and fragmented groups which have sought to negotiate influence in a limited way. Indeed as one leading African-Caribbean community activist put it to us: 'We have Asian and African-Caribbean councillors but it is sad to say that they haven't made any impact' (Interview, February 1991). He reasoned that this was the result of their inability to overcome ethnic and cultural differences and to form themselves into a 'black caucus' within the Labour Group with a clear agenda to fight for. Whatever the explanation for the limited impact of black representatives it seems evident that there is no one-to-one correspondence between increased minority representation and radical policy change. Rather, what we have described are fractured forms of political mobilisation which are mediated through established patterns of patronage. In this sense we argue that the policy agenda is set through alliances between emerging political factions which enter into relationships with key council officers. It is at this interface where the translation, or otherwise, of policy into practice takes place. Issues of political rivalry and officer antagonism are vitally important in determining how race policies are elaborated. This complex and shifting ground provides the context in which policy priorities are established. At the same time, high-ranking officers are struggling to accommodate initiatives on racial equality producing a contradictory compound of resistance and partial change.

It is clear that the emergence of black politicians and officers has had significant consequences. Some commentators have overinflated their relevance or dismissed it completely (Sivanandan, 1983; Sewell, 1993). But it seems to us that these commentators show little awareness of the complex and contingent political environment in which they must operate. A white officer commented in an interview that the presence of black elected officials at the committee level meant that he more diligently addressed the issue of racial equality in both writing reports and in his professional priorities (Interview, October 1991). It is easy to dismiss the importance of such comments but, as we have shown, black politicians are an integral part of Birmingham's political system. To characterise black politicians as either 'ineffective apostates' or 'radical tribunes' is to miss the elaborate political struggles taking place within mainstream politics. Such an approach brings a profoundly limited understanding to the unstable forms of political incorporation we have analysed. In this respect the efficacy of black political representation with regard to issues of policy needs to be understood within the wider configurations of patronage, alliance and negotiation occurring within the local political culture.

It is also evident that during the 1990s we have seen a retreat from the equal opportunity and anti-racist initiatives of the 1980s. This has been reflected, in Birmingham, London and elsewhere, in a move towards market-oriented approaches which de-emphasise the role of interventionist social policies. One of the clear dangers of this shift within local government is that it brings with it a dangerous tendency to return to a 'colour-blind' policy orientation. This is occurring in a period where racial violence is escalating and the well-being of black communities is being threatened by economic recession. A programme of action which has an explicit focus on countering racism through social and economic measures seems a distant possibility in the present environment. In this situation there is a clear need for an understanding of how policy agendas about race and related issues are formed and the possibilities for radical change.

# 8 Democracy, civil society and racism

Do the changes described in this book amount to a significant transformation in the politics of race? Have they brought about a significant realignment in the social and political relations of race in urban environments such as Birmingham? Are we seeing the emergence of new types of minority politics in the context of urban politics? How have the politics of race been transformed as a result of the emergence of black politicians as a significant political force? *Race, Politics and Social Change* has addressed all of these questions at a number of levels. In particular, we have sought to analyse the changing dynamics of racialised political mobilisations and discourses over the past two decades and to explore some likely scenarios for the future. By exploring processes and transformations in one particular political environment we have attempted to go beyond abstract generalisations in order to develop an account which takes seriously the everyday processes that have helped to shape wider social understandings of race and politics in British society. At the same time we have tried to link our analysis to broader debates about the impact of multiculturalism on contemporary politics, the role of minorities in political life and the limits of democratic institutions. In attempting to deal with all these issues we have no doubt been more successful in dealing with some than with others. This is, after all, for the reader to judge. But what is striking to us is that even in the short period since we started this research the key issues we have looked at have come to the fore of political debate in a wide variety of national and local environments.

In this concluding chapter we want to take the opportunity to reflect back upon some of the broader issues raised by our research and relate them to another key question: namely, the place of racialised minorities in the changing political environment of contemporary societies. Any rounded analysis of this issue needs to include the political dimension as one of its main concerns, as can be seen from developments in a wide variety of societies in recent years. In particular, the growing political influence of racist movements, combined with attempts to mobilise anti-racist movements, has given added weight to the need to understand the dynamics of racialised political processes at both macro and micro levels. We hope this is precisely what we have helped to do through the detailed analysis to be found in this volume.

All these issues link up in one way or another with some of the key political dilemmas about race and ethnicity that confront us at the present time. There can be little doubt, for example, that in virtually all advanced industrial societies a key area of public debate is the question of the social and political rights of minorities. Whether one looks at the media, official reports or the agendas of major research centres, the question of the political impact of racialised minority communities has come to the fore of the political agenda and is likely to grow in importance in the future. At the same time it is also clear that attempts by minorities to mobilise politically on the basis of ethnic and religious identities have led to widespread concern about the present and future position of minorities in many Western democratic societies.

Yet we know surprisingly little about the political mobilisations, conflicts and accommodations that have in one way or another produced the present situation. This is why we have concentrated in this volume on providing a critical analysis of the changing dynamics of these processes through a study of processes of change and transformation in one specific political environment. Using theoretical, historical and ethnographic material we have covered key dimensions of political and social change in Birmingham over the past few decades. While making no claim that the processes at work in Birmingham are characteristic of other urban localities, we do suggest that our analysis has some applicability in other environments, both in Britain and elsewhere. We are aware of the need for further detailed research on this issue before we can understand these processes more fully, but the account we have provided here does, we hope, exemplify some of the key trends and processes at work. There is a need for greater dialogue and research on the issues we have covered in this volume if we are to begin the rather difficult task of researching the racialisation of political culture and debate that has been so evident in recent years.

It is in the spirit of this wider concern that we want to use the conceptual and empirical material we have outlined in previous chapters as a basis for reflecting on how we have reached the present situation, the likely course of future developments and possible avenues for progressive political change. This is particularly pertinent in view of the debates that have emerged over the past few years, most notably in Britain, Western Europe and the United States about the whole question of the political participation and the representation of minority communities in political institutions. Such debates have raised important questions about the limits of democracy and the need for political institutions to become more fully representative of our multicultural societies. But there are many aspects of this issue that remain to be fully addressed and there are important variations in the way in which political institutions have responded to pressures for reform.

These are all major questions and it is not feasible to deal with all the dilemmas that they raise, but we shall attempt to tackle some of the key aspects that specifically relate to this study. In particular, we shall concentrate on four dimensions. First, the changing context within which racial politics is operating and the consequences for the representation of minority interests. Second, the impact of the transformations that we have analysed in this study on electoral politics and political parties. Third, some comparative trends in the political participation of racialised minorities. Finally, we shall suggest some likely future developments and ways in which some of the most pressing dilemmas that we face can be tackled.

## THE NEW CONTEXT OF RACIAL POLITICS

A central proposition organising this volume is that in order to understand the pronounced political changes in the role of black communities in Britain over the past two decades we need to examine fundamental aspects of what is happening within particular political processes, at both the local and national levels. Our key concerns in this volume can be summarised as: (i) the analysis of the changing terms of political discourses about race in a particular political environment, (ii) an account of the reasons why we have seen the development of a new politics of race in the past two decades, and (iii) an evaluation of the impact of increasing black participation and involvement in mainstream party politics and political institutions. By exploring all three dimensions together, in the particular environment of Birmingham, we wanted to provide an analysis that explored the new context of racial politics.

Whatever the merits of the account of these processes we have provided here it seems evident that in the immediate future the questions we have addressed are likely to gain even greater priority and to pose important dilemmas for those concerned with the political role of minorities in Britain and other West European societies. In Britain, for example, there has been a vigorous public debate in recent years about the changing balance between civil society and the state, particularly in relation to the need to redefine citizenship rights to take account of the claims by minority communities to specific religious and cultural identities (Parekh, 1991; Asad, 1990b). Part of this debate has been reflected in a questioning by both the left and the right about what it really means to call Britain a multiracial or a multicultural society and in a sense of scepticism about of the possibility of achieving such a society in any meaningful sense through the policies and initiatives that have been pursued by successive governments. It has also led to vigorous debates about how far the economic and social position of racialised minorities is characterised by social exclusion and discrimination.

Moreover, it seems indisputable that in the present political environment the question of race is one of the underlying concerns of key debates about politics and social policy. Take, for example, current debates about the changing parameters of citizenship and identity in multicultural societies, or, the debates about poverty and the underclass in the United States and increasingly in other advanced industrial societies. Although the racial and ethnic dimension of such debates is not clearly articulated all the time, there can be little doubt that the social and political position of racialised minorities has come over the past few decades to symbolise wider social concerns about the limits of democracy and equality in societies such as our own.

Yet, as we have argued throughout this volume, perhaps the single most important issue that confronts societies such as our own today is the role of racial minorities in political institutions. After all, how can a society claim to be a truly multicultural one if minorities do not feel included in its political institutions? How can social and economic equality be achieved without political equality? It is as a result of questions such as these that an increasingly important aspect of this debate is the issue of how to respond to the claims by minorities for greater access to representative institutions, for the selection of minority candidates to representative positions and for a greater say in the determination of policy agendas. Political debates about these claims have come to the fore in recent years, and have led to the articulation of counter-claims and opposition.

In a sense, the story we have reconstructed in this book about recent trends and developments in racialised politics in Birmingham can be seen as a microcosm of these broader debates. Certainly, as we have argued in Chapters 3 through 6, the question of minority participation in politics has come to symbolise the often contradictory forms that the incorporation of minority politicians can take in practice. Both Labour and Conservative politicians have developed their own responses to and interpretations of racialised politics, and specifically the role of Asian and African-Caribbean politicians. Such responses are by no means uniform and unchanging, as can be seen in the range of racialised discourses about race that are articulated by local councillors and activists from both parties.

It would be wrong, however, to see the contemporary politics of race simply through the prism of the language and actions of white politicians and activists. This would at best provide a partial view of the politics of race, and at worst ignore the role that minority politicians have played in the construction of a racialised politics. Yet what is clear from research about national and local politics is that a key voice in contemporary debates about race is that of black and ethnic minority politicians who are increasingly involved in mainstream politics. This is why in Chapter 6 we talk of the emergence of a 'new black politics' within localities such as Birmingham. By this we are referring not only to the growing number of black politicians within the local authority, but the wider social and cultural impact of black political mobilisation.

Additionally, as we have argued in some detail in previous chapters it would be misleading to see the growing number of black politicians and activists as sharing a common political ideology about either racial or wider social and economic questions. Quite the contrary. Apart from the fact that black and minority political participation is increasingly a feature of all the main political parties, it is also evident that there is little prospect of black politicians coalescing around a shared set of values and policies. Indeed, in terms of everyday politics it is clear that political identities are not formed simply on the basis of race. As we attempt to show in Chapter 6 it is equally important to take issues of class, religion, gender and ethnicity into account when analysing the political ideologies and actions of black politicians. This becomes all the more evident when one looks at the debates surrounding the Salman Rushdie affair and the role of religious identities in political life.

Such debates have linked with a growing preoccupation in academic studies of this field with questions of culture and identity (Rutherford, 1990; Grossberg,

Nelson and Treichler, 1992). Within the context of the changing dynamics of racial relations in Britain one reflection of this concern has been the growing literature on the relationship between racial, religious and gender identities (Grewal *et al.*, 1989; Brah, 1993; Anthias and Yuval-Davis, 1992; James, 1992; James and Harris, 1993). It is also interesting to note that many radical writers in this field have begun increasingly to point to the need to analyse the dynamics of racial and ethnic identities in Britain and other European societies (Hall, 1991a; Gilroy, 1991; Rattansi, 1992). Additionally, a number of writers have begun to question whether the usage of a general category like black to describe all racial minorities in British society has the effect of simplifying the complex ethnic, cultural and religious identities that characterise minority communities.

In this context there has been a tendency to conceptualise the contemporary situation in terms of notions of difference and identity, particularly in terms of ethnic and religious identities. Given the complex forms of political mobilisation that have emerged in recent years this tendency is not surprising, and it has led to a vigorous debate in Britain and other West European societies about the development of a politics constructed around hybrid 'new ethnicities' which go beyond political identities shaped by ethnic, cultural and religious background.

An interesting attempt to conceptualise the changing politics of race and identity by taking account of the role of new forms of political identity and social movements is to be found in Hall and Held (1989). Taking as their starting point the need to broaden out the conception of citizenship in order to make it less class reductionist they argue that:

> A contemporary 'politics of citizenship' must take into account the role which the social movements have played in expanding the claims to rights and entitlements to new areas. [This means addressing] questions of membership posed by feminism, the black and ethnic movements, ecology and vulnerable minorities like children. But it must also come to terms with the problems posed by 'difference' in a deeper sense: for example, the diverse communities to which we belong, the complex interplay of identity and identification in modern society and the differentiated ways in which people now participate in social life. The diversity of arenas in which citizenship is being claimed and contested today is essential to any modern conception of it because it is the very logic of modern society itself.
>
> (Hall and Held, 1989: 176)

This attempt to broaden conceptions of citizenship to include a plurality of 'differences' has led in recent years to a veritable explosion of writings on and around this issue. Such studies have done much to highlight the political dilemmas we face in developing a new politics that can deal with the politics of multiculturalism and ethnicity. They have also served to highlight the contingent and constantly changing forms of racialised politics that have emerged and taken root in recent years.

But there are clear dangers in the emerging focus on politics of identity and difference. As Homi Bhabha has warned, part of the problem with this focus is that there is a constant danger of constructing notions of difference in fixed and unchanging terms:

> The representation of difference must not be hastily read as the reflection of *pre-given* ethnic or cultural traits set in the fixed tablet of tradition.
>
> (Bhabha, 1994: 2)

But while he rejects such '*pre-given*' notions of difference it is also clear that Bhabha is articulating his own vision through the language of difference. He goes on to argue:

> The social articulation of difference, from the minority perspective, is a complex, on-going negotiation that seeks to authorise cultural hybridities that emerge in moments of historical transformation.
>
> (Ibid.)

It is important to note here that Bhabha is both criticising a fixed and unchanging conception of 'ethnic and cultural traits' and articulating an alternative perspective on the 'social articulation of difference'. But although Bhabha's critique of fixed notions of difference is highly pertinent in the present environment, we should not lose sight of the continuing, and in some senses growing, influence of essentialist and absolutist definitions of 'ethnic and cultural' difference. Whether one looks at the political language used by racist movements or certain political movements within racialised minority communities there is a clear tendency to rely on fixed and unchanging notions of community, culture and identity. At the level of practical politics the emergence of forms of political fundamentalism within Muslim and Hindu communities in Britain is perhaps the most widely discussed example of this trend. But it is by no means the only one.

What these trends suggest is that there is a clear need for an understanding of how it is that political identities around race and ethnicity are constantly formed and re-formed. We need to explore the complex dynamics through which such political identities are influenced in one way or another by other forms of identity based on categories such as religion, gender, ethnicity and locality.

## THE BURDEN OF REPRESENTATION

Chapters 3 through 7 of this volume have sought to address the question of the origins and impact of minority representation within the political system. Claims to increased representation of minorities within political institutions and parties are made of course for a variety of ideological and strategic reasons. In exploring the politics of race and social change one of the issues that we have faced throughout our research has been the question of how we can conceptualise processes of political representation in a context in which race and ethnicity have become important influences on patterns of political mobilisation, whether locally or nationally. A key theme in the discourses of black and minority activists was summarised by the question which was often posed to us: Who represents us? This was a question we confronted at all stages of our research, and in one way or another it is at the heart of the attempts made by black communities from the 1970s onwards to gain greater access to political institutions, whether through the Labour Party or the Conservative Party. Yet it is also clear that, simple as it is, this question raises a whole array of issues in its wake about the politics of representation in political systems that are becoming increasingly multicultural.

A central concern of much of the political mobilisation by minorities within the Labour Party over the past decade, for example, has been the need to increase the number of black and minority political representatives. As we have shown in the case of Birmingham, they have to a large extent been successful in achieving this objective if we look simply at the number of local politicians who are from minority backgrounds. But this is clearly not the whole story, particularly if one is not simply concerned with numerical equality but with more complex issues such as political power and influence. The growth in political participation is the result of patterns of recruitment which have brought some communities into politics while leaving others behind. In this sense we have also shown that it is important to be modest about claims of wide ranging change. There are sections of Birmingham's black communities which have not seen an increase in councillor representation. In particular this is true for the Bangladeshi community. It is quite clear, for example, if we look at the internal dynamics of local political institutions in Birmingham that the growth of black representation cannot be simply read as an indication of 'empowerment'. As we showed in our account of the changing forms of racialised politics in Chapters 5 and 6, it is important to contextualise the growth of minority representation within an analytic framework that takes account of (i) the complex balance of influence and patronage that structure the internal dynamics of political institutions, and (ii) the dynamics of party politics and ideologies. From this perspective it is important to move away from a simple numerical notion of black representation by examining both the responses of white politicians to the emergence of a new political elite and the role of black politicians and activists as political actors. This focus has enabled us to produce an account of the changing politics of race which gives due weight to the growing presence of black and minority politicians within the political system, without making assumptions about what this phenomenon means in terms of the social and political position of racialised minorities at a wider level.

The core empirical chapters of this book are therefore an attempt to establish the whole array of processes and issues that have facilitated the construction of a particular politics of race in major urban conurbations such as Birmingham over the past two decades. This kind of analysis has been largely absent from accounts of the politics of race in British society, in contrast to the wealth of detailed research on the urban politics of race in the United States. But there is a need to develop this kind of analysis if we are going to provide a dynamic account of the complex ways in which race impacts on political institutions and on everyday political processes within political parties. This explains the focus on both micro- and macro-political processes in this part of the book, which allowed us both to listen to the voices of political actors and to account for the role of institutional processes in shaping the possibilities for change and reform.

Part of the everyday tension that arises in relation to the growth of black representation in political institutions, whether at a national or local level, is the question of the responsibility of both black and white elected representatives to their constituents. As one leading black political figure has argued:

> As politicians they have responsibilities for their constituents, that's a bottom line whether you are parliamentarians or local councillors, and you've got to be seen to be doing what's right for the people that elected you or even those people who haven't elected you. Your concern is about your constituents, that's your major task.
>
> (Interview, March 1988)

This type of argument is of course not universally accepted, as our own account in previous chapters has shown. But it neatly captures perhaps one of the key dilemmas we face when exploring the changing boundaries of political representation in multicultural societies.

Along with the wider political transformations we have explored in this study, a key question remains to be fully addressed, namely: What impact, if any, do the processes covered in this volume have on the development of new policies and agendas about racial exclusion and discrimination? We have argued that the dynamics of race policy initiatives need to be analysed within the context of complex political alliances both within political parties and between politicians and bureaucrats. Beyond this, we have demonstrated that there is no simple one-to-one relationship between the emergence of black politicians and an increase in policy dynamism, arguing that the efficacy of black politicians needs to be understood within the wider patterns of political patronage operated by predominantly white political elites. In short, black representation and the politics of race must be evaluated by examining the structures of alliance found within the wider framework of local political cultures.

Another important factor that needs to be considered is the growth of racism in the context of electoral politics. The impact of race and racism on electoral politics has been a recurring theme in accounts of racial relations ever since the 1960s. The experience of Powellism, the growth of the National Front in the early 1970s and the use of coded language about immigration and race in mainstream party politics helped to highlight the role that racism could play in shaping political mobilisation. In this study, however, we have attempted to go a step further and look more closely at how specific discourses and patterns of mobilisation help to shape the politics of race in the electoral sphere. Our argument is that current trends do not point towards the emergence of a truly multiracial democracy. Rather, we have demonstrated that new forms of racialisation are occurring within the specific context of electoral politics. While these developments incorporate elements from previous forms of racial discourse, they are taking on a new life in the political domain. These political racisms are being generated in a context where the emergence of black politicians is producing clashes over the control of party agendas and where political power is being contested. The results, we argue, are new struggles over the meaning of electoral representation in a context where minorities have become increasingly politically active and begun to make some impact on established political parties, particularly at the local level.

## RACE, ETHNICITY AND POLITICS IN COMPARATIVE PERSPECTIVE

The focus of our research has been on the changing dynamics of racialised politics in the contemporary British situation. But it is also clear that the question of political participation is at the heart of contemporary debates about the role of migrant and long-established minority communities in a variety of countries. In countries all over Western Europe the question of political mobilisations by minority communities has been at the heart of many of the recent controversies and debates about immigration and racism. In countries as diverse as Belgium, Holland, France and Germany there is evidence of various kinds of political and social mobilisation by minorities. This has taken a number of forms. On the one hand, we have seen evidence of growing involvement and interest in the institutions of mainstream politics and attempts to gain access to political representation. On the other hand, there is strong evidence that minorities are also seeking to exert political influence through the development of ethnically or religiously based organisations and movements. This is particularly the case where minorities are largely excluded from and marginalised by mainstream party politics.

Quite apart from these forms of political involvement, it has become clear that the politicisation of race has taken on quite divergent forms in different societies. There is a wide body of research across the major West European societies that suggests that questions about immigration have come to occupy an important role in political debate at both the local and national levels. Migrant communities have sought to exercise political influence both through mainstream politics and through the formation of voluntary associations concerned with specific social and political issues. In other words, they have sought to mobilise politically in order to ensure that their interests were not marginalised as a result of political exclusion. These mobilisations have led to pressure on political parties and institutions to respond to the social, cultural and religious demands of migrant communities.

The reasons for this pressure are of course by no means uniform and one has to bear in mind the diverse political cultures and institutions at work. But it is clear that what we are looking at is a process that encompasses a range of societies, albeit in different ways. In a context in which patterns of migration, settlement and the development of ethnic communities have substantially transformed the social and political structures of these societies, the meaning of citizenship and national identity is being rapidly transformed. As Castles and Miller (1993) have shown in their study of international migration current trends point to the globalisation of patterns of migration:

> The age of migration has already changed the world and many of its societies.

> Most highly-developed countries and many less-developed ones have become far more culturally diverse than they were even a generation ago. A large proportion, indeed the majority, of nation states must face up to the reality of ethnic pluralism.
>
> (Castles and Miller, 1993: 271)

Yet what is also clear is that how different societies respond to this challenge varies enormously according to the wider social and political context (Wrench and Solomos, 1993). Indeed, there are clear examples of the ways in which responses vary within nation-states, according to political values, locality and region. Moreover, it is evident that there are competing ideologies both about the meaning of multiculturalism and ethnic pluralism and the political strategies necessary to achieve greater equality for minority communities. At the same time, it is also evident that political mobilisation among minority communities has taken on new forms in recent years. One example of this is the growing number of black political representatives who have been elected at both the local and national levels. But it is also reflected in the changing forms of political discourses about race and ethnicity that have been articulated at all levels of the political system.

## POSSIBILITIES FOR THE FUTURE

Do the transformations we have analysed make a difference? The evidence presented in this book suggests that they make a noticeable difference and that there has been a pronounced transformation characterised by a major realignment of political relations. Writing as we do at a time when race and ethnicity are coming to the fore in new patterns of political mobilisation, it is important that we do not lose sight of the need to look forward as well as backwards. Although it would be unwise to make hard and fast predictions about the likely course of racialised politics in the future, it is incumbent on us to at least reflect on this issue if we are to come to terms with the potential dangers that lie ahead. Indeed, what has become even more clear to us in the course of doing the research on which this book is based is that as academics working on these issues we have to actively engage with the ethical and political dilemmas which are an inextricable component of public debates about race and ethnicity. This is perhaps the most difficult question we have to deal with, given all the conflict and confusion that surrounds contemporary political debates about race. Nevertheless, it is important to try to reflect on at least some aspects of this question in order to be able to comment on some of the dilemmas which confront countries such as our own today.

What then are the likely routes of development as we look forward to the next century? This is in many ways the key question that underlies much of the analysis in this volume. But we are aware that there is a need to be careful about making easy predictions and we have eschewed the temptation to make glib generalisations. From our perspective it is vital that research should focus on the ways in which particular avenues of change are possible as a result of specific political, cultural, social and economic contexts. This means that there is an urgent need to move beyond abstract generalities and examine in greater detail developments in cities and towns such as Birmingham if we are to comprehend the changing forms of minority participation in politics and their impact on political institutions.

It is also clear that we need to know more about the changing political identities within minority communities. This is an issue which has led to much debate in recent years. Stuart Hall has captured an important element of this process when he writes of the need to understand the complex 'new ethnicities' that are being formed at the present time and of the need to go beyond the innocent notion of the essential 'black subject' (Hall 1988: 28). He has argued that there is a need to look more closely at the diverse cultural identities which compose the category 'black', pointing to the shifts and tensions surrounding the construction of blackness as an organising category that referenced common experiences of racism and marginalisation. Tariq Modood, writing from a very different position, has also been vociferous in recent years in arguing that the political notion of 'black' has had damaging consequences for 'Asians'. Modood argues that the racial dualism of 'black' and 'white' is not appropriate to the complex ethnic and racial identities that characterise British society, and that it is necessary to establish a viable ethnic pluralism (*Guardian*, 22 May 1989). He rejects the assertion that he is promoting a divisive retreat into absolute racial particularity:

> The choice, then, is not between a separatist Asian ethnicity and unity of the racially oppressed; the choice is between a political realism which accords dignity to ethnic groups on their own terms and a coercive ideological fantasy.
> (Modood, 1988: 403)

From this perspective the whole notion of a 'black politics' has to be replaced by a perspective which privileges the different routes taken by various ethnic groups in terms of social mobility and political mobilisation.

Such arguments have unfortunately remained at a level of abstraction where they do not address the changing terms of minority political participation in everyday political processes. It is noticeable that although both Hall and Modood place a strong emphasis on the emergence of new and complex forms of ethnic identity they tell us very little about the role of political actors in shaping everyday struggles and mobilisations. Although we would not want to impose a coercive racial ontology, it is important not to lose sight of the political conditions which have led to the construction of specific political identities. As we showed in some detail in Chapter 6, the articulation of new forms of minority political mobilisation within the Labour Party, and to some extent the Conservative Party, cannot be understood simply through the notion of specific types of 'Asian' and 'African-Caribbean' politics. While Hall and Modood may be right to question simplistic notions of a unitary and essential model for identity, we still need to understand how the notion of 'black' can serve as an organising category in contemporary political life. As we have tried to show in Chapter 6, blackness remains an important organising theme within political life. The politicians we talked to in the course of our research have demonstrated other alternatives to this, while at the same time recognising that the communities from which they come are subject to discrimination and racism. Thus, while it is necessary to question esentialist and simplistic notions of blackness, it is important to retain a political and analytical notion of blackness as a way of describing points of convergence and volatile alliances. As Pnina Werbner (1991) has pointed out, the contemporary political situation requires a conceptual language that can cope with the possibility of 'division within unity'. The notion of a new black politics provides an analytical category to describe political implosion as well as nascent transcultural alliances.

There are two final points that need to be made. One concerns the intersection between the growth of black political representation and political change. The trends we have outlined in this book point to the need for more analysis of this important dimension of political life in our major cities. One of the conclusions that we draw from our research in Birmingham is that the contemporary politics of race and ethnicity in societies such as Britain are in flux. Thus we do not see either a simple process of exclusion or inclusion as being the likely outcome of the current situation. Rather, we see the need to analyse the possibility of political change by taking fully into account the actual historical and political context within which specific struggles over access to political power and influence take place. It is only through such accounts of the local and national contexts within which the politics of race are shaped over time that we can begin to understand both the possibilities for transformation and the limits to reform. The second point we want to emphasise concerns the changing forms of political identities around race that are emerging at the present time. It is evident that in recent years we have seen the emergence of a complex range of identities shaped by socially constructed notions of race, ethnicity, culture and religion. Given the present political environment, we need to explore and understand more clearly how these identities are both formed and transformed. We hope that the account we have provided in this volume has helped to stimulate debate and further analysis of what is after all a key question as we look to the future of racism in Britain and other societies.

# Appendix 1: Research strategy and sample

The empirical research for this book was conducted between 1990 and 1993. Les Back was employed as a full-time Research Officer for most of this period and conducted interviews, participant observation and archival research. From the outset the research aimed to examine racialised social processes *in action*. We wanted to construct a picture of the way race and racism featured in the vernacular cultures of political life. We wanted to follow the developments within local politics over a period of time, avoiding the tendency of much of the research in this field to ignore any detailed discussion of micro-political struggles around issues of race and politics (Anwar, 1986; Ben-Tovim, *et al.* 1986; Goulbourne, 1990). We also wanted to represent the diachronic quality of local politics. In particular, we wanted to examine the meanings which politicians, officials and activists give to their actions and the structures within which they operate (Jeffers, 1991).

We used a range of qualitative research tools to examine these political processes. Semi-structured tape-recorded interviews provided a core technique for eliciting accounts from councillors and political activists. The research aimed to find out what politicians in positions of influence felt about issues such as the emergence of black politicians, race policies and related issues. As a result all of the 117 councillors on Birmingham City Council were approached in late 1989 and asked if they would agree to be interviewed. Beginning in February 1990 we conducted interviews with seventy-five councillors from the three main political parties in the city. The majority of these interviews were conducted in 1990 and 1991, with follow-up interviews in 1992, and the final interview took place in December 1993. The interviews covered a range of themes including the informants' political biography, attitudes to key events, the position of ethnic minorities in the political process, the emergence of black politicians, the race and equal opportunity policies of the City Council and the prospects for change in the 1990s. The interviews varied in terms of length and frequency: some lasted one hour while others were as long as five hours. Many of the politicians were only interviewed once, whilst key informants were interviewed repeatedly – in one case as many as seven interviews – over the three-year research period. Semi-structured interviews were also carried out with a small number of Members of Parliament and Members of the European Parliament.

In addition to the interviews with politicians we also met with a range of party activists, community relations officers and members of the black voluntary sector. However, the chief sample – in addition to politicians – was drawn from City Council officers working within various service departments. These interviews aimed to explore the ways in which race policies were being developed and implemented. These interviews covered the professional biography of officers, the relationship between politics and policy, Birmingham City Council's race and equal opportunities policy, local government structure and policy, the significance and position of black officers in the authority and prospects for future institutional change.

In most cases these interviews were conducted in public offices including Birmingham's Council House, party offices or municipal departments. Participants were also offered the opportunity to talk at home, particularly in circumstances where it was difficult to talk about confidential issues at work or other semi-public places. In addition to this, a small number of interviews were conducted at the University of Warwick where Les Back had an office at the Centre for Research in Ethnic Relations. Where possible we tried to achieve a gender balance within our sample. However, owing to the male-biased demography of political parties, council departments and political organisations in general, our sample is gender imbalanced and representative of the political groups we were studying. The overall breakdown of the sample is given in detail below.

**Sample Breakdown**

*Members of Parliament/Members of European Parliament* (Total 6)

MPs (total 4)

| | Labour | Conservative |
|---|---|---|
| (m) | 2 | 1 |
| (f) | 1 | – |

MEPs (total 2)

| | Labour | Conservative |
|---|---|---|
| (m) | 1 | – |
| (f) | 1 | – |

*Councillors* (Total 75)

| | Labour | |
|---|---|---|
| | white | black |
| (m) | 24 | 20 |
| (f) | 9 | 3 |
| | Conservative | |
| (m) | 12 | – |
| (f) | 5 | – |
| | Liberal Democrats | |
| (m) | 2 | – |
| (f) | – | – |

*Party Activists* (Total 26)

| | Labour | |
|---|---|---|
| | white | black |
| (m) | 10 | 6 |
| (f) | 4 | – |
| | Conservative | |
| (m) | 1 | 4 |
| (f) | – | 1 |

*Council Officers* (Total 32)

| | white | black |
|---|---|---|
| (m) | 17 | 10 |
| (f) | 3 | 2 |

*Community Relations Council* (Total 6)

| | white | black |
|---|---|---|
| (m) | 3 | 2 |
| (f) | 1 | – |

*Black Community Organisations* (Total 7)

| | |
|---|---|
| (m) | 6 |
| (f) | 1 |

*Other* (Total 2)

| | |
|---|---|
| (m) | 2 |
| (f) | – |

**Total Interviews**: 154

The interview data was augmented with extended participant observation. This included attending council meetings, election campaigns, demonstrations and related forums. This dimension of the research aimed to provide an insight into how issues of race featured in the daily workings of the local state and the forms of dialogue and consultation that were taking place between the local political sphere and minority organisations and representatives.

The research was not merely confined to the contemporary machinations of political life. It also sought to place current developments within a historical context. Following on from this commitment, an extensive archival search of council committee reports and local and national press material was conducted. A range of related historical sources was also examined, including political pamphlets, trade union papers, voluntary sector documentation and Community Relations Council records. In the course of the research personal letters and other private communications relating to particular political conflicts were also made available to us.

In reconstructing our account of the politics of race in Birmingham we have triangulated these three data sets (i.e. interview, observational, archival). We attempted to situate and evaluate the reliability of the accounts that were offered in the context of interviews and in other texts. One of the crucial problems we faced was that political struggles were often being enacted in the recounting of the events themselves. As we point out in Chapter 5, this meant that each account had to be carefully evaluated in the context of the wider processes of generating a political folklore which was intimately related to the position of the speaker within the political sphere. Our strategy was to treat each individual account as a discourse to be evaluated and scrutinised in relation to other available verbal and written accounts. Thus, our interpretation of the data was situated in the context of our wider participation in Birmingham's political culture and the other sources that were available to us.

# Appendix 2: Black councillors on Birmingham City Council (1979–1994)

The first black councillor to be elected to Birmingham City Council was Dr Dhani Prem, who served on the authority between 1945–1950. But black councillors did not emerge as a substantial political force until some thirty years later. What follows records the chronology of this development and includes details of significant positions held by black councillors, such as chair and vice-chair of committees.

Birmingham City Council consists of 117 elected officials. These councillors are elected on a four-year cycle with one-third of the members coming up for re-election each year: one year in every four there are no elections. We have listed below the black councillors elected since 1979 when Egbert Carliss and Prem Singh Kalsi were the first to be elected since Dhani Prem. We have also noted the party in control of the council each year and the ward represented. All of the councillors mentioned below are representatives for the Labour Party.

*1979–1980: Conservative control*

Egbert Carliss (Aston), Prem Singh Kalsi (All Saints)

*1980–1981: Labour control*

Egbert Carliss (Aston), Prem Singh Kalsi (All Saints)

*1981–1982: Labour control*

Egbert Carliss (Aston), Prem Singh Kalsi (All Saints)

*1982–1983: Conservative control*

Saeed Abdi (Handsworth), Muhammad Afzal (Aston), Egbert Carliss (Aston), Khushi Ram Jhumat (Handsworth), Sardul Singh Marwa (Soho)

*1983–1984: Conservative control*

Saeed Abdi (Handsworth), Muhammad Afzal (Aston), Egbert Carliss (Aston)

[Vice-chair of Appeals], Sharon Hunte (Handsworth), Amir Kabil Khan (Sparkhill), Sardul Singh Marwa (Soho)

*1984–1985: Labour control*

Saeed Abdi (Handsworth), Muhammad Afzal (Aston), Egbert Carliss (Aston) [Chair of Appeals], Najma Hafeez (Fox Hollies), Sharon Hunte (Handsworth), Amir Kabil Khan (Sparkhill), Sardul Singh Marwa (Soho) [Chair of Race Relations and Equal Opportunities], Phillip Murphy (Sandwell)

*1985–1986: Labour control*

Saeed Abdi (Handsworth), Muhammad Afzal (Aston), Egbert Carliss (Aston) [Chair of Appeals], Najma Hafeez (Fox Hollies), Sharon Hunte (Handsworth), Amir Kabil Khan (Sparkhill), Sardul Singh Marwa (Soho) [Chair of Race Relations and Equal Opportunities], Phillip Murphy (Sandwell), Partap Singh (Soho)

*1986–1987: Labour control*

Saeed Abdi (Handsworth), Muhammad Afzal (Aston) [Chair of Urban Renewal], Egbert Carliss (Aston) [Chair of Appeals], Najma Hafeez (Fox Hollies), Paul Haymeraj (Acocks Green), Sharon Hunte (Handsworth), Amir Kabil Khan (Sparkhill), Gulbahar Khan (Small Heath), Gurdev Singh Manku (Sandwell), Sardul Singh Marwa (Soho), Phillip Murphy (Sandwell) [Vice-chair of Race Relations Equal Opportunities], Mushtaq Rabbani (Handsworth), Partap Singh (Soho), Sybil Spence (Soho) [Vice-chair of Race Relations Equal Opportunities, replacing Phillip Murphy]

*1987–1988:Labour control*

Saeed Abdi (Handsworth) [Chair of Joint Consultative], Muhammad Afzal (Aston) [Chair of Urban Renewal], Egbert Carliss (Aston) [Chair of Appeals], Najma Hafeez (Fox Hollies) [Vice-chair of Education), Paul Haymeraj (Acocks Green) [Vice-chair of Personnel and Equal Opportunities], Bakhshish Singh Karnana (Soho), Ghazanfar Khan (Handsworth), Gulbahar Khan (Small Heath), Gurdev Singh Manku (Sandwell), Phillip Murphy (Sandwell), Mushtaq Rabbani (Handsworth), Abdul Rashid (Small Health), Bhagat Singh (Sparkbrook), Partap Singh (Soho), Sybil Spence (Soho)

*1988–1989: Labour control*

Saeed Abdi (Handsworth) [Chair of Joint Consultative], Muhammad Afzal (Aston) [Chair of Urban Renewal], Egbert Carliss (Aston) [Chair of Appeals], Mohammed Fazal (Sparkhill), Najma Hafeez (Fox Hollies) [Vice-chair of Education], Paul Haymeraj (Acocks Green) [Vice-chair of Personnel and Equal Opportunities],

Bakhshish Singh Karnana (Soho), Ghazanfar Khan (Handsworth), Gulbahar Khan (Small Heath), Gurdev Singh Manku (Sandwell), Phillip Murphy (Sandwell), Mushtaq Rabbani (Handsworth), Abdul Rashid (Small Health), Bhagat Singh (Sparkbrook), Sybil Spence (Soho), Raja Suleman Khan (Sparkhill)

*1989–1990: Labour control*

Saeed Abdi (Handsworth) [Chair of Joint Consultative Committee], Muhammad Afzal (Aston) [Chair of Urban Renewal Committee], Egbert Carliss (Aston) [Chair of Appeals Committee], Mohammed Fazal (Sparkhill), Najma Hafeez (Fox Hollies) [Chair of Social Services], Paul Haymeraj (Acocks Green), Bakhshish Singh Karnana (Soho), Ghazanfar Khan (Handsworth), Gulbahar Khan (Small Heath), Raja Suleman Khan (Sparkhill), Gurdev Singh Manku (Sandwell), Phillip Murphy (Sandwell), Mushtaq Rabbani (Handsworth), Abdul Rashid (Small Health) [Vice-chair of Personnel and Equal Opportunities], Bhagat Singh (Sparkbrook) [Vice-chair of Technical Services], Sybil Spence (Soho) Dorothy Wallace (Soho)

*1990–1991: Labour control*

Saeed Abdi (Handsworth) [Chair of Joint Consultative Committee], Muhammad Afzal (Aston) [Chair of Urban Renewal Committee], Egbert Carliss (Aston) [Chair of Appeals Committee], Mohammed Fazal (Sparkhill), Najma Hafeez (Fox Hollies), Bakhshish Singh Karnana (Soho), Mohammed Amin Kazi (Handsworth), Ghazanfar Khan (Handsworth), Gulbahar Khan (Small Heath) [Vice-chair of Housing], Raja Suleman Khan (Sparkhill), Khalid Mahmood (Sparkbrook), Gurdev Singh Manku (Sandwell), Phillip Murphy (Sandwell), Abdul Rashid (Small Heath) [Vice-chair of Personnel and Equal Opportunities], Bhagat Singh (Sparkbrook), Sybil Spence (Soho) [Vice-chair of Urban Renewal], Dorothy Wallace (Soho)

*1991–1992: Labour control*

Saeed Abdi (Handsworth) [Chair of Joint Consultative Committee], Muhammad Afzal (Aston), Raghib Ahsan (Sparkhill) – October 1991 by-election replaced Maria Kaye after her death), Mohammed Azam (Handsworth), Nam Dev Bagla (Soho) [Vice-chair of Commercial Services], Egbert Carliss (Aston) [Vice-chair of Housing], Mohammed Fazal (Sparkhill), Najma Hafeez (Fox Hollies) [Chair of Social Services], Mohammed Kazi (Handsworth) [Chair of the Race Relations sub-committee of Community Affairs, Vice-chair of National Exhibition Centre and International Convention Centre], Gulbahar Khan (Small Heath), Raja Suleman Khan (Sparkhill), Khalid Mahmood (Sparkbrook) [Chair of the Race Relations Sub-committee of Community Affairs], Gurdev Singh Manku (Sandwell), Phillip Murphy (Sandwell), Abdul Rashid (Small Heath) [Vice-chair of Personnel], Bhagat Singh (Sparkbrook) [Chair of Joint Consultative Committee], Sybil Spence (Soho) [Vice-chair of Social Services], Dorothy Wallace (Soho)

*1993–1994: Labour control*

Muhammad Afzal (Aston) [Chair of Personnel], Raghib Ahsan (Sparkhill), Dr Aleem Akhtar (Washwood Heath), Mohammed Azam (Handsworth), Namdev Bagla (Soho) [Vice-chair of Commercial Services], Egbert Carliss (Aston) [Vice-chair of Economic Development], Fazal Ellahi (Sparkhill), Mohammed Fazal (Sparkhill) [Vice-chair of Community Affairs], Najma Hafeez (Fox Hollies) [Chair of Community Affairs], Paul Haymeraj (Small Heath), Mohammed Kazi (Handsworth) [Vice-chair of National Exhibition Centre and International Convention Centre], Gulbahar Khan (Small Heath), Khalid Mahmood (Sparkbrook) (replaced in April 1993), Abdul Malik (Nechells) [Vice-chair of Urban Renewal], Gurdev Manku (Sandwell), Phillip Murphy (Sandwell), Mustaq Rabbani (Handsworth), Abdul Rashid (Small Heath), Sybil Spence (Soho) [Chief Whip of the Labour Group], Dorothy Wallace (Soho) [Vice-chair of DLO Contract Services], Bhagat Singh (Sparkbrook).

# Bibliography

This bibliography does not list the interviews, internal council documents and newspaper sources which are referred to in the course of the analysis in various chapters. These are referenced directly in the text. We have limited this bibliography to secondary sources and publicly available reports.

Anthias, F. and Yuval-Davis, N. (1992) *Racialized Boundaries* London: Routledge.

Anwar, M. (1986) *Race and Politics* London: Tavistock.

Asad, T. (1990a) 'Ethnography, literature, and politics: some readings and uses of Salman Rushdie's *The Satanic Verses*' *Cultural Anthropology* 5, 3: 239–269.

—— (1990b) 'Multiculturalism and British identity in the wake of the Rushdie affair' *Politics and Society* 18, 4: 455–480.

Back, L. (1992) 'Gendered participation: masculinity and fieldwork in a South London community' in Caplan, P., Bell, D., and Karim, W. J. (eds) *Gendered Fields* London: Routledge.

Back, L. and Solomos, J. (1992) 'Who represents us? Racialised politics and candidate selection' *Research Papers*, No. 3, Department of Politics and Sociology, Birkbeck College.

—— (1993) 'Doing research, writing politics: the dilemmas of political intervention in research on racism' *Economy and Society*, 22, 2: 178–199.

Balibar, E. (1991) 'Es Gibt Keinen Staat in Europa: Racism and Politics in Europe Today' *New Left Review* 186: 5–19.

Ball, W. and Solomos, J. (eds) (1990) *Race and Local Politics* London: Macmillan.

Barker, M. (1981) *The New Racism* London: Junction Books.

Ben-Tovim, G., Gabriel, J., Law, I. and Stredder, K. (1986) *The Local Politics of Race* London: Macmillan.

Bhachu, P. (1991) 'Culture, ethnicity and class amongst Punjabi Sikh women in 1990s Britain' *New Community* 17, 3: 401–412.

Billig, M., Condor, S., Edwards, D., Gane, M., Diddleton, D. and Redley, A. (1988) *Ideological Dilemmas: A Social Psychology of Everyday Thinking* London: Sage.

Birmingham City Council (BCC) (1991) *Racial equality in Birmingham* Birmingham: BCC Race Relations Unit.

—— (1992a) *Racial Equality Strategy* Birmingham: BCC.

—— (1992b) *Value Statement* Birmingham: BCC.

Blackstone, T., Cornford, J., Hewitt, P. and Milliband, D. (1992) *Next Left: An Agenda for the 1990s* London: Institute for Public Policy Research.

Bourne, J. (1980) 'Cheerleaders and ombudsmen: the sociology of race relations in Britain' *Race and Class* 21, 4: 331–352.

Brah, A. (1993) 'Difference, diversity, differentiation: processes of racialisation and gender' in Wrench, J. and Solomos, J. (eds) *Racism and Migration in Western Europe* Oxford: Berg.

Braham, P., Rattansi, A. and Skellington, R. (eds) (1992) *Racism and Antiracism* London: Sage.

Brar, H. S. and Keith, M. (1991) 'The politics of blackness' Paper given at the New Issues in Black Politics Conference, University of Warwick, 14–16 May 1990.

Browning, R. P., Marshall, D. R. and Tabb, D. H. (1984) *Protest Is Not Enough: The Struggle of Black and Hispanics for Equality in Urban Politics* Berkeley: University of California Press.

—— (1986) 'Protest is Not Enough: A Theory of Political Incorporation' *PS* XIX, 3: 576–581.

—— (1990) *Racial Politics in American Cities* New York: Longman.

Brubaker, R. (1992) *Citizenship and Nationhood in France and Germany* Cambridge, Mass.: Harvard University Press.

Button, J. W. (1989) *Blacks and Social Change: Impact of the Civil Rights Movement in Southern Communities* Princeton, N.J.: Princeton University Press.

Castells, M. (1983) *The City and the Grassroots* London: Edward Arnold.

Castles, S. and Miller, M. (1993) *The Age of Migration* London: Macmillan.

Centre for Contemporary Cultural Studies (CCCS) (1982) *The Empire Strikes Back* London: Hutchinson.

Clifford, J. and Marcus, G. E. (eds) (1986) *Writing Culture: The Poetics and Politics of Ethnography* Berkeley: University of California Press.

Cockburn, C. (1991) *In the Way of Women* London: Macmillan.

Cohen, P. (1988a) 'Popular racism, unpopular education' *Youth and Policy* 24: 8–12.

—— (1988b) 'Tarzan and the Jungle Bunnies: class, race and sex in popular culture' *New Formations* 5: 25–30.

—— (1991) *Monstrous Images, Perverse Reasons: Cultural Studies in Anti-Racist Education* Centre for Multicultural Education, Institute of Education, University of London.

Cohen, P. and Bains, H. (eds) (1988) *Multi-Racist Britain* London: Macmillan.

Conservative Political Centre (1962) *Helping the Immigrants* London: CPC.

Deakin, N. (1970) *Colour, Citizenship and British Society* London: Panther.

Dear, G. (1985) *Handsworth/Lozells, September 1985: Report of the Chief Constable, West Midlands Police* Birmingham: West Midlands Police.

Dunleavy, P. (1980) *Urban Political Analysis: The Politics of Collective Consumption* London: Macmillan.

Dyson, M. E. (1993) *Reflecting Black: African-American Cultural Criticism* Minneapolis: University of Minnesota Press.

Fanon, F. (1967) *Towards the African Revolution* New York: Monthly Review Press.

Fitzgerald, M. (1984) *Political Parties and Black People* London: Runnymede Trust.

—— (1990) 'The emergence of black councillors and MP's in Britain: some underlying questions' in Goulbourne, H. (ed.) *Black Politics in Britain* Aldershot: Avebury.

Gates, H. L. Jr (ed.) (1986) *'Race', Writing and Difference* Chicago: University of Chicago Press.

—— (1992) *Loose Canons: Notes on the Culture Wars* New York: Oxford University Press.

Geschwender, J. (1977) *Class, Race and Worker Insurgency* Cambridge: Cambridge University Press.

Gilroy, P. (1980) 'Managing the "underclass": a further note on the sociology of race relations in Britain' *Race and Class* XXII, 1: 47–62.

—— (1982) 'Steppin' out of Babylon: race, class and autonomy' in CCCS *The Empire Strikes Back* London: Hutchinson.

—— (1987) *There Ain't No Black in the Union Jack* London: Hutchinson.

—— (1990) 'One nation under a groove: the cultural politics of "race" and racism in Britain' in Goldberg, D. T. (ed.) *Anatomy of Racism* Minneapolis: University of Minnesota Press.

—— (1991) 'It ain't where you're from, it's where you're at . . . The dialectics of diasporic identification' *Third Text*, 13: 3–16.

—— (1992) 'Cultural studies and ethnic absolutism' in Grossberg, L. *et al.* (eds) *Cultural Studies* London: Routledge.

—— (1993a) *The Black Atlantic: Modernity and Double Consciousness* London: Verso.

—— (1993b) *Small Acts: Thoughts on the Politics of Black Cultures* London: Serpent's Tail.

Goldberg, D. T. (ed.) (1990) *Anatomy of Racism* Minneapolis: University of Minnesota Press.

Goldberg, D. T. (1992) 'The Semantics of Race' *Ethnic and Racial Studies* 15, 4: 543–569.

—— (1993) *Racist Culture* Oxford: Blackwell.

Goulbourne, H. (1990) 'The contribution of West Indian groups to British politics' in Goulbourne, H. (ed.) *Black Politics in Britain* Aldershot: Avebury.

Goulbourne, H. (ed.) (1990) *Black Politics in Britain* Aldershot: Avebury.

Green, D. G. (1990) *Equalizing People: Why Social Justice Threatens Liberty* London: IEA Health and Welfare Unit.

Grewal, S., Kay, J., Landor, L., Lewis, G. and Parmar, P. (1989) *Charting the Journey* London: Sheba.

Griffiths, P. (1966) *A Question of Colour* London: Leslie Frewin.

Grossberg, L., Nelson, C., and Treichler, C. (eds) (1992) *Cultural Studies* London: Routledge.

Hall, S. (1980) 'Race, articulation and societies structured in dominance' in UNESCO *Sociological Theories: Race and Colonialism* Paris: UNESCO.

—— (1988) 'New ethnicities' in Mercer, K. (ed.) *Black Film British Cinema: ICA Documents 7* London: British Film Institute.

—— (1991a) 'Old and new identities, old and new ethnicities' in King, A. D. (ed.) *Culture, Globalization and the World System* London: Macmillan.

—— (1991b) 'The local and the global: globalization and ethnicity' in King, A. D. (ed.) *Culture, Globalization and the World System* London: Macmillan.

Hall, S., Critcher, C., Jefferson, T., Clarke, J. and Roberts, B. (1978) *Policing the Crisis: Mugging, the State, and Law and Order* London: Macmillan.

Hall, S. and Held, D. (1989) 'Citizens and citizenship' in Hall, S. and Jacques, M. (eds) *New Times: The Changing Face of Politics in the 1990s* London: Verso.

Hall, S. and Jacques, M. (eds) (1989) *New Times: The Changing Face of Politics in the 1990s* London: Lawrence and Wishart.

Hall, S. and Jefferson, T. (eds) (1976) *Resistance Through Rituals* London: Hutchinson.

Harris, C. (1991) 'Configurations of racism: the Civil Service, 1945–60' *Race and Class* 33, 1: 1–30.

Harvey, D. (1989) *The Condition of Postmodernity* Oxford: Blackwell.

Hewitt, R. (1986) *White Talk, Black Talk: Inter-Racial Friendship and Communication Amongst Adolescents* Cambridge: Cambridge University Press.

—— (1991) 'Language, youth and the destabilisation of ethnicity' Paper given at the 'Conference on Ethnicity in Youth Culture: Interdisciplinary Perspectives', Fittjagard, Botkyrka, Sweden, 3–6 June 1991.

Hodge, M. (1991) *Quality, Equality, Democracy* Fabian Pamphlet 549, London: Fabian Society.

hooks, b. (1992) *Black Looks: Race and Representation* London: Turnaround.

James, W. (1992) 'Migration, racism and identity: the Caribbean experience in Britain' *New Left Review* 193: 15–55.

James, W. and Harris, C. (eds) (1993) *Inside Babylon: The Caribbean Diaspora in Britain* London: Verso.

Jeffers, S. (1991) 'Black sections in the Labour Party: the end of ethnicity and "Godfather politics" in Werbner, P. and Anwar, M. (eds) *Black and Ethnic Leaderships: The Cultural Dimension of Political Action* London: Routledge.

Jenkins, R. and Solomos, J. (eds) (1989) *Racism and equal opportunity policies in the 1980s* Cambridge: Cambridge University Press.

Jouhl, A. (1992) 'No quality without equality – a community perspective' Paper presented at the 'Quality and Equality Seminar', 9 October 1992, Birmingham City Council, Birmingham.

Kahn, P. and Meehan, E. (eds) (1992) *Equal Value/Comparable Worth in the UK and the USA* London: Macmillan.

Katznelson, I. (1976) *Black Men, White Cities* Chicago: University of Chicago Press.

—— (1981) *City Trenches: Urban Politics and the Patterning of Class in the United States* New York: Pantheon.

Keith, M. (1989) 'From punishment to discipline? Racism, racialisation and social control' Paper presented the PSA Conference, University of Warwick.

—— (1990) 'Misunderstandings?: Policing, reform and control, co-optation and consultation' in Goulbourne, H. (ed.) *Black Politics in Britain* Aldershot: Avebury.

—— (1992) 'Angry writing: (re)presenting the unethical work of the ethnographer' *Society and Space* 10: 551–568.

—— (1993) *Race, Riots and Policing: Lore and Disorder in a Multi-racist Society* London: UCL Press.

—— (1994) 'Street Sensibility? Negotiating the political by articulating the spatial' Paper presented at conference on Migration, Social Exclusion and the European City, University of Utrecht, 14–16 April.

Keith, M. and Cross, M. (1993) 'Racism and the postmodern city' in Cross, M. and Keith, M. (eds) *Racism, the City and the State* London: Routledge.

Keith, M. and Pile, S. (eds) (1993) *Place and the Politics of Identity* London: Routledge.

Ladner, J. (ed.) (1973) *The Death of White Sociology* New York: Vintage Books.

Lawrence, E. (1981) 'White sociology, black struggle' *Multi-Racial Education* 9: 3–17.

—— (1982) 'In the Abundance of Water the Fool is Thirsty: Sociology and Black "Pathology" in CCCS' (1982) *The Empire Strikes Back* London: Hutchinson.

Layton-Henry, Z. (1992) *The Politics of Immigration* Oxford: Basil Blackwell.

Levin, M., Paul, E. F., Conway, D., Papps, I., Taylor, J. K. and McElroy, W. (1992) *Equal Opportunities: A Feminist Fallacy* London: IEA Health and Welfare Unit.

McCrudden, C., Smith, C. and Brown, C. (1991) *Racial Justice at Work* London: Policy Studies Institute.

Marable, M. (1983) *How Capitalism Underdeveloped Black America* London: Pluto Press.

—— (1985) *Black American Politics* London: Verso.

Marshall, T. H. (1950) *Citizenship and Social Class* Cambridge: Cambridge University Press.

Melucci, A. (1989) *Nomads of the Present* London: Radius.

Messina, A. M. (1989) *Race and Party Competition in Britain* Oxford: Clarendon Press.

Miles, R. (1982) *Racism and Migrant Labour* London: George Allen and Unwin.

—— (1984) 'Marxism versus the "sociology of race relations"?' *Ethnic and Racial Studies* 7, 2: 217–237.

—— (1986) 'Labour migration, racism and capital accumulation in Western Europe' *Capital and Class* 28: 49–86.

—— (1988) 'Racism, Marxism and British politics' *Economy and Society* 17, 3: 428–460.

—— (1989) *Racism* London: Routledge.

—— (1993) *Racism after 'race relations'* London: Routledge.

Miles, R. and Phizacklea, A. (1979) 'Some introductory observations on race and politics in Britain' in Miles, R. and Phizacklea, A. (eds) *Racism and Political Action in Britain* London: Routledge and Kegan Paul.

—— (1984) *White Man's Country: Racism in British Politics* London: Pluto Press.

Modood, T. (1988) 'Black, racial equality and Asian identity' *New Community* XIV, 3: 397–404.

Morrison, T. (ed.) (1993) *Race-ing Justice, En-gendering Power* London: Chatto and Windus.

Mosse, G. (1985) *Toward the Final Solution: A History of European Racism* Madison, Wis.: University of Madison Press.

Myrdal, G. (1969a) *Objectivity in Social Research* London: Duckworth.

—— (1969b) *An American Dilemma: The Negro Problem and Modern Democracy* New York: Harper and Row.

Narayan, R. (1977) *Black England* London: Doscarla Publications.

Newton, K. (1976) *Second City Politics: Democratic Politics and Decision Making in Birmingham* Oxford: Clarendon Press.

Ohri, S. K. and Phillips, L. (eds) (1986) *A Different Reality: An account of Black people's experiences and their grievances before and after the Handsworth Rebellions of September 1985* Birmingham: West Midlands County Council.

Omi, M. and Winant, H. (1986) *Racial Formation in the United States* New York: Routledge and Kegan Paul.

Parekh, B. (1991) 'British citizenship and cultural difference' in Andrews, G. (ed.) *Citizenship* London: Lawrence and Wishart.

Parmar, P. (1981) 'Young Asian women: a critique of the pathological approach' *Multiracial Education* 9, 3: 19–29.

Patterson, S. (1969) *Immigration and Race Relations in Britain 1960–1967* London: Oxford University Press.

Phillips, A. (1991) *Engendering Democracy* Cambridge: Polity Press.

Phillips, M. (1983) 'Danger! Astrologers at work: a note on the narrow orthodoxy of race relations research' *Community Development Journal* 18, 3: 263–269.

Phizacklea, A. and Miles, R. (1980) *Labour and Racism* London: Routledge and Kegan Paul.

Plant, R. and Barry, N. (1990) *Citizenship and Rights in Thatcher's Britain: Two Views* London: IEA Health and Welfare Unit.

Pohlmann, M. D. (1990) *Black Politics in Conservative America* New York: Longman.

Prem, D. (1966) *The Parliamentary Leper* Delhi: Everest Press.

Rae, D. (1981) *Equalities* Cambridge Mass.: Harvard University Press.

Rattansi, A. (1992) 'Changing the subject?: Racism, culture and education' in Donald, J. and Rattansi, A. (eds) *'Race': Culture & Difference* London: Sage.

Reed, A. (1988) 'The black urban regime: structural origins and constraints' in Smith, M. P. (ed.) *Power, Community and the City* Comparative Urban and Community Research, Vol. 1, New Brunswick, N. J.: Transaction Books.

Reeves, F. W. (1989) *Race and Borough Politics* Aldershot: Avebury.

Rex, J. (1968) 'The sociology of the zone of transition' in Pahl, R. (ed.) *Readings in Urban Sociology* London: Pergamon Press.

—— (1970) *Race Relations and Sociological Theory* London: Weidenfeld and Nicolson.

—— (1973) *Race, Colonialism and the City* London: Routledge and Kegan Paul.

—— (1979) 'Black Militancy and Class Conflict' in Miles, R. and Phizacklea, A. (eds) *Racism and Political Action in Britain* London: Routledge and Kegan Paul.

—— (1981) 'A Working Paradigm for Race Relations Research' *Ethnic and Racial Studies* 4, 1: 1–25.

—— (1986a) *Race and Ethnicity* London: Open University Press.

—— (1986b) 'The Role of Class Analysis in the Study of Race Relations – A Weberian Perspective' in Rex, J. and Mason, D. (eds) *Theories of Race and Ethnic Relations* Cambridge: Cambridge University Press.

—— (1988) *The Ghetto and the Underclass: Essays on Race and Social Policy* Aldershot: Avebury.

—— (1989) 'Some notes on the development of the theory of race and ethnic relations in Britain' Unpublished discussion document, Centre for Research in Ethnic Relations, University of Warwick.

—— (1990) 'The relationship between theoretical and empirical work in the Centre' Unpublished discussion document, Centre of Research in Ethnic Relations, University of Warwick.

Rex, J. and Mason, D. (eds) (1986) *Theories of Race and Ethnic Relations* Cambridge: Cambridge University Press.

Rex, J. and Moore, R. (1967) *Race, Community and Conflict* London: Oxford University Press.

Rex, J. and Tomlinson, S. (1979) *Colonial Immigrants in a British City* London: Routledge and Kegan Paul.

Rich, P. (1986) *Race and Empire in British Politics* Cambridge: Cambridge University Press.

Rose, E. J. B. and Associates (1969) *Colour and Citizenship: A Report on British Race Relations* London: Oxford University Press.

Rutherford, J. (ed.) (1990) *Identity: Community, Culture, Difference* London: Lawrence and Wishart.

Saggar, S. (1992) *Race and Politics in Britain* London: Harvester Wheatsheaf.

Sewell, T. (1990) '"New Realism": black political participation in the 1990s', Paper presented at the New Issues in Black Politics Conference, University of Warwick, 14–16 May.

—— (1993) *Black Tribunes: Black Political Participation in Britain* London: Lawrence and Wishart.

Shukra, K. (1990a) 'Black sections in the Labour Party' in Goulbourne, H. (ed.) *Black Politics in Britain* Aldershot: Avebury.

—— (1990b) 'Black sections in the 1990s?' Paper presented at the New Issues in Black Politics Conference, University of Warwick, 14–16 May.

Silverman, J. (1986) *Independent Inquiry into the Handsworth Disturbances September 1985* Birmingham: Birmingham City Council.

Sivanandan, A. (1982) *A Different Hunger* London: Pluto Press.

—— (1983) 'Challenging Racism: strategies for the eighties' *Race and Class* 25, 2: 1–12.

—— (1990a) 'All that melts into air is solid: the hokum of new times' *Race and Class* 31, 3: 1–30.

—— (1990b) *Communities of Resistance: Writings on Black Struggles for Socialism* London: Verso.

Smith, S. J. (1989) *The Politics of Race and Residence: Citizenship, Segregation and White Supremacy in Britain* Cambridge: Polity Press.

Soja, E. (1989) *Postmodern Geographies* London: Verso.

Solomos, J. (1988) *Black Youth, Racism and the State* Cambridge: Cambridge University Press.

—— (1993) *Race and Racism in Britain* 2nd edition, London: Macmillan.

Solomos, J. and Back, L. (1991a) 'The Politics of Race and Social Change in Birmingham: Historical Patterns and Contemporary Trends' *Research Papers*, No. 1, Department of Politics and Sociology, Birkbeck College.

—— (1991b) 'Black Political Mobilisation and the Struggle for Equality' *Sociological Review* 39, 2: 215–237.

—— (1995) *Racism and Society* London: Macmillan.

Solomos, J., Findlay, B., Jones, S. and Gilroy, P. (1982) 'The organic crisis of British capitalism and race: the experience of the seventies' in CCCS *The Empire Strikes Back* London: Hutchinson.

Staples, R. (1976) *Introduction to Black Sociology* New York: McGraw Hill.

Stanfield, J. H. II and Dennis, R. M. (eds) (1993) *Race and Ethnicity in Research Methods* Newbury Park, Cal.: Sage.

Touraine, A. (1981) *The Voice and the Eye: An Analysis of Social Movements* Cambridge: Cambridge University Press.

van Dijk, T. A. (1984) *Prejudice and Discourse: An Analysis of Ethnic Prejudice in Thought and Talk* Amsterdam: Benjamins.

—— (1987) *Communicating Racism: Ethnic Prejudice in Thought and Talk* London: Sage.

Wainwright, H. (1987) *Labour: A Tale of Two Parties* London: Hogarth Press.

Werbner, P. (1991) 'Black and ethnic leadership in Britain: a theoretical overview' in Werbner, P. and Anwar, M. (eds) *Black and Ethnic Leaderships: The Cultural Dimension of Political Action* London: Routledge.

West, C. (1993) *Race Matters* Boston: Beacon Press.

Wetherall, H. and Potter, J. (1986) 'Discourse analysis and the social psychology of racism' *Newsletter of the Social Psychology Section of the British Psychological Society* 15: 24–29.

Wieviorka, M. (1993) 'Tendencies to racism in Europe: does France represent a unique case, or is it representative of a trend?' in Wrench, J. and Solomos, J. (eds) *Racism and Migration in Western Europe* Oxford: Berg.

Williams, E. N. (1982) 'Black Political Progress in the 1970s' in Preston, M. B. *et al.* (eds) *The New Black Politics* London: Longman.

Wrench, J. and Solomos, J. (eds) (1993) *Racism and Migration in Western Europe* Oxford: Berg.

# Index